Payment Methods and Fir Trade

Sang Man Kim

Payment Methods and Finance for International Trade

 Springer

Sang Man Kim
International Trade
Duksung Women's University
Seoul, Korea (Republic of)

ISBN 978-981-15-7041-4   ISBN 978-981-15-7039-1   (eBook)
https://doi.org/10.1007/978-981-15-7039-1

This Springer imprint is published by the registered company Springer Nature Singapore Pte Ltd.
The registered company address is: 152 Beach Road, #21-01/04 Gateway East, Singapore 189721,
Singapore

Preface

This book covers various methods of payment in international trade and trade finance schemes for international trade. In addition, this book also overviews the concepts, purposes, features, and risks of international trade.

Companies engage in international trade transactions for various purposes. Maximizing corporate value by increasing revenues and profits will be the ultimate goal for most companies. Companies engaging in international trade transactions are likely to gain more revenue and profits.

International trade transactions, however, bring various risks that originate from the features of international trade transactions. Exporters may not get paid even after the performance of a contract. The risk of non-payment is largely dependent on the method of payment.

In international trade, the number of documents required will vary depending on the individual transaction. Documents come in two types: financial documents and commercial documents. Financial documents mean bills of exchange, promissory notes, checks, or other similar instruments used for obtaining the payment of money, while commercial documents mean invoices, transport documents, documents of title, or other similar documents.

The basic methods of payment in international trade are "payment in advance" (cash in advance), "open account", "documentary collection", and "documentary credit" (letter of credit). Other types of method of payment, such as "consignment", "netting", and "bank payment obligation", are also used. Each of the methods of payment has advantages and disadvantages to the respective parties.

Some methods of payment might bring detrimental losses rather than profits, and also cause cash flow problems. In negotiating methods of payment, companies need to consider trade finance as well as non-payment risk. There are various types of trade finance normally used in international trade: pre-shipment finance, post-shipment finance, export working capital financing, negotiation of bills of exchange (or discounting invoices), export factoring, international forfaiting, export credit insurance (export credit guarantee), etc.

The understanding of various methods of payment in international trade together with the relevant trade finance scheme is a key factor for a successful international trade transaction. The understanding of the features and risks of international trade will help to understand the various methods of payment.

For the successful completion of an international trade transaction, depending on the terms of the transaction, both parties need access to funds. Small and Medium-Sized Enterprises (SMEs), compared to large companies, often face difficulties in raising capital or funds. Financing an international trade transaction is often key to successful completion. There are various financing mechanisms available for international trade transactions. Besides financing ability, the choice of a proper financing mechanism is also important for the successful completion of an international trade transaction.

For successful completion of an international trade in goods or services, depending on the payment terms and other conditions of a particular transaction, both exporters and importers need access to funds. Thus, it is important to understand the trade finance mechanisms for the successful completion of an international trade. The ability to allow longer payment terms has become a competitive factor in international trade. However, long payment terms bring cash flow shortage to an exporter. Thus, an exporter needs to obtain trade finance in order to make up the cash flow shortage arising out of an international trade transaction with long payment terms.

Exporters preparing the performance of export transactions are frequently in need of finance for the performance of the transactions (or for delivery of the goods). Such finance is called pre-shipment finance. Exporters are also in need of finance after the performance of the transactions (or after delivery of the goods) because they get paid long after transactions are completed. Such finance is called post-shipment finance. Post-shipment finance includes negotiation of bills of exchange and/or documents, forfaiting, and factoring.

Export credit insurance (or export credit guarantee) is very useful for the facilitation of pre-shipment finance and of post-shipment finance. Therefore, it is considered one of the financing mechanisms available in international trades.

Many countries have established export credit agencies to promote exports through various support mechanisms, including export credit insurance (or export credit guarantee). Its main aim is to promote exports by protecting exporters from commercial and political risks.

Export credit insurance (or export credit guarantee) promotes a country's exports by giving a variety of advantages to its exporters. The key functions of export credit insurance include reducing non-payment risks, offering competitive payment terms, increasing exports with reduced non-payment risk and competitive payment terms, creating easy and accessible trade financing solutions, etc. When an export credit insurance (or export credit guarantee) backs an exporter's foreign receivables, commercial banks are often willing to lend to an exporter with favorable terms against foreign receivables, otherwise excluded from the borrowing base.

This book provides a comprehensive treatment of methods of payment in international trade accessible to those less familiar with the subject matter. This book provides various examples and figures for trade documents, each method of payment, trade finance scheme, etc.

This book will be a valuable reference for experienced managers and bankers in international trade. This book can be used as a guide book or a manual for new employees in trading companies. It can also be used as a college textbook for a one-semester course for upper-level undergraduate or graduate students.

This book is based on the author's practices as a legal consultant and underwriter for export trades, and researches as a professor of international trade. The figures were created or modified by the author.

Seoul, Korea (Republic of)   Sang Man Kim

Contents

About the Author

Sang Man Kim

Attorney at Law (New York, USA)
Professor (Duksung Women's University, Seoul, South Korea)
Arbitrator/Mediator (Korean Commercial Arbitration Board)
Former Deputy Director (Korea Trade Insurance Corp.)

Sang Man Kim is a Professor of International Trade at Duksung Women's University in Seoul, South Korea. He is also an attorney at law (New York, USA), and an arbitrator and mediator at the Korean Commercial Arbitration Board.

In his former role as a deputy director at the Korea Trade Insurance Corporation (a Korean Government-owned official export credit agency), Prof. Kim worked as an underwriter and legal consultant for Korean international trades for a period of 15 years (1995–2010).

Professor Kim graduated with a B.A. in law and an M.D. in international business transactions law from Korea University. Professor Kim further pursued and completed LLM (M.D.) from the University of Minnesota Law School, and a Ph.D. in commercial law from Korea University.

Over the past 25 years, Prof. Kim has practiced and researched international trade, and has published over 80 articles and 11 books on the topic.

Chapter 1
Introduction to International Trade

1.1 Concept of International Trade

International trade can be defined by its various purposes. International trade can be defined as the "transaction of goods and/or services between two or more countries". It can also be defined as the "transaction of goods and/or services across national boundaries". Goods are generally something tangible, while services are intangible. Here are examples of international trade. An American seller sells automobiles to a Chinese buyer. The automobiles will be transported from the USA, across national boundaries to China, and the funds for the payment will be transferred from China to the USA. This is an example of international trade in goods.

The American seller requests a Greek shipping company to transport automobiles to China, and the Greek shipping company transports the automobiles ("cargo") from the USA to China. This is an example of international trade in services.

Very often, the international trade in goods and the international trade services go hand in hand in international trade transactions. International trade is the first type of international business activity for most enterprises.

International trade has grown dramatically in the past 70 years due to the reduction of trade barriers and the promotion of free trade. Since 2011, the international trade in services has been expanding rapidly, at a faster pace than the international trade in goods.[1] The value of world merchandise trade in 2018 reached USD 19.67 trillion, while the value of world trade in commercial services in 2018 reached USD 5.3 trillion.[2]

Occasionally, the term "international transaction" is erroneously used for the term "international trade". An "international transaction", or cross-border transaction,

---

[1]WTO (2019a), p. 7.
[2]WTO (2019b), pp. 8–9.

S. M. Kim, *Payment Methods and Finance for International Trade*, https://doi.org/10.1007/978-981-15-7039-1_1

can be defined as a transaction between two or more countries. The term "international transaction" covers financial transactions (e.g. foreign investment, international loans, financial instruments, etc.) besides international trade. International trade is thus part of international transaction. International trade is the most traditional and/or typical form of international business activity.

1.2   Purposes of Engaging in International Trade

This section discusses for what purposes companies engage in international trade activities. Companies do so for various purposes. Maximizing corporate value by increasing revenues and profits is the ultimate goal for most companies that undertake international business transactions. As the international market is much larger than the domestic market, international trade transactions will help to increase revenues.[3] Thus, companies engaging in international trade transactions are likely to gain more revenues and profits.

An international trade transaction will bring various benefits to the parties concerned, and to the countries as well. Exporting companies and importing companies respectively undertake international trade for various purposes. Exporting companies can increase sales and profits through exporting goods and/or services to foreign countries, sometimes selling at a higher price. In the USA, exporting companies make 17% more profit than non-exporting companies.[4] Exporting companies will increase production, which will also bring an employment increase and will lead to growth of gross domestic product (GDP) in the exporting country.

Importing companies can make profits by selling imported goods in the domestic market, which may bring an employment increase. Importing companies may import raw materials that will be used to manufacture exporting goods. Such imports will bring growth of GDP and also contribute to increased export.

Further, consumers can also enjoy incidental benefits from international trade. Consumers are able to purchase goods at a lower price owing to import from the countries rich in those goods. Consumers can purchase goods that are not produced at all in an importing country.

1.2.1   To Increase Revenues and Profits: The Exporter's Perspective

Making profit is common in every trade: both in domestic trade and international trade. But international trade will help to increase revenues as the international market is much larger than the domestic market. A company can increase its volume of

---

[3]Hill et al. (2016), p. 530.
[4]US Commercial Services (2015), p. 5.

sales through international trade. The population of the USA is 328 million (0.33 billion) and the world population is 7.7 billion. An American company is theoretically able to increase the maximum volume of sales by 23 times through participating in international trade activities. A company is thus able to increase sales and revenues through international trade, which will result in maximizing the corporate value as well as the corporate profits. In general, companies engaging in exports make 17% more profit than those companies that do not.[5]

1.2.2 To Use Production Capability Fully and Sell Excess Products: The Exporter's Perspective

A company is able to sell its excess products in foreign markets. For example, a company could produce goods for export by using its excess production capacity. Suppose a company manufactures two million automobiles, and the maximum domestic demand is one million automobiles. One million automobiles will exceed the domestic demand, and will not be sold in the domestic market, and the auto manufacturer thus needs to export one million automobiles to foreign countries.

1.2.3 To Learn or Acquire Advanced Technology: The Importer's Perspective

When a company imports high-technology products such as aircraft or industrial plant, the contract usually includes training program and aftercare assistance. Accordingly, the technology and services come together with the product, and the importing country will learn the advanced technology.

1.2.4 To Meet Domestic Demand: The Importer's Perspective

Consumers may need some goods that cannot be supplied in the domestic market. Manufacturing companies may also need raw materials or components such as oil, gas, or semi-conduct chips, that cannot be supplied from the domestic market.

Companies need to provide goods and services quickly and efficiently to meet the domestic demands or needs. In addition, they must do so as competitively as possible. In the absence of international trade, can English people eat trophic fruits such as bananas, pineapples, coconuts, mangos etc.? The answer will be "absolutely not".

---

[5]Ibid., p. 5.

1.3   Features of International Trade

Regardless of the purposes for engaging in international trade activities, companies must be aware of the various features of international trade, and must understand the distinctions between international trade and domestic trade.

These features of international trade bring companies engaging in international trade risks as well as benefits. Therefore, it is necessary to maximize the benefits and minimize the risks to achieve the purposes of international trade. An understanding of the features of international trade will be the starting point for companies engaging in international trade transactions.

1.3.1   Different Laws and Standards

As an international trade is a transaction between two or more countries, the national laws differ between the parties. Industry standards also differ between the parties. Every authority applies particular laws and standards to a specific instance. A court normally uses a "choice of law" rule[6] to determine the laws applicable to a dispute.[7] When a German exporter enters into a contract for the sale of automobiles with an American importer, it is necessary to decide which law governs the contract (American or German law, or sometimes a third country's law). The law governing a contract or legal matters is called the "governing law" or the "applicable law".

In reality, American law differs from German law. No matter which country's law governs a contract for sale of automobiles between a German exporter and an American importer, American laws and standards for automobile safety will apply to the automobiles driven in America. Therefore, the automobiles for American import should be manufactured in compliance with American laws and standards.

Prior to exporting to a foreign country, an exporting company should be aware of any law of an importing country that might affect the export transaction. Basic information on that law can often be obtained from an importing company or a distributor in an importing country, but further detailed and specific information can be obtained by legal opinions from a local lawyer.

1.3.2   Government Control and Intervention

An international trade has material effects on the national interest of both countries, the exporting country and the importing country. Thus, governments are inclined to intervene in and control international trade transactions.

---

[6]Choice of laws rules are normally enacted in the "private international law" of each nation.

[7]August et al. (2009), p. 149.

As goods move across national boundaries, each country inspects the goods and controls the movement of the goods. An export declaration is required in an exporting country, and an import declaration is required in an importing country. Among the purposes of such controls is to protect the local economy and national health (e.g. against infection from COVID 19, Ebola virus, or MERS, etc.).

Moreover, transactions with foreign governments, government agencies, or public entities often require specialized procedures and documentation (e.g. public competitive bidding, compliance with invitation to bidding, bank guarantees, numerous certifications, etc.). In many countries, imports by the government exempt import licenses, or customs duties.

1.3.3 Complex Documents

As an international trade is a transaction between two or more countries, complex documents are required. In an international trade in goods, various documents (e.g. bill of lading, air waybill, certificate of origin, packing list, inspection certificate, marine insurance policy, etc.) are required. Many of these documents are not normally required in a domestic trade. Furthermore, either of an exporter or importer in an international trade in goods concludes incidental contracts with, e.g. a shipping company, an insurance company, an inspecting company, banks, etc. Therefore, an international trade in goods involves various contracts and documents other than a contract for sale.

1.3.4 Different Customs and Cultures

As an international trade is a transaction between two or more countries, customs and cultures will differ between the parties. Customs will differ country to country and region to region. Customs may apply to an international business transaction as a gap-filling of the laws. An exporting company should be aware of the customs of an importing country for the successful completion of a transaction.

An international business transaction involves parties in different countries and in different cultures. Cultural difference might bring misunderstanding and an adverse effect to a transaction. A deep and refined awareness of cultural differences is required for success in international negotiations. Understanding and appreciating the culture of a foreign party is a necessary foundation for negotiating international trade transactions.

1.3.5 Different Languages

As an international trade is a transaction between two or more countries, the languages will, in many cases, differ between the parties. English is commonly used in international trade, and correspondence and documents are normally made in English.

1.3.6 Different Currencies

As an international trade is a transaction between two or more countries, the currencies may differ between the parties. It is inevitable that the contract currency will differ from (at least) one of the parties' national currencies. Soft currencies can fluctuate erratically or depreciate against hard currencies, and a transaction with a soft currency can thus cause bigger problems for the other party.[8] In an international trade transaction, hard currencies (such as the US dollar, the euro, British sterling, or Japanese yen) are normally used.

1.3.7 Long Distance

As an international trade is a transaction between two or more countries, the parties may be located a long distance apart. It will take time for the parties to meet for negotiation of the transaction. The goods will be transported to a foreign country across national borders, and thus the transportation distance may be very long. Accordingly, additional time for transportation is required in the performance of an international business transaction.

1.4 Risks in International Trade

1.4.1 Introduction

Companies engaging in international trade confront seemingly never-ending challenges and risks.[9] Some of the risks are attributable to the counter party, and others are not. Although those risks can be mitigated by relevant measures, no international trade transaction can be undertaken without risks. It is essential to understand what ultimate effects each risk will have on the respective parties.

---

[8]Hill et al. (2016), p. 530.
[9]Johnson and Bade (2010), p. xi.

Risks can be reduced and adjusted with proper assessment and measures. Exporting to other countries does not always bring a higher risk than selling in the domestic market. Each of the different foreign markets has different levels of risk.[10]

Generally, an exporter is concerned about payment, while an importer is concerned about the delivery of goods. However, even seemingly simple international trade transactions can go wrong, and sometimes *really* go wrong. There are many reasons why international trade transactions go wrong. Absence of risk assessment, or wrong risk assessment, would be the most direct reason.

What is the best action that we can take? The right risk assessment can reduce and minimize the risks. Risk assessment can be conducted with the following steps.

- Find what risks can be assessed in a specific transaction?
- Find what risks can be covered (or reduced) through terms of payment, payment guarantees, and/or export credit insurances.
- Find whether the buyer is likely to accept these terms of payment and/or payment guarantees.
- Find whether the other risk factors are acceptable (considering the importance of a specific transaction).
- If the other risk factors are acceptable, prepare for the transaction. If not, find another transaction.

In some countries, what the seller thought was a contract may not be a contract, but just a memorandum of understanding (MOU). Although an MOU is an agreement, it is not legally binding nor enforceable. A signed contract may not be considered as a valid contract, because it was signed by an unauthorized low-ranked person, instead of by an authorized person of higher position.

When the parties do not use the same terminology, or do not focus on the details of the agreed terms of payment, this can lead to future disputes. Even though such errors do not always result in non-payment, they will be likely to cause delays in payment, or bring disputes.

Unclear or undefined terms of payment will be likely to bring claims on the buyer, who will take the opportunity to deduct payment unilaterally. For instance, when a contract stipulates "the contract price is 200,000 Dollars", there may be a dispute regarding the meaning of "Dollars". "Dollars" can be argued as Hong Kong dollars instead of US dollars.

The choice of currency could be of great importance, particularly in an increasingly competitive market. The fluctuation of exchange rate might bring unexpected loss or profit, which is a significant risk in international trade.

Any successful negotiation must take reasonable and equal consideration of the demands of both parties in order to find a compromise and avoid unnecessary discussions or misunderstandings.

---

[10]US Commercial Services (2015), p. 5.

1.4.2 Risk Factors

While risk is a factor in all business transactions, international trade involves additional risks.[11] Most of the features of international trade bring some risks. Before starting an international trade transaction, the parties must first consider the various risks to which they will be exposed, and they must assess the risks. Many of the risks will be the same regardless of whether they are exporting or importing. This section will overview the factors that can bring risks in international trade transactions.

1.4.2.1 Foreign Exchange and Currency

If payment is going to be made in a currency other than that in which the seller incurs their costs, a new currency risk will arise. In most cases, the seller's main costs are paid in their own local currency, which automatically creates currency risk if invoicing an export transaction in another currency. The size of that risk will depend on the currency and the outstanding period until payment.

Foreign exchange and currency risks bring a huge risk for a company, and may result in actual monetary loss or damage. A fluctuation of exchange rate might bring unexpected loss or profit, which is a significant risk in international trade transactions. Foreign exchange risk management has been one of the significant concerns for most exporters, in particular for SMEs.

Depreciation in the contract currency will present the exporter with unexpected loss, while appreciation in the contract currency will present the importer with unexpected loss. The volume of exchange risk depends on the particular currency and the period of payment. Soft currency will normally bring bigger risk as it fluctuates more. Transaction with a soft currency can be a problem for the other party.[12] In some cases, the choice of currency for a contract is more important than the contract price (or unit price) itself.

There are various methods of hedging foreign exchange risk, but the parties to an international trade transaction find many of them unacceptable or impracticable. By using forward exchange or future exchange, the parties to an international business transaction can reduce foreign exchange risk. But such an exchange hedge incurs transaction costs. Some export credit agencies operate "foreign exchange risk insurance" (or foreign currency guarantee), and a foreign exchange risk insurance operated by an export credit agency has been well accepted for foreign exchange risk hedging.

Case study
Let us review an example of German export to the USA. In the local supply contract for local supply in Germany, the contract price is Euro 1 million, and

---

[11] Jimenez and Guillermo (2012), p. 13.
[12] Hill et al. (2016), p. 530.

in the export contract for German export, the contract price is USD 1.3 million. Suppose that the current EUR/USD exchange rate is @1.140 at the time of the export contract. If converted, the contract price in the export contract will be equal to Euro 1.14 million, Euro 14,000 over the contract price in a local supply contract. In this export transaction, a profit of Euro 14,000 is expected.

However, should the EUR/USD exchange rate rise to @1.340 at the time of payment, then the contract price in the export contract will turn out Euro 0.970, Euro 30,000 below that in the local supply contract. Consequently, the export transaction will result in Euro 30,000 unexpected loss. In the event that the EUR/USD exchange rate drops at the time of payment, the result will be the reverse, bringing unexpected profit.

This example will be sufficient to show the importance of currency in international trade transactions. A change in exchange rate can create an unexpected loss or profit to the parties involved, which is a significant risk to the parties. Soft currencies such as the Vietnam VND or the Thai Baht may fluctuate more, and cause bigger risks than har currencies such as the US dollar or the euro. Still worse, some countries may impose restrictions on foreign currency exchange, or on foreign currency transfer, which will cause bigger risks and damages.

1.4.2.2 Different Laws and Legal System

The legal system and laws vary greatly from country to country. Each country has different laws, thus it is very rare that two different parties' laws are the same. The difference of laws and legal system may cause unexpected trouble or dispute.

Common law system Versus Civil law system

There are two main legal systems: the "Common law system", better known as English-American law, and the "civil law system", better known as continental law.

The common law system is based on tradition, precedent, and court cases (court decisions) rather than having written statutory laws. The common law system evolved in England and is found in most of Great Britain's former colonies and the USA. The common law system has much flexibility and allows judges to interpret a dispute in the light of the prevailing situation.

The civil law system is based on written statutory laws. The courts interpret and apply the written statutory laws. Most countries in the world, including China, Germany, Japan, Russia, France and Korea, operate with the civil law system.

Just as the economic system of a country is influenced by the prevailing political system, the legal system of a country is influenced by the prevailing political system.[13]

Every country has its own levels and standards of laws. For instance, automobile safety standards vary considerably country to country. In a developed country, food hygiene policy is likely to be more strict than that in an underdeveloped country. Each country has its own consumer protection laws, which differ country to country.

Awareness is required of the laws that govern the transactions to complete international trade successfully. Legal advice from a local lawyer may be needed, without which unexpected loss or damage may be suffered.

The United Nations Convention on Contracts for the International Sale of Goods (CISG or the Vienna Convention) may govern a specific transaction in addition to the governing law chosen. As of March 2020, 93 countries are parties to the CISG.

1.4.2.3 Finance Concern

For successful completion of an international trade transaction, depending on the terms of the transaction, the parties concerned need access to funds. SMEs, in contrast to large companies, often face difficulties in raising capital or funds. Financing an international trade transaction is often key to successful completion.

In a credit terms transaction (or in a long payment terms transaction), the exporter will be in need of trade finance, while in a cash payment terms transaction (or in an advance payment terms transaction), the importer will be in need of trade finance.[14] The ability of the exporter to allow long payment terms has become a key competitive factor in international trade. However, long payment terms normally brings cash flow shortage to the exporter. Thus, the exporter needs to obtain trade finance in order to make up the cash flow shortage arising out of an international trade transaction with credit terms (or long payment terms).

The "working capital cycle" is the amount of time it takes to turn the net current assets and current liabilities into cash. The longer the cycle is, the longer a company is tying up funds in its working capital without earning a return on it. In reality, the working capital cycle depends on the terms of payment. The working capital cycle in an international trade transaction is normally longer than that in a domestic transaction. Therefore, companies strive to reduce the working capital cycle by collecting receivables quicker. Companies may be able to shorten the working capital cycle with favorable payment terms. If the working capital cycle is short, a company is able to increase sales and revenue. There is no doubt that every company prefers a shorter working capital cycle.

Working capital cycle case study

---

[13] Ibid., p. 44.
[14] Belay (2009), pp. 306–307.

This is an example that shows the length of the working capital cycle. An exporter buys goods from a local supplier. The local supplier demands cash in advance for the payment terms. The exporter sells the goods to a foreign buyer (importer) on an open account of 90 days from bill of lading date because the exporter has to grant extended sales terms to offer competitive payment terms.

It takes three months for the manufacture of the goods, and the exporter thus takes delivery of the goods after three months from the payment to the local supplier. Then, the exporter ships the goods and sends the shipping documents to the importer. The importer pays three months after shipment. In this case, the working capital cycle would be six months (from the date of payment to the local supplier to the date of payment from the importer).

1.4.2.4 Language Difference

As international trade is a transaction between two different countries, the languages are generally different between the parties concerned. The difference of language brings us some risks. Although English is the standard language in international trade, disputes may arise out of English communication or documents, in particular when one or both of the parties' first language is not English. While English is considered the standard language of international trade, its use is not universal and the level of understanding will vary from country to country and business to business.

1.4.2.5 Culture Difference

As international trade is a transaction between two different countries, the cultures are generally different between the parties. Expectations of courtesy and manners can influence the negotiation of an international trade transaction.

The difference of culture may bring unexpected troubles or disputes. For example, in some countries people do not like the colors red or yellow. In those countries, the red and yellow branding of the American fast food chain McDonald's will offend people's feeling and will give the wrong image. This may well adversely affect their business. For further examples, in Brazil the "O.K. finger sign" means "blame" and not "Yes".

1.4.2.6   Longer Distance and Transportation

In international trade, transportation involves greater distances, with cargo often undergoing prolonged storage or changing hands;[15] transshipment is often inevitable. The greater periods and distances of transportation can bring greater risk of damage (or decay) to or loss of the cargo than a domestic trade, and disputes often occur out of the contracts of carriage. During the long period of transportation, the prices of the goods can greatly fluctuate. The transportation cost may be high due to long transportation. And there are other risks. For example, the vessel may be robbed by sea robbers, such as Somalia pirates.

1.4.3   Commercial Risk and Country Risk

The parties to an international trade transaction are exposed to various risks. Some of the risks are attributable to the counter party and others are not. Credit risk can largely be classified as a commercial risk and country risk (or political risk). Country risks normally bring more immense and significant impacts on international business transactions than commercial risks. Other than commercial risk and country risk, the parties are also exposed to exchange risk.

1.4.3.1   Commercial Risk

Commercial risk refers to the risk solely attributable to the party itself.[16] Typical commercial risks to an exporter would be:

- The importer cannot make payment due to insolvency or bankruptcy.
- The importer raises a market claim (or malicious claim) regardless of the quality of the goods.
- The importer delays payment due to cash flow shortage.

  Typical commercial risks to an importer would be:

- The exporter delivers non-conforming goods.
- The exporter does not deliver the goods at all.
- The exporter delivers the goods behind schedule.

  In order to mitigate commercial risk, it is necessary to conduct thorough credit investigation and evaluate the creditworthiness of the other party. Some risks can be reduced by obtaining favorable contract terms. Unfortunately, it may be necessary to give up other terms in return for obtaining the favorable terms, as the terms of a contract are normally zero-sum game. Export credit insurance (or export credit

---

[15]Jimenez and Guillermo (2012), p. 13.
[16]Grath (2014), p. 19.

guarantee) is mainly designed for non-payment risk. Thus, export credit insurance (or export credit guarantee) can be useful for mitigating commercial risks, but it charges a premium.

1.4.3.2 Country Risk

Country risk (or political risk) means the risk attributable to the country that are not the responsibility of the parties.[17] Country risk includes war, civil disorder, country default, foreign exchange reserve running out, restriction on foreign currency exchange, restriction on foreign currency transfer, etc. Country risk also includes non-payment by public authorities or by private enterprises acting on the state's behalf.[18] Change of political regime, government legislation or monetary policy can also be country risks.[19] Most export credit insurances (or export credit guarantees) also cover country risk.[20]

The OECD's Arrangement on Officially Supported Export Credits provides in Article 25 the five elements of country credit risk:

- general moratorium on repayments decreed by the obligor's/guarantor's government or by that agency of a country through which repayment is effected;
- political events and/or economic difficulties arising outside the country of the notifying participant or legislative/administrative measures taken outside the country of the notifying participant that prevent or delay the transfer of funds paid in respect of the credit;
- legal provisions adopted in the obligor's/guarantor's country declaring repayments made in local currency to be a valid discharge of the debt, notwithstanding that, as a result of fluctuations in exchange rates, such repayments, when converted into the currency of the credit, no longer cover the amount of the debt at the date of the transfer of funds;
- any other measure or decision of the government of a foreign country that prevents repayment under a credit; and
- cases of force majeure occurring outside the country of the notifying participant, e.g. war (including civil war), expropriation, revolution, riot, civil disturbances, cyclones, floods, earthquakes, eruptions, tidal waves and nuclear accidents.

---

[17] Stephens (1999), p. 102; Belay (2009), p. 132; Anders (2014), p. 24.
[18] Ray (1995a), p. 18.
[19] Willsher (1995), p. 128.
[20] Stephens (1999), p. 102.

Each export credit agency (ECA) has developed its own system for assessing commercial risk and country risk,[21] and provides export credits (export credit insurance/guarantee, direct loan, etc.) based on their assessment. The OECD's Arrangement on Officially Supported Export Credits illustrates country risk mitigation techniques in Annex XIII (Criteria and Conditions Governing the Application of Country Risk Mitigation Techniques and Buyer Risk Credit Enhancements).

1.4.3.3   Exchange risk

Measures to restrict foreign currency exchange or restrict foreign currency transfer are taken by and are attributable to government. Thus, restriction on foreign currency exchange or restriction on foreign currency transfer is a type of country risk. However, exchange risk is not directly attributable to government, although it is, in some way, affected by the national economy and politics.

References

August, R., et al. (2009). *International Business Law* (15th ed., p. 149). USA: Pearson Education, Upper Saddle River.

Grath, A. (2014). *The Handbook of International Trade and Finance* (3rd ed., p. 19). London, U.K.: Kogan Page.

Hill, C. W. L., et al. (2016). *International Business (Asia Global Edition)* (2nd ed., p. 530). McGraw-Hill Education: Singapore.

Jimenez, G. C. (2012). *ICC Guide to Export/Import: Global Standards for International Trade*, 4th ed., ICC Publication No. 686, Paris, France, p. 13.

Johnson, T. E., & Bade, Donna L. (2010). *Export Import Procedures and Documentation* (4th ed.). New York, USA, p. xi.: AMACOM.

Ray, J. E. (1995a). *Managing Official Export Credits* (p. 18). Institute for International Economics: Washington D.C., USA.

Ray, J. E. (1995b). *Managing Official Export Credits* (p. 20). Institute for International Economics: Washington D.C.

Seyoum, B. (2009). *Export-Import Theory, Practices, and Procedures* (2nd ed., pp. 306–307). New York, USA: Routledge.

Stephens, M. (1999). *The Changing Role of Export Credit Agencies* (p. 102). IMF Washington: Washington D.C., USA.

Stephens, Malcolm (1999), *The Changing Role of Export Credit Agencies*, IMF Washington, Washington D.C., USA, p. 102; Seyoum, Belay (2009), *Export-Import Theory, Practices, and Procedures*, 2nd ed., Routledge, New York, USA, p. 132; Grath, Anders (2014), *The Handbook of International Trade and Finance*, 3rd ed., Kogan Page, London, U.K., p. 24.

US Commercial Services. (2015). *A Basic Guide to Exporting* (11th ed., p. 5). US Commercial Services: Washington D.C., USA.

WTO (2019a), *World Trade Report 2019*, WTO, p. 7.

WTO (2019b), *World Trade Statistical Review 2019*, WTO, pp. 8–9.

Willsher, R. (1995). *Export Finance: Risks* (p. 128). U.K.: Structures and Documentation, Macmillan Press, Basingstoke.

---

[21] Ray (1995b), p. 20.

Chapter 2
International Trade Contracts

2.1 Concept of a Contract

A contract is an agreement between two or more parties creating legally enforceable obligations. A valid contract creates legal obligations. A contract stipulates the terms and conditions of a particular transaction, and specifies the rights and obligations of the parties concerned.

Definitions of a contract

A contract is an agreement between two or more parties creating obligations that are enforceable or otherwise recognizable at law. (*Black's Law Dictionary*)

A contract is a promise or a set of promises for the breach of which the law gives a remedy or the performance of which the law in some way recognizes as a duty. (US Restatement)

A sale consists in the passing of title from the seller to the buyer for a price. (Uniform Commercial Code §2–106)

A contract of sale of goods is a contract by which the seller transfers or agrees to transfer the property in goods to the buyer for a money consideration, called price. (English Sale of Goods Act)

The first step for a contract is the process of negotiation between the parties. The second step is to draw up the contract. The third step is to enter into (conclude) the contract.

© The Editor(s) (if applicable) and The Author(s), under exclusive license
to Springer Nature Singapore Pte Ltd. 2021
S. M. Kim, *Payment Methods and Finance for International Trade*,
https://doi.org/10.1007/978-981-15-7039-1_2

Whenever disputes arise out of an international contract, there is the question of which country's law to apply. An international contract is governed by the national laws of a specific country. If a court decides that it possesses jurisdiction in an international dispute, then a further question, concerning the "choice of law", must be considered.[1] The choice of governing law in an international contract will usually be made by a contract clause in a specific contract.[2] Such choice of law may not be recognized by the court. In a specific dispute, the governing law is finally decided by the private international law of the competent jurisdiction. The governing law may be decided by an international convention or rule, if any. For instance, in the European Union, the Rome I Regulation[3] decides on the law applicable to contractual obligations and the Rome II Regulation[4] decides on the law applicable to non-contractual obligations. Private international law directs which country's laws (substantive laws, not procedural laws) are to apply to a specific dispute. Normally, the laws of a certain nation, as a governing law, applies to an international dispute. Nevertheless, this does not necessarily mean that only the laws of only one nation are applicable, for different aspects of a dispute can be governed by different laws.[5]

The domestic laws of each country vary considerably. Thus, which country's laws governs a contract is critical in an international contract. For instance, most English-American laws require "consideration" for a contract to be valid and enforceable, whereas most continental laws (including German, French, Chinese, Japanese, and Korean) do not. To resolve the problem of different laws, many countries have ratified international conventions (e.g. the CISG, United Nations Convention on the Carriage of Goods by Sea (the Hamburg Rules)), and international uniform rules (e.g. UCP 600, Incoterms 2020, URDG 758, URC 522, etc.) are normally incorporated into international contracts.

The governing law governs contract enforcement, and the parties to a contract normally resort to the governing law when the other party has breached the contract. The parties' interests vary depending on the respective governing law (or applicable law). Thus, in many cases, agreeing on the governing law in the negotiation of contract terms is a very difficult process.

As the common law system has the tendency to be relatively less specific, contracts in the common law system tend to be expressed in detail, with all contingencies clearly spelled out. On the other hand, contracts in the civil law system tend to be less specific and much shorter, as many of the legal issues are already stipulated in the relevant statutory civil code. Thus, drawing up a contract in a common law jurisdiction could cost more.

---

[1] Fawcett and Carruthers (2008), p. 8.

[2] Carr (2010), p. 567.

[3] Regulation (EC) No. 593/2008 of the European Parliament and of the Council of 17 June 2008 on the law applicable to contractual obligations (Rome I).

[4] Regulation (EC) No. 864/2007 of the European Parliament and of the Council of 11 July 2007 on the law applicable to non-contractual obligations (Rome II).

[5] Fawcett and Carruthers (2008), p. 8.

2.2 Formation of a Contract

2.2.1 Requirements for the Formation of a Valid Contract

A typical process for a contract formation will be (1) request for proposal (RFP) or request for quote (RFQ), (2) offer, and (3) acceptance. A contract is concluded at the moment when an acceptance of an offer becomes effective (see Article 23 of the CISG). Once a contract is concluded, subsequent communications may be construed as proposals to modify or change the contract, and such modifications (or changes) require mutual consent.

Concluding a contract normally involves more than signing a contract. A typical process for drafting and concluding a contract will be (1) negotiating the terms and conditions of the contract, (2) drawing up the contract, (3) reviewing the contract, (4) signing the contract, and (5) executing the contract (where formal requirement for a contract is required). Where any dispute arises between the parties, reference to the contract will be the first recourse. Drafting the contract is the key to managing the various legal risks in an international trade transaction. Accordingly, it is important to draft a contract with a precise manner and careful attention.

Although completely written contracts would be best in international trade transactions, contracts can also be concluded orally or electronically. For instance, the CISG provides (Article 11): "A contract of sale need not be concluded in or evidenced by writing and is not subject to any other requirement as to form. It may be proved by any means, including witnesses."

A valid contract is formed when the following requirements are met:

- there must be an "offer";
- there must be an "acceptance" of that offer;
- *Offer and acceptance constitute an agreement.*
- there must be an intention to create a contract;
- there must be "capacity" to conclude a contract;
- *The nature of the business should be within the objectives set out in the company's articles of incorporation. Infants or mentally ill parties have no capacity to conclude a contract.*
- consent must be freely given without duress;
- consent must be given without being based on false information;
- the purpose of the contract must be "legal";
- consent must be freely given without duress;
- consent must be given without being based on false information;
- the purpose of the contract must be "legal";
- *A contract for the sale of human organs, for example, is illegal in most countries. An agreement to commit a crime is also illegal, and thus invalid.*
- there must be "consideration" (under English-American laws only).

- *Each party must provide something to the other party to meet the consideration requirement. A contract without consideration is not enforceable under English-American law.*

The requirements for a valid contract will differ in each legal system (or each national law) around the world. Sometimes local laws will apply irrespective of the governing law chosen in the contract, because the governing law in a specific dispute is finally decided by the private international law of the competent jurisdiction. Furthermore, if some provisions of the chosen law in a contract are against the public policy of the jurisdiction, the court applies its local law instead. Thus, local legal advice should be taken to ensure formation of a valid contract in an international trade transaction.

Most large trading companies have various model contracts that set standard contract terms. Each time, a model contract appropriate for the particular transaction is chosen. The expansion of international trade has brought the need for universally acceptable standard contracts of global acceptance. Most SMEs cannot seek legal advice for every contract. The International Chamber of Commerce (ICC) has published various model contracts and guides to international contracting. However, the model contracts need to be modified or changed to suit the specific circumstances and to reflect the relative bargaining powers (or commercial strengths) of the parties.

A valid contract imposes obligations and confers rights. The two main obligations in a sales contract are the delivery of goods by the seller and the payment by the buyer.

Defective contracts

- **Void contract** A void contract is totally without any legal effect from the beginning. (e.g. an agreement to commit a crime, a contract for the sale of human organs).
- **Voidable contract** A voidable contract is one that one or both parties may elect to avoid or to ratify a contract (e.g. a contract of an infant or mentally ill party).
- **Unenforceable contract** An unenforceable contract is an agreement that is otherwise valid, but that may not be enforceable due to various defenses extraneous to contract formation (e.g. a statute of limitations, lack of consideration).

2.2.2 The Process of Offer and Acceptance

In international trade transactions, a contract is basically formed by an offer and an acceptance of that offer.

An offer is a proposal to conclude a contract, and "a proposal for concluding a contract addressed to one or more specific persons constitutes an offer if it is sufficiently definite and indicates the intention of the offeror to be bound in case of acceptance" (Article 14(1) of the CISG). To be deemed an offer, a proposal must not only indicate an intention to be bound by an acceptance but also must be sufficiently definite. A proposal is sufficiently definite if it indicates the goods and expressly or implicitly fixes or makes provision for determining the quantity and the price (Article 14(1) of the CISG).

Elements of offer under the CISG
The CISG provides the concepts and elements for an "offer" in Article 14. The elements for an "offer" are:
- an offer must be for concluding a contract;
- an offeree(s) must be a specific person(s);
- an offer must be sufficiently definite;
- an offeror must be bound in case of acceptance.

When the seller offers to sell goods to the buyer, the buyer may then:
- give an acceptance without change or reservation. This constitutes an acceptance, and a contract is thus concluded. While an acceptance is normally made by written or oral statement, it may also be made by conduct that begins to perform a contract (e.g. transferring payment, delivering the goods, etc.);
- give an acceptance with modifications or conditions. This is a rejection of the offer and constitutes a counter offer, not an acceptance. This counter offer will have to be considered by the seller who may then accept the counter offer or go back with a further reoffer for the buyer to consider. Modifications or conditions relating, among other things, to the price, payment, quality, and quantity of the goods, place and time of delivery, extent of one party's liability to the other party or the settlement of disputes, are considered to be a counter offer (CISG Article 19(3)).
- reject entirely. Then the offer becomes invalid. Once a rejection is made, the offer cannot thereafter be accepted.

Elements of acceptance under the CISG

The CISG provides the concepts and elements for an "acceptance" in Article 18 and 19. The elements for an "acceptance" are:
- an acceptance can be made by a statement or by other conduct;
- an acceptance must indicate assent to an offer;

An acceptance must not include additions, limitations, or other modifications. An acceptance that contains additions, limitations, or other modifications is not an acceptance, but a rejection of an offer and constitutes a counter offer.

Once the parties reach a final agreement and sign a contract, the contract is binding upon both parties—seller and buyer. Any further amendments to the contract require the consent of both parties.

It is common for an individual agreement for a contract to be made by the use of a pro-forma invoice or purchase order instead of a complete contract.

2.2.3   Information Included in an International Sale Contract

Usually an international contract for a sale of goods includes the following:

- description of the goods;
- quantity of the goods
- contract price (and currency);
- delivery terms (including Incoterms 2020 Rules);
- time of delivery;
- payment conditions;
- inspection of the goods (and inspection requirements);
- documents;
- packing requirements;
- retention of title;
- force majeure; and
- dispute resolution; governing law, jurisdiction, litigation/arbitration.

See, for example, the ICC Model International Sale Contract.

Standard arbitration clauses

- **International Chamber of Commerce (ICC)** All Disputes arising out of or in connection with the contract shall be finally settled under the Rules of Arbitration of the International Chamber of Commerce by one or more arbitrators appointed in accordance with the said Rules.
- **London Court of International Arbitration (LCIA)** Any dispute arising out of or in connection with this contract, including any question regarding its existence, validity or termination, shall be referred to and finally resolved by arbitration under the Rules of the London Court of International Arbitration, which Rules are deemed to be incorporated by reference into this clause.
- **American Arbitration Association (AAA)**
  (1) The parties can provide for arbitration of future disputes by inserting the following clause into their contracts:
  "Any controversy or claim arising out of or relating to this contract, or the breach thereof, shall be settled by arbitration administered by the American Arbitration Association under its Commercial Arbitration Rules, and judgment on the award rendered by the arbitrator(s) may be entered in any court having jurisdiction thereof."
  (2) Arbitration of existing disputes may be accomplished by use of the following:
  "We, the undersigned parties, hereby agree to submit to arbitration administered by the American Arbitration Association under its Commercial Arbitration Rules the following Controversy: (describe briefly). We further agree that the above controversy be submitted to (one) (three) arbitrator(s). We further agree that we will faithfully observe this agreement and the rules, that we will abide by and perform any award rendered by the arbitrator(s), and that a judgment of any court having jurisdiction may be entered on the award."
- **Korean Commercial Arbitration Board (KCAB)** Any dispute arising out of or in connection with this contract shall be finally settled by arbitration in Seoul in accordance with the International Arbitration Rules of the Korean Commercial Arbitration Board and laws of Korea.

2.2.4 Ordering Process

The practical process of ordering in an international trade will usually begin with an inquiry. When the seller receives an inquiry from a foreign buyer, the seller has to determine whether the inquiry is acceptable and whether they are able to perform the forthcoming order. If it is an initial transaction with the buyer, the seller must conduct due diligence to find how creditworthy the buyer is.

The seller can send a pro-forma invoice or offer sheet as a reply to an inquiry. If so, the pro-forma invoice or offer sheet will constitute an offer in a legal sense. If the seller sends a reply to an inquiry in a form other than an offer sheet, the buyer will place an order. Where the seller receives a purchase order following an inquiry, it represents a contractual offer from a potential buyer. The seller then decides whether to accept the purchase order as submitted, to negotiate changes, or to refuse. The seller undertakes an export-costing exercise to decide whether the transaction would be commercially viable.

2.3 Performance of a Contract

2.3.1 Obligations

Once a contract is concluded and signed, the parties must comply with all the terms of the contract. If any of the terms are not complied with, there will be a breach of contract. The two main obligations in a sale contract are delivery of goods by the seller and payment by the buyer. To perform a contract, team effort is required and everyone involved must handle their parts of the transaction with care to ensure that the goods are made in accordance with the relevant contract.

2.3.2 Breach of Contract

If the parties do not perform any of the contract terms, there will be a breach of contract. Typical breaches of contract by the seller are (1) delivery of non-complying goods (e.g. inferior goods, defective goods), (2) late shipment, (3) non-delivery, and (4) failure to carry out the other obligations.

Typical breaches of contract by the buyer are (1) delayed payment, (2) non-payment, (3) market (or malicious) claims, and (4) failure to carry out the other obligations.

A breach of contract by one party usually entitles the other party (aggrieved party) to make a legal claim for any losses suffered, or damages incurred. Material (or substantial) breach entitles the other party to cancel (void) a contract. In most cases the parties will attempt to resolve the disputes by themselves. If an amicable resolution is not reached (or they do not reach mutual agreement), they will take the dispute to an arbitration or a court to recover (redress). It is said litigation (lawsuit) is generally more expensive and time-consuming than arbitration.

2.3.3 Various Examples of Contract

2.3.3.1 Complete Contract

Sales Agreement

This Agreement ("Agreement") is made this 1st day of June 2019 by and between Paris Tea Co. Ltd. with its registered office at [*address*] FRANCE ("Buyer") and Hankook Ginseng Product Co. Ltd., with its registered office at [*address*] KOREA ("Seller")

WITNESSETH

WHEREAS, the Buyer desired to purchase from the Seller and the Seller desired to sell to the Buyer the goods specified on article 1.

NOW, THEREFORE, in consideration of the premises and covenants herein contained, the parties hereto agree as follows:

Article 1. Goods, Quantity, Price, Free Sample

1.1 Unit Price and Transportation

The agreed unit price of each goods shall be based on FOB Korean port.

1.2 Free Sample and Promotional Material Only For This Time Order

The Seller provide the agreed 20% of free sample for each product to the buyer. These free samples shall be same as Table 2.2 and shipped together with Goods specified on Table 2.1 by free of charge.

Table 2.1 (Currency: Euro)

Goods	Size	Quantity	Unit price	Amount
Korean red ginseng extract	30 g × 3 bottles	1,500	13.38	20,070.00
Total	–	1,500	–	20,070.00

Table 2.2

Goods	Size	Quantity
Korean red ginseng extract	30 g × 3 bottles	300

Article 2. Payment

2.1 Currency & Payment method

Except otherwise agreed by the parties, all the payment for the Goods shall be made in Euro 20,070.00.

60% T/T: before preparing goods.

40% T/T: 120 days after arrival of goods.

2.2 Shipment

Shipment will be done within 30 days after sending 60% T/T by the Buyer.

But if possible, the Seller tries to reduce time.

2.3 Partial Air-Shipment

In the event that the Buyer request the partial air shipment, the all airfreight shall be borne by the Buyer.

Article 3. Force Majeure

The Seller shall not be responsible for non-delivery or delay in delivery resulting from causes by acts of god such as fire, flood, typhoon and earthquake or by reason of riots, strike and wars.

Article 4. Arbitration

All disputes, controversies, or differences which may arise between the parties, out of or in relation to or in connection with this contract or for the breach thereof, shall be finally settled by arbitration in Seoul, Korea in accordance with the commercial arbitration rules of the Korean Commercial Arbitration Board. The award rendered by the arbitrator(s) shall be final and binding upon both parties concerned.

Article 5. Effective Date and Term

This agreement shall become effective upon signing of the duly authorized representatives of both parties and remain in full force and effect up to 1st day of June 2020 unless terminated earlier pursuant to the written consent.

IN WITNESS WHEREOF, the parties hereto have executed this Agreement as of the day and year first above written.

By: By:
TXXX TXXX VXX   SXXX Lee

2.3.3.2   Offer Sheet

SUNGHWA CORPORATION
Exporter & Manufactures

Messrs.   Our Ref. XXXX

                                                        Seoul July 1. 2019

OFFER SHEET

We are pleased to offer the under-mentioned article(s) as per conditions and details
described as follows

Items No.	Commodity & Description	Unit	Quantity	Unit price	Amount
	100% Nylon Fabrics				
NB-1	19" length	yd	500	US$0.6	US$ 300
NB-2	20" length	yd	500	US$1.0	US$ 500
NB-3	25" length	yd	500	US$0.8.	US$ 400
NB-4	26" length	yd	500	US$0.9.	US$ 450

Delivery Term   : CFR N.Y., USA
Shipment   : Within 1 month after receipt of L/C
Shipping port   : Busan, Korea
Destination   : New York, USA
Inspection   : Maker's inspection shall be final
Origin   : Republic of Korea
Packing   : Export standard carton packing
Payment   : By irrevocable at sight L/C, in favor of us
Offer Validity   : Until end of July, 2019
Remarks   : Subject to our final confirmation

Looking forward to your valued order for the above offer, we are,

Yours Faithfully,

                                                    SUNGHWA Corp.
                                                        Seoul, Korea

                                                    CXX-SXX Kim / Director

2.3.3.3   Purchase Order

MAKS Tech (M) Sdn Bhd
(Co. No.554882-X)

No. 108A 2nd Floor, JXXX KXXX 23, Bandar Puchong Jaya
471000 Puchong, Selangor Darual Ehsan, Malaysia.
Tel No: 6 03 8070 XXXX; Fax No: 6 03 8070 XXXX; Email: vstjong@makstech.com

PURCHASE ORDER

Mobile Air-Conditioning Service Technology Co. Ltd.	Purchase Order No. PO-0202/2019
#102-107 Byeiksan Megatrium, 999, Dapsipri-dong	Your Ref No.
Dongdaemun-gu, Seoul, Korea	Date 10 September 2019
Tel No: 822-2242-XXXX	Payment Terms T/T 60 Days
Fax No: 822-2242-XXXX	Delivery Due Date December 2019
Email: ksc@mobileair.com	Contact Person Vincent ST Jong
Attn: Mr. Seok-Chang Kim	

Please enter our order as follows and return the countersigned duplicate copy to us for our reference.

Item	Qty	Description	Unit Price (USD)	Total Price (USD)
1	100	MAKS CLINIC A/C charging MC MF260 HS Code : 8421.39-9090	3,000.00	300,000.00
2	100	MAKS CLINIC A/C charging MC MF200C HS Code : 8421.39-9090	2,000.00	200,000.00
3	1,000 Box (24 packs/box)	PAG Oil Charge (PAG 64)	90 / Box	90,000.00
		(US Dollar : Five Hundred and Ninety Thousand Only)		
		TOTAL AMOUNT		590,000.00

Notes : 1. Notification of delivery must reach us before shipping.
        2. Suppliers to summit the Original Invoice c/w a copy of our Purchase Order to us.

SELLER'S CONFIRMATION   For MAKS Tech (M) Sdn Bhd

_____   _____

Signature, Stamp   Authorised Signature

2.3.3.4   Pro-Forma Invoice

♧ HANKOOK

HANKOOK PRESION INDUSTRY CO. LTD.

June 3, 2019

TMPO-19–0603–01

Name of Seller   HANKOOK PRECISION INDUSTRY CO., LTD.

Address: XXX, XXX, XXX City, Kyeonggi-Do, Korea

Contact No.:   Tel: +82–31-841-XXXX   Fax: +82-31-841-XXXX

             Mobile: +82–10–9351-XXXX

Email Address: lsm@hpi.co.kr

Name of Buyer   TEPPA MARKETING

Address: XXX, XXX, XXX City, France

Contact No.:   Tel: 33–235–196-XXX   Fax: 33–235–196-XXX

             Mobile: XX-XX-XXX-XXX

Email Address: sales@teppaarketing.com

ATTENTION: TOMMY SANCHEZ

             General Manager

**SUBJECT: BRAND NEW 1000 GALLONS CAPACITY ROAD CLEANING
TRUCK**

PROFORMA INVOICE

I. Model

Item	Specification	Qty	Unit price	Total unit price
1	**Brand new 1000 gallons capacity road cleaning truck**	100	USD 50,500	USD 5,050,000
	1,000 Gallons Capacity Road Cleaning Trucks Note: General Requirements and description of 1,000 Gallons Capacity Road Cleaning Trucks is based on the Technical Specification No. BFP-TC-2018–01 (As of December 20, 2018)			

II. Payment Terms

- Partial shipment is allowed.
- Drawdown against BL copy and Commercial Invoices
- LC shall be payable 75 days upon receive from the B/L dates.
- Required a Draft LC for confirmation before issuance of Final LC
- All charges related to any required amendment after Final LC has been issued will be for the account of whom requires to.

III. Delivery
A. Delivery commitment of the seller will commence after discussion with BFP.

IV. Bank Details
ADVISING BANK: XXX BANK XXX BRANCH
SWIFT CODE: HVBKKRSEXXX

References

Carr, Indira. (2010). *International Trade Law* (4th ed., p. 567). Abingdon, UK: Routledge-Cavendish.
Fawcett, James, & Carruthers, Janeen M. (2008). *Private International Law* (14th ed., p. 8). Oxford, U.K.: Oxford University Press.

Chapter 3
Documents for International Trade

3.1 Introduction

In international trade, the number of documents required and the nature of the documentation will vary greatly depending on the underlying contract (e.g. sales contract), the nature of the goods, the value of the cargo, the complexity of the export sale, the shipment/transport required and the rules, restrictions and trade agreements of the countries concerned.

The key documents in an international trade for goods are a contract of sale, bill of lading (or other transport document), commercial invoices, payment-related documents (a documentary credit, bill of exchange, bank guarantee, bank draft, promissory note, etc.), insurance documents, etc. The parties are required to enter into a number subsidiary agreements with, for example, transporting companies, insurance companies, and banks, depending on the respective contract of sale. An international trade transaction requires the parties to carefully manage a number of documents, and the parties should be familiar with the correct usage and potential pitfalls concerning the documents.[1]

According to the URC 522 (the Uniform Rules for Collections, 1995 Revision, ICC Publication No. 522), documents come in two types: "financial documents" and "commercial documents". The URC 522 defines financial documents and commercial documents as follows (Article 2 of the URC 522):

1. **"Financial documents"** means bills of exchange, promissory notes, cheques, or other similar instruments used for obtaining the payment of money;
2. **"Commercial documents"** means invoices, transport documents, documents of title or other similar documents, or any other documents whatsoever, not being financial documents.

---

[1] Jimenez et al. (2012).

S. M. Kim, *Payment Methods and Finance for International Trade*, https://doi.org/10.1007/978-981-15-7039-1_3

3.2 Commercial Documents

3.2.1 Transport Documents

In international trade for goods, either the seller or the buyer needs to conclude a contract for carriage with a carrier or freight forwarder. SMEs commonly prepare the shipment by a contract with a freight forwarder. A freighter books space for the cargo and, in many cases, conduct customs formalities in addition.

Where the goods are delivered to a carrier or freight forwarder, a shipper receives transport documents from the carrier or freight forwarder. Where a freight forwarder (or non-vessel-operating common carrier (NVOCC)) issues a bill of lading, the bill is in particular called a freight forwarder's bill of lading or house bill of lading. A freight forwarder (or NVOCC) plays dual positions in the transportation of the goods; a carrier to its shippers and a shipper to the vessel-operating common carrier (VOCC).

Transport documents evidence the contract of carriage, the receipt of goods, and the details of the transport. Transport documents come in two main groups: those that give title to the goods ("negotiable documents") and those that do not give title to the goods ("non-negotiable documents"). A bill of lading is a negotiable document, while an air waybill is a non-negotiable document.

3.2.1.1 Bill of Lading

A bill of lading, as a negotiable document, acts as a receipt of the goods, and confers the title to the goods by constituting the contractual rights of the holder in due course against the carrier. A bill of lading is not only an acknowledgement that the goods have been loaded on board the ship (or that the goods have been received by the carrier in a received bill of lading), but also a separate contract with the shipping company, which includes the title to the goods. The buyer cannot get access to the goods under a bill of lading without possession of this document. A bill of lading is issued by a shipping company and has negotiable status. As well as evidencing the contract of carriage terms and the receipt of goods, they provide entitlement to receive the goods.

A consignee or holder to whom the bill of lading has been endorsed can collect the goods against presentation of an original bill of lading. Banks usually require the bill of lading to be made to the bank's order, or to the shipper's order and endorsed by them, thus ensuring that either the bank or the buyer can collect the goods. The negotiable status of a bill of lading allows the goods to be sold while in transit. Bills of lading are, in practice, issued in three originals, and the number of bills of lading issued is specified on the bill of lading. Once the goods are released against one original bill of lading, the others in the set become worthless.

The seller will either (1) send the bills of lading to a foreign buyer (or his agent), or (2) present them through the banking system for collection (or for payment by documentary credit). Where the buyer does not receive the bill of lading before the goods are unloaded, the buyer may suffer demurrage charges, namely storage costs, which the buyer will seek to recover from whoever caused the delay.

Bills of lading with negotiable status are also issued as:

- "through bills of lading", such as combined transport bills of lading or multi-modal bills of lading used when goods are transported by container from an inland terminal to an export port, on to a destination port and finally to another inland terminal in an importing country. The "multi-modal transport operator" who issues a combined transport bill of lading must either sign as the agent for a named carrier or as the actual carrier;
- "liner bills of lading" for regular shipping services between two ports where the carrying vessel has a designated berth;
- "short-form bills of lading". These do not contain the full contract of carriage details. The reverse side of a bill of lading is blank and does not state shipping contract.

The bill of lading will give a general description of the cargo with the statement "XX boxes/crates shipped on board in apparently good condition". However, the shipping company may add adverse comments declaring defective condition of the goods or the packing such as "carton No. 20 split and broken". Such a bill of lading is called as a "dirty bill of lading", or a "foul bill of lading", in contrast with a "clean" bill of lading that is without such clause. The buyer and their banks will expect to receive a "clean" bill of lading, and a dirty bill of lading will normally not be accepted under a documentary credit.

3.2.1.2 Air Waybill

An air waybill is a receipt for the goods by an air carrier or agent and evidence of the contract of transport. However, an airway bill is not a document of title to the goods and, therefore, it is not a negotiable document. Air waybill should be issued in at least nine copies, of which the first three copies are classified as originals. The first copy is retained by the issuing carrier, the second copy by the consignee, and the third copy by the shipper.

The goods in the air consignment are normally consigned directly to the named consignee. Unless the goods are consigned to a third party like the issuing bank, the buyer can obtain the goods from the carrier at destination. An air consignment note may be issued instead of an air waybill.

3.2.1.3 Sea Waybill

A sea waybill describes the goods and contains a contract of carriage, but is not negotiable. A sea waybill does not evidence title to the goods. The goods will be released to the consignee specified on a sea waybill. For short duration of transportation, sea

waybills are issued since there will normally be no time for a negotiable bill of lading
to get to the buyer for prompt clearance of the goods for import.

3.2.1.4   Charter Party Bills of Lading

A charter party bills of lading is issued where the exporter has chartered a carrying
vessel. Because of the non-standard nature of the carriage contract and the potential
claims against the cargo by the ship owner if the charter is not paid for, these bills of
lading are not normally accepted as being quasi-negotiable.

3.2.1.5   Missing Bills of Lading

It often happens that the cargo arrives at an importing country before the bills of
lading are in the buyer's hands. The buyer will have received notification that the
goods are ready for collection and that failure to collect will incur demurrage charges.
     The buyer will ask a bank to issue a "letter of guarantee" (or an indemnity) to the
carrier, requesting the release of the goods and undertaking to reimburse the carrier
if the carrier suffers loss as a result of releasing the cargo without the original bill
of lading. If the bank accepts the risk of doing so, the buyer (bank's customer) will
naturally have to sign a counter indemnity agreeing to reimburse the bank if any
claim is made against the bank. The buyer will also undertake to deliver the bills of
lading to the bank when the buyer comes to have them in hand.
     If the seller is expecting to receive payment on a documentary collection or docu-
mentary credit basis, the buyer will also have to undertake to pay the collection on
receipt or accept any bill of exchange drawn on them.

3.2.2   Commercial Invoices and Other Documents

Once a contract has been entered into and shipment of the goods is ready, some of
the following documents will be required, depending on the terms of the contract
and the rules and regulations of the countries concerned.

3.2.2.1   Commercial Invoice

A commercial invoice is the bill issued by the seller to the buyer. A commercial
invoice is to be produced by the seller in accordance with the contract (and/or the pro-
forma invoice). A commercial invoice will normally be issued in the same currency
as that in the contract or the documentary credit, and contain a description of the
goods. The accuracy of a commercial invoice is of vital importance in a documentary
credit. The description of the goods in a commercial invoice must correspond with

that appearing in the documentary credit concerned (Article 18(c) of UCP 600). An English court found that "machine shelled groundnut kernels" in the commercial invoice was not the same description as "Coromandel groundnuts" in the documentary credit, although it was understood by traders that machine-shelled groundnut kernels were the same good as Coromandel groundnuts.[2]

For exports to some countries, consular invoices are required in the form laid down and signed by the appropriate official in the embassy or agency of the country concerned or customs invoices in the form laid down by the customs office in the importing country.

3.2.2.2 Packing List

A packing list is used to describe how the goods are packaged for shipment. Packing list forms are available through commercial stationers or packing companies. A packing list lists the shipper/exporter, the consignee, and the notifying party, and indicates the details of the weight, serial numbers, and markings placed on the packing. Some countries may set specific requirements for the packaging for goods. A packing list is used for filing insurance claims when there is damage or casualty to the cargo during transportation.

3.2.2.3 Certificate of Origin

A certificate of origin certifies the country in which the goods were produced or originated, or the preponderance of value that was added or manufactured. Certificates of origin are normally issued by a chamber of commerce in the exporting country, but some countries require another official body or even a consul at the port of departure to sign or issue them. In many cases, the exporter's own certification is accepted.

3.2.2.4 Inspection Certificate

An inspection certificate may be required by the rules of the importing country to ensure that goods conform to local regulations. Buyers may also call for such certificates to ensure the quality of the goods. However, inspection certificates do not guarantee that the goods inspected conform to the contract. SGS, Intertek International, Cotecna and Bureau Veritas are the most famous inspecting agencies. Inspection certificate are not mandatory, but are often required in a documentary credit transaction or between unfamiliar parties.

---

[2]*J. H. Rayner and Co. Ltd. v. Hambro's Bank, Ltd* (1943) 1 K.B. 36.

3.2.3   Specimen and Examples

3.2.3.1   Specimen Bill of Lading

3.2.3.2   Specimen Sea Waybill

1. Subject to the terms and conditions set forth herein, the Goods to be carried subject to the terms and conditions provided for in the Carrier's applicable Bill of Lading and its tariff, both of which may be inspected at the Carrier's offices or at those of his authorized agents. Every reference in the Carrier's applicable Bill of Lading and its tariff to the words "Bill(s) of Lading" shall mean "Non-negotiable Waybill(s)" and the terms and conditions thereof shall be read and construed accordingly.

2. This Non-negotiable Waybill shall have effect subject to all the provisions of the Carriage of Goods by Sea Act of the United States of America, approved April 16, 1936, or subject to the provisions of any legislation relating to the carriage of goods by sea that incorporates the Hague Rules contained in the International Convention for the Unification of Certain Rules Relating to Bills of Lading, dated the 25th August, 1924, or to similar effect, including amendments thereto dated Brussel, 23rd February 1968, as may be compulsorily applicable under the laws of the locality where the Waybill is issued or the Goods are to be delivered, as if set forth herein. The defenses and limitations of said Act or such legislation shall apply to the Goods whether carried on or under deck and before the Goods are loaded on and after they discharged from the vessel and throughout the entire time the Goods are in the actual custody of Carrier.

3. Neither the Carrier nor the ship shall in any event be or become liable for any loss or damage to or in connection with the transportaion of goods to and or from ports of the United States in an amount exceeding US $500 per package lawful money of the United States, or in case of goods not shipped in packages, per customary freight unit, or the equivalent of that sum in other currency, unless the nature and value of such goods have been declared by the shipper to the Carrier before shipment and inserted in the Non-Negotiable Waybill and extra freight and other charges paid as provided for by the Carrier's tariff.

4. In the event of any claim for loss or damage, the Carrier and the ship shall be discharged from all liability in respect of such loss or damage unless suit is brought within one year after delivery of the Goods or the date when the Goods should have been delivered.

5. (a) When the Goods are held in the Carrier's custody and only before the Consignee claims their delivery after their arrival at the place of delivery, the Shipper may request the Carrier, on production of the full sets of the Waybill and also by paying to the Carrier such reasonable remuneration as demanded by the Carrier and indemnifying him against all expenses, loss and damage which may be incurred by him by complying with such request to re-route the Goods, and to deliver the Goods to some other person than the Consignee indicated in the Waybill at any stage of the transit as well as to change the place of delivery the Goods.

   (b) However, the Carrier may refuse the above requests if the requests interfere with his normal or intended operations, or if they are not practically possible to comply with at the time when the requests reach the Carrier, or if damage or substantial inconvenience would be caused to him or to Consigness of other consignments.

   (c) Notwithstanding paragraph 5 (a) above, the Shipper may make an irrevocable declaration in writing to the Carrier that the Consignee will make, in place of the Shipper, those requests stipulated in paragraph 5(a) to the Carrier; and if the Carrier thereafter comply with such requests, the

3.2.3.3   Specimen Air Waybill

Shipper's Name and Address	Shipper's Account Number	Not negotiable Air Waybill issued by	KOREAN AIR
		Copies 1, 2 and 3 of this Air Waybill are originals and have the same validity	
Consignee's Name and Address	Consignee's Account Number	It is agreed that the goods described herein are accepted in apparent good order and condition (except as noted) for carriage SUBJECT TO THE CONDITIONS OF CONTRACT ON THE REVERSE HEREOF. THE SHIPPER'S ATTENTION IS DRAWN TO THE NOTICE CONCERNING CARRIER'S LIMITATION OF LIABILITY. Shipper may increase such limitation of liability by declaring a higher value for carriage and paying a supplemental charge if required.	
Telephone :			
Issuing Carrier's Agent Name and City			
		Accounting Information	
Agent's IATA Code	Account No.		

Airport of Departure(Addr. of First Carrier) and Requested Routing														
TO	By First Carrier	Routing and Destination	to	by	to	by	Currency	CHGS Code	WT/VAL PPD COLL	Other PPD COLL	Declared Value for Carriage	Declared Value for Customs		

Airport of Destination	Flight/Date	For Carrier Use Only	Flight/Date	Amount of Insurance	INSURANCE-If Carrier offers Insurance, and such insurance is requested in accordance with conditions on reverse hereof, indicate amount to be insured in figures in box marked 'amount of Insurance'.

Handling Information

No. of Pieces RCP	Gross Weight	kg lb	Rate Class		Chargeable Weight	Rate	Charge	Total	Nature and Quantity of Goods (incl. Dimensions or Volume)
			Commodity Item No.						

Prepaid	Weight Charge	Collect	Other Charges
	Valuation Charge		
	Tax		
	Total Other Charges Due Agent		Shipper certifies that the particulars on the face hereof are correct and that insofar as any part of the consignment contains dangerous goods, such part is properly described by name and is in proper condition for carriage by air according to the applicable Dangerous Goods Regulations.
	Total Other Charges Due Carrier		
			Signature of Shipper or his Agent
Total Prepaid		Total Collect	
Currency Conversion Rates		CC Charges in Dest. Currency	
			Executed on(date) at(place) Signature of Issuing Carrier or its Agent
For Carrier's Use Only at Destination	Charges at Destination	Total Collect Charges	

ORIGINAL 3(FOR SHIPPER)

3.2.3.4   Commercial Invoice Example 1

COMMERCIAL INVOICE

	Issue Date & No. of Invoice
Shipper / Export HANKOOK GINSENG PRODUCTS CO. LTD XXX XXX-RO XXX-GU XXX-SI XXX-DO REPUBLIC OF KOREA	January 21, 2019 Kone-190121-02 **T/T** 30% T/T : before preparing goods 30% T/T : sending by buyer before 11th February, 2019 40% T/T : 2 months after arrival of goods
Consignee XXX TEA CO. LTD. ○○ XXX XXX PARIS FRANCE	**Notify** LXXX VXXX(att Silvana) Tel:XXXX Rue de XXXX - BP 38 xxx@lxxvxx.fr
Remarks FOB KOREAN PORT	**Applicant** XXX TEA CO. LTD. ○○ XXX XXX PARIS FRANCE
Port of Loading BUSAN PORT, SOUTH KOREA	**Final Destination** LE HAVRE PORT, FRANCE
Carrier XX BREMERHAVEN 0012W	**Departure Date** January 29, 2019

Marks	Description	Quantity (BOX)	Unit Price (EUR)	Total Amout (EUR)
	KOREAN RED GINSENG EXTRACT 30g × 3 bottles(wooden box)	1,500	13.20	19,800
	Promotional Items			
	KOREAN RED GINSENG EXTRACT 30g × 3 bottles(wooden box)	300	0.90	270
	GROSS TOTAL	1,800	EUR	20,070
	Gross Total Amount		EUR	20,070

XXXX GINSENG PRODUCTS CO. LTD.

(SIGNATURE)

SXXX WXXX, KIM PRESIDENT

3.2.3.5   Commercial Invoice Example 2

COMMERCIAL INVOICE

① Shipper/Seller SXXX CORP. 13 JONG-RO, JONGRO-GU SEOUL, KOREA	⑧ Invoice No. & Date 191012 OCT. 20, 2019
	⑨ L/C No. & Date 266001LC190821 OCT 10, 2019
② Consignee QXXX CO., LTD. A20 No.8, XIANGGANG ROAD CENTRAL QUINDAO CHINA	⑩ L/C Issuing Bank XXX BANK
③ Nortify Party QXXX CO., LTD. A20 No.8, XIANGGANG ROAD CENTRAL QUINDAO CHINA	⑪ Remarks: CONTRACT NO. QXXX 190721

④ Port of Loading PUSAN, KOREA	⑤ Final Destination QUINDAO CHINA	
⑥ Carrier XIANG XXX V 8070	⑦ Sailing on or about OCT. 20, 2019	

⑫ Marks and number of packages	⑬ Description of Goods	⑭ Quantity/Unit	⑮ Unit-price	⑯ Amount
				⑰ CIF QINGDAO
N/M SEA FROZEN POLLOCK H AND G		535..018 MT	@$1,555	USD 831,952.99 SIZE : 25CM UP
	PACKING : 2 × 11KG/BAGS OF EXPORT STANDARD PACKING			

⑱ C.P.O. Box :
   Cable Address   :
   TEL   :
   FAX   :   ⑲ Signed By :

3.2.3.6   Packing List Example

PACKING LIST

① Shipper/Seller SXXX CORP. 13 JONG-RO, JONGRO-GU SEOUL, KOREA		⑧ Invoice No. & Date 191012 OCT. 20, 2019	
② Consignee QXXX CO, LTD. A20 No.8, XIANGGANG ROAD CENTRAL QUINDAO CHINA		⑨ Remarks: L/C NO : 266001LC190821 OCT 10, 2019 ISSUING BANK : XXX BANK	
③ Notify Party QXXX CO., LTD. A20 No.8, XIANGGANG ROAD CENTRAL QUINDAO CHINA			
④ Port of Loading PUSAN, KOREA	⑤ Final Destination QUINDAO CHINA		
⑥ Carrier XIANG XXX V 8070	⑦ Sailing on or about OCT. 20, 2019		

⑩ Marks and number of packages	⑪ Description of Goods	⑫ Quantity	⑬ Net-Weight	⑭ Gross-Weight	⑮ Mearsurement
N/M	SEA FROZEN POLLOCK H AND G SIZE : 25CM UP	535..018 MT	535,018 KGs	547,000 KGS	1,302.380 CBM
	PACKING : 2 × 11KG/BAGS OF EXPORT STANDARD PACKING				

TEL :
FAX :   Signed By :

3.3   Financial Documents

3.3.1   Bill of Exchange (Documentary Draft)

A bill of exchange (or a documentary draft) (see Fig. 3.1), is a convenient method of collecting debts internationally with a special status recognized in many jurisdictions. A bill of exchange can be defined in short as an unconditional order in writing to pay a certain money.

The Bills of Exchange Act 1882 (England) defines a "bill of exchange" as an *unconditional* order *in writing*, addressed by one person to another, signed by the person giving it, requiring the person to whom it is addressed to pay on demand or at a fixed or determinable future time a sum certain in money to or to the order of a specified person, or to bearer.

Each of these elements needs explanation:

(1) "unconditional" means that no conditions are allowed. A bill with a clause such as "If the cars are shipped by October 20, the payment will be made" is not a valid bill of exchange. Such a bill could be a mere promise or contract rather than a bill of exchange;

(2) "in writing" includes hand-writing, typewriter, and printing;

(3) in "addressed by one person", one person refers to a drawer;

(4) in "to another", "person" is omitted after "another". Thus the complete expression will be "to another person". "Another person" refers to a drawee who is to make the payment. Where a drawee "accepts" the obligation to pay a bill of exchange by signing the bill on its face with the word "accepted" (the mere signature of the drawee without additional words (i.e. "accepted") is sufficient), they will become the "acceptor" and then are legally obliged to pay (Sect. 17);

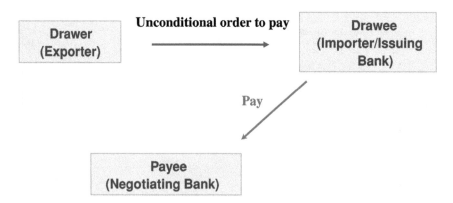

Fig. 3.1 Bill of exchange in international trade

Bills of Exchange Act 1882 (England)

3 Bill of exchange defined.

(1) A bill of exchange is an unconditional order in writing, addressed by one person to another, signed by the person giving it, requiring the person to whom it is addressed to pay on demand or at a fixed or determinable future time a sum certain in money to or to the order of a specified person, or to bearer.

(2) An instrument which does not comply with these conditions, or which orders any act to be done in addition to the payment of money, is not a bill of exchange.

(3) An order to pay out of a particular fund is not unconditional within the meaning of this section; but an unqualified order to pay, coupled with (a) an indication of a particular fund out of which the drawee is to reimburse himself or a particular account to be debited with the amount, or (b) a statement of the transaction which gives rise to the bill, is unconditional.

(4) A bill is not invalid by reason—

> (a) That it is not dated;
> (b) That it does not specify the value given, or that any value has been given therefor;
> (c) That it does not specify the place where it is drawn or the place where it is payable.

(5) "on demand or at a fixed or determinable future time" means either (a) to pay immediately (to pay at sight), or (b) to pay at a fixed future time (i.e. pay on December 1), or (c) to pay at a determinable future time (i.e. 60 days from bill of lading date of October 1);

(6) "a sum certain in money" means that the value of the bill should be fixed money, and that something other than money cannot be the payment;

(7) "to or to the order of a specified person or to bearer" means that the payee is stated in either (a) to a specified person (i.e. "to ABC Co."), or (b) to the order of a specified person (i.e. "to the order of ABC Co."), or (c) to a bearer (i.e. "to a bearer" or "to a holder").

The Bills of Exchange Act 1882 has many sections dealing with the liabilities of each party to a bill of exchange. In general, any party who signs a bill as a drawer, acceptor or endorser is legally liable to pay or recourse unless they add the words "without recourse" by their signature.

The respective responsibilities and liabilities of each party are as follow:

- **The drawer.** The drawer undertakes that a sight bill of exchange will be paid on demand, and that a term bill of exchange will be accepted and paid at maturity. In principle, to preserve the drawer's undertaking, the bill of exchange must be noted and protested if unpaid or not accepted. (section 48, 51)

- **The drawee/acceptor.** The drawee has no liability on a bill of exchange itself until they accept the bill. When they accept a bill of exchange, the drawee becomes an acceptor who is primarily liable to pay. (section 17)
- **Endorser (or indorser).** By indorsing a bill, the endorser undertakes that the acceptor will pay any other "holder in due course". The endorser takes a position similar to the drawer, and is to pay the bill in case of dishonor by the acceptor.
- **Holder.** A holder in due course has the right to demand payment on a bill of exchange against the acceptor. If the acceptor refuses to accept or fails to pay, a holder in due course can recourse to the drawee or endorsor. A "holder in due course" means a person or business that has acquired the bill of exchange for value and in good faith. The main duty of a holder is to present a bill promptly for acceptance and/or payment and to note and protest in case of non-acceptance or non-payment. Non-acceptance or non-payment must be immediately notified to the drawer or endorser to retain the recourse right.

In an international trade transaction, a drawer in a bill of exchange (or a draft) is normally the seller seeking to collect money, and a drawee is normally the buyer (or the issuing bank in a documentary credit transaction). For negotiation (or discount) of the receivables including the shipping documents, a drawer (seller) normally makes a bill of exchange payable to a negotiating bank. However, a drawer (seller) can also make a bill payable to themselves.

Bills of exchange are normally issued in sets. The Bills of Exchange Act 1882 provides that "where a bill is drawn in a set, each part of the set being numbered, and containing a reference to the other parts the whole of the parts constitute one bill" (Sect. 71).

However, if inadvertently a drawee accepts both bills in a set, a third party holder could claim payment. The parties need to be careful that only one bill in a set is in circulation. A bill of exchange in an international trade transaction looks like the examples in Fig. 3.2.

A bill of exchange is independent from the underlying contract or transaction (e.g. a sale contract, a documentary credit) under which it is drawn. Therefore, a holder in due course (a holder who takes a bill in good faith and for value) takes it free from any defect in the title regardless of any disputes out of the underlying contract. In principle, a bill of exchange is a "negotiable instrument" unless specifically stated not to be. The status of negotiable instruments is recognized in most countries.

No. 1 Bill of exchange

---

① BILL OF EXCHANGE

NO. ② __2019070101__   DATE __③ July 1, 2019__   ④ Seoul Korea
FOR ⑤ **US$2,000,000**
AT ⑥ **90 DAYS AFTER B/L July 1, 2019** OF ⑦ **THIS FIRST** BILL OF EXCHANGE (⑧ **SECOND**
OF THE SAME TENOR AND DATE BEING UNPAID) PAY TO ⑨ KOREA EXCHANGE BANK
OR ORDER THE SUM OF ⑤ **SAY US DOLLARS TWO MILLION ONLY**
⑩ VALUE RECEIVED AND CHARGE THE SAME TO ACCOUNT OF __⑪ KUHDA__
ELECTRONICS (INDIA) PVT. LTD. B-140, PHASE-12, NEW DELHI-110020   DRAWN
UNDER ⑫ **INDIAN FOREIGN BANK, F-57, JANPATH NEW DELHI**
L/C NO. ⑬ **XXXXXX**   dated ⑭ **May 20, 2019**
TO ⑮ **INDIAN FOREIGN BANK**   ⑯ **DONG-A PLASTIC CO., LTD.**
           F-57, JANPATH NEW DELHI   *ChulSooKim*
                                                              CHUL-SOO KIM
                                                              PRESIDENT

No. 2 Bill of exchange

---

① BILL OF EXCHANGE

NO. ② __2019070101__   DATE __③ July 1, 2019__   ④ Seoul Korea
FOR ⑤ **US$2,000,000**
AT ⑥ **90 DAYS AFTER B/L July 1, 2019** OF ⑦ **THIS SECOND** BILL OF EXCHANGE (⑧ **FIRST**
OF THE SAME TENOR AND DATE BEING UNPAID) PAY TO ⑨ KOREA EXCHANGE BANK
OR ORDER THE SUM OF ⑤ **SAY US DOLLARS TWO MILLION ONLY**
⑩ VALUE RECEIVED AND CHARGE THE SAME TO ACCOUNT OF __⑪ KUHDA__
ELECTRONICS (INDIA) PVT. LTD. B-140, PHASE-12, NEW DELHI-110020   DRAWN
UNDER ⑫ **INDIAN FOREIGN BANK, F-57, JANPATH NEW DELHI**
L/C NO. ⑬ **XXXXXX**   dated ⑭ **May 20, 2019**
TO ⑮ **INDIAN FOREIGN BANK**   ⑯ **DONG-A PLASTIC CO., LTD.**
           F-57, JANPATH NEW DELHI   *ChulSooKim*
                                                              CHUL-SOO KIM
                                                              PRESIDENT

---

① Title.
② Bill of exchange no.
③ Date of issue.
④ Place of issue.
⑤ Amount of bill.
⑥ Maturity date.
⑦-⑧ Two bills are issued.
⑨ Payee: A negotiating bank will be normally a payee, but the drawee itself can
   be a payee:
   – order bill: Pay to XXX Bank Or Order, Pay to the order of XXX Bank
   – named bill: Pay to XXX Bank
   – bearer bill: Pay to Bearer.
⑩ Bill of exchange can be used as a receipt that the payee duly received the
   payment.
⑪ Accountee (account party). In a documentary credit transaction, the applicant
   (buyer) will be an accountee.
⑫-⑭ Underlying contract: The underlying contract could be either a sale contract
   or a documentary credit transaction.
⑮ Drawee: The drawee will be the buyer in documentary collection, while it will
   be an issuing bank in a documentary credit transaction.
⑯ Drawer: The drawer will be the seller (creditor).

Fig. 3.2 Examples of bill of exchange in international trade

The **US Uniform Commercial Code (UCC)** defines "negotiable instrument" as follows (§ 3–104):

"negotiable instrument" means an unconditional promise or order to pay a fixed amount of money, with or without interest or other charges described in the promise or order, if it:
>   (1) is payable to bearer or to order at the time it is issued or first comes into possession of a holder;
>   (2) is payable on demand or at a definite time; and
>   (3) does not state any other undertaking or instruction by the person promising or ordering payment to do any act in addition to the payment of money, but the promise or order may contain (i) an undertaking or power to give, maintain, or protect collateral to secure payment, (ii) an authorization or power to the holder to confess judgment or realize on or dispose of collateral, or (iii) a waiver of the benefit of any law intended for the advantage or protection of an obligor.

A bill of exchange may be (1) payable on demand in trade, or may be (2) payable on some future date (or on a specified future date). A draft payable at sight is called as "sight bill" or "sight draft", while a draft payable on some future date (or on a specified future date) is called a "time bill", "time draft", "date draft", "term bill", or "term draft". A sight bill is payable on the presentation of a bill to the drawee and, therefore, the issue of acceptance does not arise.

A sight bill (or sight draft) is used in a sight payment sale, while a time bill (or time draft) is used in a credit sale. A time bill gives the drawee the time for payment after acceptance of a bill. At maturity the bill will be presented for payment to the drawee (acceptor). The bank handling a bill on behalf of the seller may act as follows:

- A negotiating bank may negotiate (or discount) the bill by paying the seller immediately the negotiated amount (face value less discount). The discount includes interest for the period between payment and the maturity date, and some other charges.
- A collecting bank may first obtain the drawee's acceptance, and then hold the bill until maturity and present the bill for payment at maturity. The payment is made at maturity, and then the collecting bank remits the money to the seller.

Drawer and drawee in a check

In the US Uniform Commercial Code – Article 3 Negotiable Instruments, a draft includes a check other than a documentary draft (a bill of exchange). Thus, a cheque is also a form of draft. But in a check, the drawer has a debt to pay to the payee and the drawee is the drawer's depositary bank (i.e. the buyer will be a drawer, while the seller will be a payee and the buyer's depositary bank will be a drawee.) Therefore, in a check, the drawer is the debtor, not the creditor, and the drawee (drawer's depositary bank) is not the debtor. The drawee, drawer's depositary bank will pay the check out of the drawer's deposit, not the bank's own money.

3.3.2 Promissory Note

A promissory note (see Fig. 3.3) is also a negotiable instrument similar to a bill of exchange except that it involves only two parties: maker and payee. A promissory note can be shortly defined as "an unconditional promise in writing to pay a certain money". The Bills of Exchange Act 1882 (England) defines a promissory note as an unconditional *promise* in writing *made* by one person to another signed by *the maker*, engaging to pay, on demand or at a fixed or determinable future time, a sum certain in money, to, or to the order of, a specified person or to bearer.

Promissory notes are widely used as debt instruments where a debtor (or buyer, borrower) issues a promissory note promising to pay the creditor (or seller, lender) on the specified due date.

Bills of Exchange Act 1882 (England)

83 Promissory note defined

(1) A promissory note is an unconditional promise in writing made by one person to another signed by the maker, engaging to pay, on demand or at a fixed or determinable future time, a sum certain in money, to, or to the order of, a specified person or to bearer.

(2) An instrument in the form of a note payable to maker's order is not a note within the meaning of this section unless and until it is indorsed by the maker.

(3) A note is not invalid by reason only that it contains also a pledge of collateral security with authority to sell or dispose thereof.

(4) A note which is, or on the face of it purports to be, both made and payable within the British Islands is an inland note. Any other note is a foreign note.

The US Uniform Commercial Code (UCC) defines "note" as follows (§ 3–104):
(e) An instrument is a "note" if it is a promise and is a draft if it is an order.

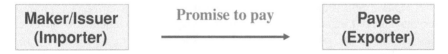

Fig. 3.3 Promissory note in international trade

Example of a promissory note

PROMISSORY NOTE

Place of issue:
Date of issue:
Value:
Issuer:

For value received, we, ABC Co. with Commercial Registration number ---------- as the issuer, unconditionally and irrevocably undertake to pay to the order of [PAYEE] the sum of US$ [   ] on demand.

The holder may obtain recourse without notice of non-payment or without protest of non-payment.

Signature of Authorized Representative of Issuer:
[NAME]

For and on behalf of

[STAMP]

3.3.3   Payment of Bill of Exchange and Promissory Note

Bills of exchange and promissory notes payable at sight must be presented promptly for payment. Time bills must be presented promptly for acceptance, and time bills must be also presented on the due date for payment.

If either a bill of exchange is not accepted or paid at maturity, or a promissory note is not paid at maturity, then special procedures are required to "note" or "protest" non-payment to preserve the holder's legal rights to recourse under the Bills of Exchange Act 1882 (England). Non-payment or non-acceptance must be immediately notified to the drawer and endorser(s) to retain their "undertakings" or "guarantees", and this procedure is called "notice (or note)". Failure to advise the drawer or endorser(s) of non-acceptance/non-payment, without a good excuse, will mean that the "guarantee(s)" of the drawer and endorser(s) are potentially discharged. Under the Bill of Exchange Act 1882 of England, when a bill has been dishonored by non-acceptance or by non-payment, notice of dishonor must be given to the drawer and each indorser, and any drawer or indorser to whom such notice is not given may be discharged (section 48).

References

Jimenez (2012). *ICC Guide to Export/Import: Global Standards for International Trade*, 4th ed., ICC Publication No. 686, Paris, France, p. 23.
J.H. Rayner and Co. Ltd. v. Hambro's Bank, Ltd. [1943] 1 K.B. 36.

Chapter 4
Overview of Payment Methods

4.1 Introduction

This chapter outlines payments in international trade, and basic methods of payment. This chapter provides a case study (or various payment clauses in international trade contracts) for the respective methods of payment.

In international trade, it is important to ensure payment from overseas buyers. The method of payment determines how payment from overseas buyers is secured. Companies run businesses to make profits and to increase the value of the companies. Profit is achieved through business activity. A sale is not a sale until payment is made, and a sale without payment would be no more than a gift. The profit is the revenue achieved by the company minus the expenditure incurred. The revenue, however, will not be achieved without payment.

International trade plays a very important role in the global economy as well as in the domestic economy. International trade is one of the best business activities to increase profit because the global market is much bigger than the domestic market.

An international trade transaction is not completed until an importer receives the goods and an exporter gets paid. An international trade transaction is completed only when the parties have each respectively performed the contractual obligations. An exporter is concerned about the payment, while an importer is concerned about the delivery of goods. Once an international sale contract is entered into, the goods must be shipped and the payment collected. The ultimate goal for each export transaction is getting paid in full and on time.

How can we secure payment in international trade? There is no simple answer. How to secure payment depends largely on the selection of a payment method. Although international trade is considered to bring more risks than domestic trade, there are numerous reliable payment methods, such as letters of credit, cash in advance, payment guarantees, etc. Payment for international trade, and finance and global banking for international trade, have evolved to the point where international trade is safe and efficient.

© The Editor(s) (if applicable) and The Author(s), under exclusive license   51
to Springer Nature Singapore Pte Ltd. 2021
S. M. Kim, *Payment Methods and Finance for International Trade*,
https://doi.org/10.1007/978-981-15-7039-1_4

The payment terms are among the most important factors in an international trade contract. The payment terms influence the cash management and finance for international trade transactions. As the advantages for the respective parties of each of the payment terms are quite distinct, the negotiation process for the payment terms is one of the most difficult processes in an international trade transaction.

The ability to allow a longer period of payment has become a major competitive factor in negotiations from the seller's perspective, because the terms of such credits are mostly to the advantage of the buyer. As a consequence, demand for longer periods of payment and more advantageous terms for the buyer has increased.

Table 4.1 Basic methods of payments

Category	Methods of payment
Payment in advance	Payment in advance • Cash in advance, payment before delivery
Open account	Open account (O/A) • Cash in arrears, T/T usance
Documentary collection	Documents against payment (D/P) • sight draft, cash against documents
	Documents against acceptance (D/A) • time draft, cash against acceptance
Documentary credit	Sight credit
	Deferred payment credit
	Acceptance credit
	Negotiation credit
Other methods	Bank payment obligation (BPO)
	Consignment
	Netting
(Other classification)	
By the technical means of payment	Telegraphic transfer (T/T) (wire transfer, bank transfer) • advance remittance • later remittance
	Credit card
	Electronic payment
	Demand draft (D/D) or check
	Mail transfer (M/T)
By the time of payment	Advance payment (Payment in advance)
	Concurrent payment • D/P (documents against payment) • CAD (cash against documents) • COD (cash on delivery)
	Deferred payment (Payment in arrears)

It is required to develop professional and undisputed terms in a contract. Accordingly, it is of great importance for both buyer and seller to know how to structure practical terms in a transaction. In practice, this often means that during negotiations the seller must be willing and able to compromise on the terms of payment. In this regard, it is important to understand the various methods of payment.

For the successful negotiation of the payment terms, the parties need to take reasonable and equal consideration of the demands of the other party. Each party needs to know how to structure the practical payment terms. In most cases, the seller must be able to compromise on terms of payment. To that end, it is important to understand the various methods of payment.

In the negotiation process for the payment terms, the seller should know the minimum requirements for the time and method of payment (i.e. when payment should be made and how payment should be made). The buyer may request the seller to offer a credit transaction instead of a cash transaction, whereas the seller would prefer cash payment or payment in advance. They should negotiate on when the payment will be made. How payment should be made depends on the banks' roles.

4.2 Basic Types of Payment Method

"How the seller gets paid by an overseas buyer" means the "method of payment". The method of payment determines:

- how payment is going to be made;
- when payment is going to be made;
- the obligations of the parties concerned; and
- The bank's role in international trade.

The methods of payment in international trade in reality do not differ from those used in domestic trade. Methods of payment can be classified into various categories by the methods or by the time. The four primary methods of payment in international trade are[1]:

- payment in advance (cash in advance);
- open account (cash in arrears, T/T usance);
- documentary collection (bank collection, bills for collection); and
- documentary credit (letter of credit).

The payment methods other than the four primary methods of payment would be[2]:

- consignment;

---

[1]Donnelly (2010), p. 79, Anders (2014), p. 33, Collyer (2007), pp. 22–23; Jimenez (2012), pp. 109–110.
[2]US Commercial Services (2015), p. 161; Seyoum (2009), pp. 239–240, US Department of Commerce/International Trade Administration (2012), p. 3, Hennah (2013).

- netting;
- bank payment obligation (BPO);
- open account backed by standby letter of credit (L/C) or bank guarantee;[3]
- electronic payment.

Five basic methods of payment used today, categorized by how the payment is actually made and by the role of the parties and the banks, are:[4]

Table 4.2 The definition of the respective methods of payment

Payment in advance	Payment is made before delivery of the goods.
Open account	The seller ships the goods to the buyer and sends the shipping documents directly to the buyer, and the buyer will pay in the future.
Documentary collection	The seller entrusts the collection of the payment to its bank ("remitting bank") by providing collection documents and a collection form, which will send the documents to the buyer's bank ("collecting bank") with a collection instruction to release the documents to the buyer against payment or against acceptance of a draft. In a documentary collection, the buyer should either pay or accept a draft before it gains the documents to take delivery of goods.
Documentary credit	A documentary credit is basically a definite undertaking (or guarantee) of an issuing bank to pay if the documents presented complies with the terms and conditions of the credit. An issuing bank will pay a beneficiary, if the documents presented complies with the terms and conditions of the credit
Bank payment obligation	A bank payment obligation (BPO) is an irrevocable and independent undertaking of an obligor bank to pay (or incur a deferred payment obligation and pay at maturity) a specified amount to a recipient bank following submission of all data sets required by an established baseline resulting in a data match or an acceptance of a data mismatch
Consignment	An exporter sends the goods to an importer (or foreign distributor) on a deferred payment basis, and the importer does not pay for the goods until it is sold to a third party Payment is sent to the seller only after the goods have been sold by the foreign distributor to the end customer. The foreign distributor receives, manages, and sells the goods for the exporter who retains title to the goods until they are sold
Netting	In a netting, the seller ships goods to their warehouse located in an importing country, and the buyer takes goods from the warehouse from time to time at this time. And the delivery of goods takes place at the time the buyer takes the goods from the warehouse Payment is made after the buyer takes the goods from the seller's warehouse located in an importing country to sell in the domestic market. A netting is basically on a credit transaction, and normally the payment date is set at a future date on which the goods are sold in an importing country

---

[3] Jimenez, Guillermo C. (2012), p. 112.
[4] Grath, Anders (2014), pp. 34–35.

- bank transfer (also referred to as bank remittance, telegraphic transfer);
- credit card;
- check payment;
- documentary collection (also called bank collection);
- letter of credit (also called documentary credits).

Mail transfer would fall into one of these methods of payment. However, it is no longer used today since the SWIFT system was introduced in 1973.

Documentary collection comes in two types:

- documents against payment (sometimes referred to as sight draft[5] or cash against documents[6]);
- documents against acceptance (sometimes referred to as time draft,[7] trade acceptance, or cash against acceptance[8]).

Documentary credit appears in four basic forms[9] (UCP 600 Article 6(b), UCP 500 Article 10(a)):

- sight credit (or sight L/C). (A draft may or may not be used in a sight letter of credit.);
- deferred payment credit (or deferred payment L/C). (A draft is not used in a deferred payment credit.);
- acceptance credit (or acceptance L/C). (A draft is used in an acceptance credit.);[10]
- negotiation credit (or negotiation L/C). (A draft may or may not be used in a negotiation credit. A negotiation credit may be payable at sight or at usance. In a negotiation credit, drafts must be drawn on a bank other than a negotiating bank.)

Article 10[11] of the UCP 500 more clearly stipulates four types of documentary credit (sight payment credit, deferred payment credit, acceptance credit, and negotiation credit.)

The methods of payment classified by time of payment would be:

- advance payment (payment in advance);
- concurrent payment;
- deferred payment (payment in arrears).

Each payment method has strengths and weaknesses for the respective parties, which would be completely distinct for the other party's perspective. The degree of risk is dependent on the method of payment.[12] A payment in advance and an

---

[5]US Commercial Services (2015), p. 161.

[6]US Department of Commerce/International Trade Administration (2012), p. 9.

[7]US Commercial Services (2015), p. 162.

[8]US Department of Commerce/International Trade Administration (2012), p. 9.

[9]Adodo, Ebenezer (2014), p. 99; Adodo, Ebenezer (2009), p. 618.

[10]Ebenezer Adodo (2014), p. 99.

[11]Article 10 Types of Credit: a. All Credits must clearly indicate whether they are available by sight payment, by deferred payment, by acceptance or by negotiation.

[12]Carr (2010), p. 463.

open account are very simple, easy to use and inexpensive. However, a payment in advance is very risky for the buyer, and an open account is very risky for the seller. A documentary credit (letter of credit) is a secure payment method for the seller and is somewhat fair both for the seller and the buyer, but it is expensive and complicated.

The ICC Banking Commission finally accepted the Uniform Rules for Bank Payment Obligations in July 2013. The fact that the ICC Banking Commission has accepted the Uniform Rules for Bank Payment Obligations means that the 'bank payment obligation' has officially been admitted and accepted as one of the payment methods in international trades. The US Department of Commerce sees "consignment" to be a method of payment. Therefore, the main payment methods in international trade could be payment in advance (cash in advance), open account, documentary collection, documentary credit, bank payment obligation, and consignment.

How payment should be made can be divided into two main categories: "clean payment" and "documentary payment". Clean payment means that the buyer must pay according to a contract after receiving the seller's invoice. Clean payments are primarily used in an open account. Documentary payments are divided into (1) documentary collections (when the buyer has to pay or accept a bill of exchange to obtain access to the documents for collection) and (2) documentary credits (where the seller is also guaranteed payment by an issuing bank.

In the following chapters, we will discuss the respective methods of payment in much greater detail.

The basic methods of payment can be listed as follows in security (safety) order (in safety order) for an exporter;[13] the order will be quite the opposite for an importer:

- payment in advance;
- documentary credit;
- bank payment obligation;
- documentary collection;
- open account;
- consignment.

---

[13]Grath, Anders (2014), pp. 32–34; US Commercial Services (2015), p. 3.

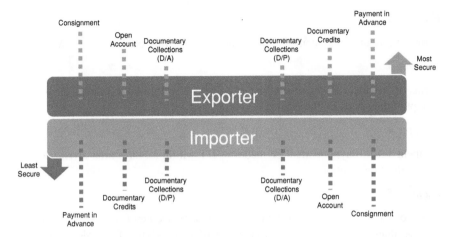

Fig. 4.1 The order of payment terms risk[14]

4.3 Case Study for Respective Methods of Payment

4.3.1 Payment in Advance (Cash in Advance)

Example 1

Payment Term: Payment shall be made within 30 days from the contract date.

Example 2

Article 2. Payment
    2.1 Currency & Payment method
    Except otherwise agreed by the parties, all the payment for the Goods shall be made in EURO 20,00.00.
    60% T/T: before preparing goods. ☞ *cash in advance*
    40% T/T: 120 days after arrival of goods. ☞ *open account.*

4.3.2 Open Account

Example 1

Terms of Payment: Payment shall be made by O/A (T/T) within 60 days after B/L date.

---

[14]US Department of Commerce/International Trade Administration (2012), p. 3; Seyoum, Belay (2009), p. 240

Example 2

Terms of Payment: Payment shall be made by T/T within 60 days after AWB date.

Example 3

Terms of Payment: Payment shall be made by T/T within 60 days after the date of receipt of the goods by the Buyer.

Example 4

Payment Term: Payment shall be made by T/T within 30 days after arrival date of the goods at destination.

Example 5

Terms of Payment: Payment shall be made by open account (T/T) immediately but not later than 3 days after the date of delivery of the goods to a forwarder designated by the Buyer.

4.3.3   Documentary Collection

Example 1

Terms of Payment: Payment shall be made by D/P collection subject to Uniform Rules for Collections, ICC Publication No. 522.

Example 2

Payment Term: Payment shall be made by D/A collection bill payable at 90 days after B/L (AWB) date, subject to ICC URC 522.

Example 3

Payment Term: Payment shall be made by D/A collection bill payable at 90 days after sight, subject to ICC URC 522.

Example 4

Article 4. Payment

4.1 The standard payment for the Goods shall be made in United States Dollars by D/A payment in favour of the Seller. The seller should issue Proforma Invoice with the payment term of D/A 90 days from the B/L date.

4.1.1 The payment currency for the shipment destined Artenius Hellas would be EURO. Both parties would settle final price with USD-EUR conversion rate on the shipment date. Temporary price for the shipment in P/I will be calculated by temporary conversion rate near the date of P/I issuing.

Example 5

    8. TERMS OF PAYMENT: D/A 60 DAYS FROM B/L DATE.
    9. DELIVERY TERMS: CIF ANTWERPEN, BELGIUM.
    10. CONTRACT PRICE: EUR 500,000.
    11. DESCRIPTION: MICRO FIBER GOODS.

Example 6

Terms of Payment: D/A 90 Days after sight.

4.3.4   Documentary Credit

Example 1

Payment: By a Documentary Letter of Credit at 60 days after sight in seller's favour

Example 2

Terms of Payment: By an irrevocable letter of credit at sight.

Example 3

Payment: Drafts to be drawn at 60 days from B/L date under an irrevocable letter of credit.

Example 4

Payment: By confirmed irrevocable letter of credit available against a sight draft.

Example 5

Terms of Payment: 100% irrevocable confirmed letter of credit at sight.

Example 6

Article 4. Payment
    Except otherwise agreed by both parties in written agreement, all the payment for the Goods shall be made in US Dollars either by Cash in advance or an irrevocable letter of credit at sight in favor of the Seller.
    4.4.5 Choosing between alternatives payment methods
    The ICC Model International Sale Contract: Manufactured Goods

A-7	PAYMENT CONDITIONS (ART. 5)

□ **Payment on open account (art. 5.1)**

Time for payment (if different from art. 5.1) __ days from date of invoice. Other ___

   □ Open account backed by demand guarantee or standby letter of credit (art. 5.6)

□ **Payment in advance (art. 5.2)**

       Date (if different from art. 5.2): _____

       □ Total price

       □ __ % of the price; remaining amount ___ % to be paid at _____

       □ Payment in advance backed by advance payment bond

□ **Documentary collection (art. 5.4)**

       □ D/P Documents against payment

       □ D/A Documents against acceptance

□ **Irrevocable documentary credit (art. 5.3)**

       □ Confirmed

       □ Unconfirmed

Place of issue (if applicable): _____ Place of confirmation (if applicable): ___

Credit available   Partial shipments: Transhipment:

□ At sight   ____ Allowed   _____ Allowed

□ By deferred payment at: ____ days ____ Not allowed _____ Not allowed

□ By acceptance of draft at: ____ days

□ By negotiation

Date on which the documentary credit must be notified to seller (if different from art. 5.3)

    _____ days before date of shipment   other: _____

□ **Irrevocable Bank Payment Obligation (art. 5.5)**

   □ Settlement by Payment

     □ Settlement by Deferred Payment Undertaking and payment at maturity.

   Deferred payment terms _____ days after sight or after date of _____

Date on which the Bank Payment Obligation must be notified to seller (if different from art. 5.5)

   _____ days before date of shipment   other:_____

□ **Other:** _____

(e.g. cheque, bank draft, electronic funds transfer to designated bank account of seller)

Seller's Bank Details

IBAN/bank account number: _____

BIC/Swift code: _____

References

Donnelly, Michele (2010), *Certificate in International Trade and Finance*, ifs School of Finance, Cantebury, U.K., p. 79; Grath, Anders (2014), *The Handbook of International Trade and Finance*, 3rd ed., Kogan Page, London, U.K., p. 33; Collyer, Gary (2007), *The Guide to Documentary Credits*, 3rd ed., ifs School of Finance, Cantebury, U.K., pp. 22–23; Jimenez, Guillermo C. (2012), *ICC Guide to Export/Import: Global Standards for International Trade*, 4th ed., ICC Publication No. 686, Paris, France, pp. 109–110.

US Commercial Services (2015), *A Basic Guide to Exporting*, 11th ed., US Commercial Services, Washington D.C., USA, p. 161; Seyoum, Belay (2009), *Export-Import Theory, Practices, and Procedures*, 2nd ed., Routledge, New York, USA, pp. 239–240; US Department of Commerce/International Trade Administration (2012), *Trade Finance Guide: A Quick Reference for US Exporters*, US Department of Commerce, Washington D.C., USA, p. 3; Hennah, David J. (2013), *The ICC Guide to the Uniform Rules for Bank Payment Obligations*, ICC Publication No. 751E, Paris, France.

Jimenez, Guillermo C. (2012), *ICC Guide to Export/Import: Global Standards for International Trade*, 4th ed., ICC Publication No. 686, Paris, France, p. 112.

Grath, Anders. (2014). *The Handbook of International Trade and Finance* (3rd ed., pp. 34–35). London, U.K.: Kogan Page.

US Commercial Services. (2015b). *A Basic Guide to Exporting* (11th ed., p. 161). US Commercial Services: Washington D.C.

US Department of Commerce/International Trade Administration. (2012a). *Trade Finance Guide: A Quick Reference for US Exporters* (p. 9). US Department of Commerce: Washington D.C.

US Commercial Services. (2015c). *A Basic Guide to Exporting* (11th ed., p. 162). US Commercial Services: Washington D.C., USA.

US Department of Commerce/International Trade Administration. (2012b). *Trade Finance Guide: A Quick Reference for US Exporters* (p. 9). US Department of Commerce: Washington D.C., USA.

Adodo, Ebenezer (2014), Letters of Credit: The Law and Practice of Compliance, Oxford University Press, Oxford, U.K., p. 99; Adodo, Ebenezer. (2009). *Establishing Purchase of Documents under a Negotiation Letter of Credit* (p. 618). Sing: J. Legal Stud.

Adodo, Ebenezer. (2014). *Letters of Credit: The Law and Practice of Compliance* (p. 99). Oxford, U.K.: Oxford University Press.

Carr, Indira. (2010). *International Trade Law* (4th ed., p. 463). Routledge-Cavendish, Abingdon: U.K.

Grath, Anders (2014), *The Handbook of International Trade and Finance*, 3rd ed., Kogan Page, London, U.K., pp. 32–34; US Commercial Services (2015), *A Basic Guide to Exporting*, 11th ed., US Commercial Services, Washington D.C., p. 3.

US Department of Commerce/International Trade Administration (2012), Trade Finance Guide: A Quick Reference for US Exporters, US Department of Commerce, Washington D.C., USA, p. 3; Seyoum, Belay. (2009). *Export-Import Theory, Practices, and Procedures* (2nd ed., p. 240). USA: Routledge, New York.

Chapter 5
Payment in Advance (Cash in Advance)

5.1 Introduction

In a "payment in advance" (also referred to as a "cash in advance") transaction, the seller gets paid before "delivery of goods"[1] (e.g. shipment of goods, arrival of goods, etc.). Payment in advance requires the buyer to pay prior to the delivery of the goods.

Payment in advance is the most favorable and advantageous method of payment for the seller. Payment in advance is also the most secure and least risky payment method for the seller. The seller does not assume risk of non-payment and/or risk of delays in payment because payment is a precondition to the delivery of the goods (and mostly a precondition to shipment).

Every seller prefers payment in advance. From the seller's point of view, receiving payment prior to the delivery (or shipment) might seem ideal as it eliminates all risks related with non-payment, and the seller has also immediate use of the payment. Payment in advance, however, is the least advantageous for the buyer. Payment in advance brings the highest risk to the buyer as the buyer is wholly dependent on the seller shipping the correct goods in accordance with the contract. The buyer is often concerned that the goods may not be sent at all if payment is made in advance, and also that he will take the delivery of correct goods. All the risks will be borne by the buyer. Hence, every buyer loathes payment in advance, and finds payment in advance unacceptable.

Payment in advance is very little used in international trade as the international trade market is very competitive. Most buyers find payment in advance totally unacceptable, except in some limited cases. It is used for products of high demand, unique products, small orders (such as spare parts), first orders, etc.

---

[1] What "delivery of goods" means is dependent upon "delivery terms" in the respective contract for sale. "Delivery terms" in a contract for sale is expressed by the Incoterms Rules (Incoterms 2020 came into force on January 1, 2020). In case of FOB, CFR, or CIF, the goods are delivered when the goods are on board the vessel (see Incoterms 2020).

© The Editor(s) (if applicable) and The Author(s), under exclusive license
to Springer Nature Singapore Pte Ltd. 2021
S. M. Kim, *Payment Methods and Finance for International Trade*,
https://doi.org/10.1007/978-981-15-7039-1_5

Fig. 5.1 Flow of payment in advance

A partial advance payment (e.g. 10–30%) may be more acceptable to the buyer and therefore more realistic, but leaves the seller exposed to the risk on the remaining balance. Full payment in advance occurs when the seller's products are in extremely high demand and a foreign buyer or an importing country are not a priority for the exporter.[2] Sellers relying on payment in advance terms are not likely to obtain large market shares. Sellers who insist on payment in advance as their sole payment method may lose out to competitors who are willing to offer more attractive payment terms.

5.2 Operation of a Payment in Advance

With the payment in advance method, the seller can eliminate the risk of non-payment since payment is received prior to delivery (or transfer of ownership) of the goods (see Fig. 5.1).

In payment in advance, the seller is relieved of collection problems and can immediately use the payment. On the other hand, payment in advance tends to create cash flow problems for the buyer as they have to borrow or prepare the funds for payment before they receive the goods and can sell the goods for money.

There are, at large, four technical methods in a payment in advance: by telegraphic transfer (or wire transfer, bank transfer), by credit card, by check, or by electronic payment. Telegraphic transfer (also known as wire transfer) is the most commonly used for payment in advance, and credit cards are also commonly used in small transactions.

The payment in a "payment in advance" transaction can be also made via documentary credit, such as under a "red clause" letter of credit.

5.2.1 Telegraphic Transfer (Bank Transfer, Wire Transfer)

International telegraphic transfer (also known as "wire transfer", or "bank transfer") is almost immediate and easy and, therefore, commonly used for international

---

[2]Jimenez (2012).

payment. It is also among the most secure and preferred technical methods in a payment in advance as well as in an open account. An exporter should provide clear routing instructions to an importer when using this method, including the receiving bank's name, address, SWIFT[3] code, routing number as well as exporter's name, address, and bank account number. The fee for an international telegraphic transfer can be paid by a sender (or importer) or it can be deducted from the receiver's (exporter's) account. Therefore, the parties should make sure who is to pay the transferring fee.

5.2.2 Credit Card

Exporters who sell directly to foreign buyers may select credit cards, especially for small consumer goods transactions. Exporters should check with their credit card companies for specific rules on international use of credit cards. Although exporters must tolerate the fees charged by credit card companies, credit cards may help the volume of sales grow because of their convenience and wide acceptance.

5.2.3 Payment by Check

Payment in advance by check using a check drawn on the importer's account and mailed to the exporter will result in a lengthy collection delay of perhaps several weeks. Therefore, this method may defeat the original intention of receiving payment before shipment. Moreover, if shipment is made before the check is collected, there is a risk that the check may be returned due to insufficient funds in the importer's account or even because of a stop-payment order by the importer. Therefore, payment by check, which was once common before telegraphic transfer was introduced, is not much used in international trade transactions.

5.2.4 Electronic Payment

Electronic payment is a way of paying for transactions by using an electronic payment system or medium, without the use of cash. The development of various electronic payment systems have facilitated the acceptance of electronic payment. The increase of internet based banking and commerce have also increased the use of electronic payment. Electronic payment is often used in small international trade transactions by replacing the use of credit card.

---

[3]SWIFT (Society for Worldwide Interbank Financial Telecommunication): established in Belgium in 1973.

5.3 Advantages/Disadvantages

5.3.1 Advantages/Disadvantages

Payment in advance is the most favorable and advantageous method of payment for the seller. Payment in advance is also the most secure and least risky payment method for the seller. The seller does not assume risk of non-payment and/or risk of delays in payment. The seller is relieved of collection problems and can immediately make use of the payment.

The buyer would be concerned that the goods may not be sent at all, or that he would not receive correct goods. Payment in advance tends to create cash flow problems for the buyer as they may have to borrow or prepare the money for payment before they sell the goods and prepare the funds for payment. Payment in advance is the most disadvantageous for the buyer, and brings the highest risk to the buyer. All the risks will be borne by the buyer.

Foreign buyers in developing markets may find it necessary to pay in advance in order to obtain high-demand or luxury goods. Creditworthy foreign buyers, who prefer greater and better cash utilization, will find payment in advance unacceptable and may stop the transaction.

5.3.2 When to Use Payment in Advance

Payment in advance is not common in international trade as the international trade market is very competitive. Payment in advance is used in very limited circumstances, namely:

- products in high demand;
- unique products, not available elsewhere;
- small orders (such as spare parts);
- the importer is a new customer (first order);
- the importer has a less-established operating history;
- the importer's creditworthiness is doubtful, unsatisfactory, or unverifiable;
- the political and commercial risks of the importer's home country are very high.

Payment in advance is recommended for use in the seller's market or in high-risk trade relationships. The seller requires payment in advance when the creditworthiness of an overseas buyer is low or unacceptable, and/or the country risk of an importing country is unstable.

The amount of payment in a payment in advance transaction varies, but a partial advance payment (e.g. 10–30% of the contract price)[4] may be more acceptable to the buyer and therefore more realistic. Where part payment is made in advance, the

---

[4]Bertrams (2013).

balance will be paid in the future by one of the other methods of payment. In an overseas construction or an export of capital goods, down payment of a minimum of 15–30% of the contract is the international practice. The OECD "Arrangement on Officially Supported Export Credits"[5] requires that the subject of official support is to make downpayments of a minimum of 15% of the contract value.

The OECD Arrangement on Officially Supported Export Credits.

10. Down Payment, Maximum Official Support and Local Costs

(a) The Participants shall require purchasers of goods and services which are the subject of official support to make down payments of a minimum of 15% of the export contract value at or before the starting point of credit as defined in Annex XV. For the assessment of down payments, the export contract value may be reduced proportionally if the transaction includes goods and services from a third country which are not officially supported. Financing/insurance of 100% of the premium is permissible. Premium may or may not be included in the export contract value. Retention payments made after the starting point of credit are not regarded as down payment in this context.

References

Bertrams, R. F. (2013). *Bank guarantees in international trade* (4th ed., p. 39). Netherlands: Kluwer Law International, Hague.
Jimenez, G. C. (2012). *ICC guide to export/import: Global standards for international trade* (4th ed., p. 112). ICC Publication No. 686, Paris, France.

---

[5]The Arrangement applies to all official support provided by or on behalf of a government for export of goods and/or services, including financial leases, which have a repayment term of two years or more. The Arrangement applies to the export of capital goods, overseas construction, shipbuilding contract, etc., but does not apply to sale of consumer goods.

Chapter 6
Open Account

6.1 Introduction

In an open account transaction, the seller ships (or delivers) goods and sends the shipping documents including invoice directly (not using a banking system) to the buyer without receiving payment, and the buyer will pay at a future due date. The seller extends credit to the buyer by allowing them to pay in arrears.

An open account transaction allows a foreign buyer to make payments at some future date, and the buyer does not issue any negotiable instrument evidencing his legal commitment to pay at the appointed time. These terms are most common when the buyer has a strong credit history and is well-known to the seller.

An "open account" is conceptually the opposite of a "payment in advance". In an open account transaction, the seller delivers goods without any guarantee or security for payment—such as bills of exchange, documentary credits, or payment guarantees—and therefore, they are relying on the buyer's payment at a future due date. Once the seller ships goods and sends bills of lading to the buyer, they cannot get the goods back. The seller loses all control of the goods and relies on the buyer to pay at due date.

The only recourse in case of non-payment is taking legal action against the buyer, which is a time-consuming and expensive process. An open account is well used when the buyer has a long and favorable payment record or is creditworthy.[1] The most practical method to mitigate the risks associated with an open account would be conducting a thorough credit investigation and credit evaluation of the buyer, and purchasing export credit insurance from an export credit agency (ECA) in an exporting country.

Although an open account is very risky to the seller, it is the most common payment method in international trade as the international trade market is very competitive and tends to be a buyer's market. Many buyers often press sellers for open account

---

[1] US Commercial Services (2015), p. 162.

payment terms. Therefore, sellers who do not offer open account terms will lose out to their competitors and will not take a lot of market share. An open account transaction is very simple, easy to use, and inexpensive. An open account can be a convenient payment method if the buyer has a good payment record and is reliable.

The expressions that indicate the existence of an open account in a sale contract are "T/T 60 Days from B/L date", "O/A (or T/T) 90 Days from B/L date", "Wire Transfer 60 Days from B/L date" etc.

6.2   Operation of an Open Account

In an open account transaction (see Fig. 6.1), the seller ships goods according to a contract for sale and sends shipping documents directly to the buyer, and the buyer will pay in the future. The seller delivers goods to the buyer without receiving payment or any other legally binding security (such as a bill of exchange, payment

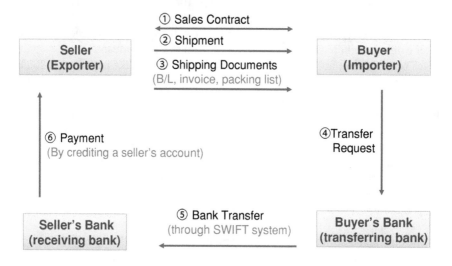

① The seller and buyer conclude a contract for sale, for which the payment method is an open account.
② The seller ships the goods according to a contract for sale.
③ The seller sends shipping documents (transport document (bill of lading or air waybill), invoice, packing list) directly to the buyer.
④ The buyer simply instructs its bank to transfer the amount by depositing funds or by debiting his account. This is the same as a normal bank transfer in domestic trade transactions.
⑤ The buyer's bank transfers funds to the seller's bank by crediting the seller's bank account or by debiting their account with the seller's bank.
⑥ The seller's bank gives the funds to the seller by crediting the seller's account with the bank.

Fig. 6.1   Flow of open account

guarantee, documentary credit) at the time of delivery, and the buyer is expected to pay in the future (typically 30, 60, or 90 days later).

An open account is a very simple and convenient payment method. The bank's role is limited to transferring the money to the seller at the request of the buyer. An open account is the most common payment method in international trade transactions. Shipping documents are sent directly to the buyer, not through the banking system. The shipping documents usually include a bill of lading (or other transport document, such as air waybill, sea waybill), invoice, packing list, certificate of origin, insurance policy etc., but not a bill of exchange (a documentary draft). The shipping documents required under an open account transaction must be clearly stated in a contract for sale.

Once the buyer receives the shipping documents, the buyer will take the goods with the shipping document. The buyer will check the goods upon taking delivery of them, and raise a claim in case of any breach of a contract, such as non-conformity of the goods or defective goods. Typical forms of claim would be replacement of defective goods, reduction of price, or refusal of payment. In case of a fundamental breach of a contract, the buyer is entitled to terminate a contract.

- Fundamental breach

"A breach of contract committed by one of the parties is fundamental if it results in such detriment to the other party as substantially to deprive him of what he is entitled to expect under the contract, unless the party in breach did not foresee and a reasonable person of the same kind in the same circumstances would not have foreseen such a result". (Article 25 of the CISG).

In the absence of breach of a contract, the buyer will sell the goods in the domestic market, and pay the seller with the funds from the sale in the domestic market. The buyer will transfer the payment by telegraphic transfer (bank transfer). The buyer can conduct an import transaction without working capital (or without using his own working capital). On the other hand, the seller has to use his own working capital, which may bring cash flow problems to the seller. The seller will try to make use of trade finance techniques, such as negotiation or factoring, by selling the account receivable to financial institutions. However, such trade finance techniques are not easy to acquire, because the payment from the buyer is not secured. An open account is the most disadvantageous to the seller, while it is most advantageous to the buyer.

If goods are shipped by sea, bills of lading will be sent directly to the buyer. Once the seller sends the draft of lading to the buyer, he cannot get the draft of lading or the goods back. If goods are shipped by air, then the buyer will be a consignee of an air waybill (i.e. the goods will be consigned directly to the buyer). The seller will lose all control of the goods and rely on the buyer to pay at a future due date.

6.3 Features and Advantages/Disadvantages

6.3.1 Features (Comparison with a Documentary Collection)

The seller sends shipping documents directly to the buyer, and the buyer will pay at a future due date. A bill of exchange (or documentary draft) is not issued. The bank's role is very limited: purely transferring funds to the seller by telegraphic transfer (e.g. SWIFT) at the request of the buyer. The bank does not send shipping documents on behalf of the seller, does not collect money from the buyer, and does not guarantee payment. Therefore, an open account is considered an inexpensive, convenient, and fast method of payment.

The features of an open account can be better understood by comparison with a documentary collection. The seller sends shipping documents directly to the buyer in an open account, while the seller sends shipping documents through the banking system (with the assistance of a remitting bank, a collecting bank, or a presenting bank) to the buyer in a documentary collection. In an open account, the bank's role is limited to transferring funds to the seller by telegraphic transfer, while in a documentary collection the bank's role is one of sending and presenting shipping documents and collecting payment from the buyer (i.e. presenting and releasing shipping documents to the buyer against payment or acceptance of a draft, collecting money from the buyer, and transferring funds to the seller.). A bill of exchange (documentary draft) is not used in an open account, while it is used in a documentary collection.

6.3.2 Advantages and Disadvantages

In an open account, goods will be sent to the buyer, the payment will be due sometime in the future, and all the risks will be borne by the seller. An open account is considered as the most disadvantageous for the seller, while it is considered as the most advantageous for the buyer.

The disadvantages for the seller would be as follow:

- The seller will lose control of goods without payment.
- The seller will lose control of goods without security for payment, such as a bill of exchange (a documentary draft), promissory note, payment guarantee, documentary credit.
- The seller can hardly use trade finance techniques such as negotiation, factoring, or forfaiting.
- The seller will suffer cash flow problem.
- The seller has to pursue collection abroad in case of non-payment.
- The seller may not get paid by reason of market claim by the buyer.

The advantages for the buyer would be as follow:

- The buyer will be relieved of cash flow problem.
- The buyer has time to inspect goods before payment.
- The buyer can save costs, such as the letter of credit issuing fee, collection fee etc.

In return for offering an open account, and to set-off those disadvantages, the seller needs to try to acquire better contract conditions—such as a higher contract price, large sales volume, better delivery terms etc.

An open account is not a well-balanced payment method for the parties, because it is the most disadvantageous for the seller and the most advantageous for the buyer. However, an open account is the most widely used payment method in international trade. So, why is the open account nowadays widely used in international trade? The answer would be:

- Credit information and country information are much more reliable, and much easier to get.
- The global market is very competitive today, much to the benefit of the buyer.
- Most sellers offer open account simply to meet the competition.
- Export credit insurance against commercial risks and political risks is available.

Reference

US Commercial Services. (2015). *A basic guide to exporting*, 11th ed., US Commercial Services, Washington D.C., USA, p. 162

Chapter 7
Documentary Collection

7.1 Introduction

A documentary collection (also sometimes referred to as a "bank collection",[1] or a "bill for collection"[2]) is a payment method whereby the seller entrusts the collection of payment to its bank ("remitting bank") by providing collection documents and a collection form, which will forward those documents to the buyer's bank ("collecting bank') with a collection instruction to release the documents to the buyer against payment or against acceptance of a documentary draft (bill of exchange).

In a documentary collection, the seller ships goods and sends the collection documents (e.g. bill of lading, commercial invoice, packing list, bill of exchange) and the draft to the buyer through the banking system, and the buyer pay the draft. In a documentary collection, the seller does not send the draft and the documents directly to the buyer. Rather, the seller will request their bank to send the draft and the collection documents through the banking channel for the purpose of collecting the payment from the buyer.

In a documentary collection, the seller's bank and the buyer's bank assist by forwarding documents to the buyer against payment or against acceptance of the drafts, and by transferring payment to the seller. In a documentary collection, the seller does not send shipping documents directly to the buyer. Instead, the seller sends them via a remitting bank and the collecting bank. This is big difference to an open account, where the seller sends shipping documents directly to the buyer.

---

[1] Grath (2014), p. 47.
[2] Bishop (2006), p. 17.

© The Editor(s) (if applicable) and The Author(s), under exclusive license
to Springer Nature Singapore Pte Ltd. 2021
S. M. Kim, *Payment Methods and Finance for International Trade*,
https://doi.org/10.1007/978-981-15-7039-1_7

A documentary collection involves a bill of exchange (a documentary draft), of which the face value the buyer is to pay at sight or at a specified future date. A draft payable at sight is called a sight bill (or sight draft), while a draft payable at a specified future date is called a time bill (or time draft, term bill). The buyer should either pay a sight bill or accept a time bill before it gains the shipping documents to take delivery of goods.

Payment (or acceptance) of the draft is obtained from the buyer in exchange for the shipping documents, and the payment will be remitted to the seller through a banking system. A documentary collection is also referred to as a "bank collection" as a bank will collect payment from the buyer.

A documentary collection comes in two forms, "documents against payment" (D/P) and "documents against acceptance" (D/A);

- In a documents against payment, the collecting bank releases shipping documents to the buyer against payment of a bill of exchange (namely sight bill), and the collecting bank will remit the payment to the seller through the remitting bank. As the collecting bank will hold the documents unless the buyer pays a bill of exchange, the seller will not lose control of goods without payment. A documents against payment could be considered as concurrent payment (or simultaneous payment) because the documents (including transport document, title to the goods) are exchanged for payment simultaneously.
- In a documents against acceptance, the collecting bank releases the documents to the buyer against acceptance of a bill of exchange (namely time bill), and the buyer will pay the bill of exchange on a specified future date. When a collecting bank receives payment from the buyer on the future due date, they will remit the payment to the seller through the remitting bank. Therefore, the seller loses control of the documents and the goods in exchange for an accepted bill of exchange only. It may happen that the seller loses goods without receiving payment. A documents against acceptance could be considered as deferred payment because payment is made at a future date long after the documents are released to the buyer.

A documentary collection is governed by the Uniform Rules for Collections (URC 522) and all collection forms and/or collection instructions thus bear reference to the URC 522.

Under the URC 522 (Article 2(a)), "collection" means the handling by banks of documents in accordance with collection instructions received, in order to:

- obtain payment and/or acceptance; or
- deliver documents against payment and/or against acceptance; or
- deliver documents on other terms and conditions.

In a documentary collection, neither the remitting bank nor the collecting bank undertakes to pay the seller. The remitting bank's role is purely forwarding the documents to the collecting bank for collection, and the collecting bank's role is to present the documents to the buyer for collection of payment. A documentary collection involves no guarantee for payment. However, a documentary collection is considered a more secure alternative than an open account in that it involves a draft that is to be accepted by the buyer prior to the release of documents. Once a draft is negotiated to a third party (i.e. a negotiating bank), the buyer is not allowed to raise any claim out of an underlying contract for sale. The buyer's payment obligation under a documentary draft is not affected by the underlying contract for sale, and is independent of the underlying contract for sale.

7.2 Operation of a Documentary Collection

7.2.1 Overview

In a documentary collection, the seller entrusts the collection of the payment to its bank (the "remitting bank") by providing collection documents (including shipping documents and documentary drafts) and a collection form, which will forward those documents to the buyer's bank (the "collecting bank") with a collection instruction to release the documents to the buyer against payment or against acceptance of a documentary draft (bill of exchange).

The seller and the buyer would first agree on the payment method of a documentary collection. The sale contract must clearly describe a payment method of either documents against payment or documents against acceptance. The sales contract must specify the documents required. The documents required will vary depending on the respective contract for sale. The documents usually include transport documents (bill of lading or air waybill), commercial invoices, packing lists, inspection certificates, bill of exchange, etc.

As aforementioned, a documentary collection comes in two types: "documents against payment" and "documents against acceptance". Most of the procedures are common to the two types, except that the documents are released "against payment" of a draft in a documents against payment, while the documents are released "against acceptance" of a draft and payment is made at a future date in a documents against acceptance.

7.2.2 Parties to a Documentary Collection

In a documentary collection, the principal (the seller) entrusts the collection of the payment to the remitting bank (the seller's bank) by providing collection documents and a collection form. The remitting bank forwards those documents to the collecting bank (the buyer's bank) with a collection instruction, and the collecting bank (the presenting bank) presents the collection documents to a drawee (the buyer) against payment of a draft (in D/P) or against acceptance of a draft (in D/A).

The main parties to a documentary collection are the principal (the seller), the remitting bank (the seller's bank), the collecting bank (the buyer's bank), the presenting bank (the buyer's bank, normally the same as the collecting bank), and the drawee (buyer):

- **The principal** is the party entrusting the handling of the collection to the bank and is normally the seller.
- **The remitting bank** is the bank to which the principal has entrusted the handling of the collection. The remitting bank is the seller's bank based in the exporting country and acts as the agent of the principal.
- **The collecting bank** is any bank other than the remitting bank involved in processing the collection. The collecting bank will normally present the documents to the drawee for collection, in which case the collecting bank is called the presenting bank. The collecting bank is the buyer's bank based in the importing county and is normally a correspondent bank of the remitting bank. The collecting bank acts as the agent of the remitting bank.
- **The presenting bank** is the collecting bank making presentation to the drawee. The presenting bank notifies the drawee of the arrival of the collection and requests payment. The collecting and presenting bank is normally one and the same, but does not have to be.
- **The drawee** is the party to whom the presentation for collection is to be made in accordance with the collection instruction. The drawee is normally the buyer in a documentary collection.

The remitting bank acts for the seller as per the instruction given by the seller, and acts as an agent of the seller. The remitting bank will firstly examine what has been received. Once the remitting bank receives the documents, it will inspect the documents to find whether the documents conform to the collection instruction form. In case of conformance, they will entrust the collection of payment to the collecting bank by forwarding the documents. In most cases, the seller requests the remitting bank, instead of making a collection request, to negotiate (or purchase) the draft together with the documents in order to cash the draft for working capital. When the remitting bank decides to negotiate the draft, they will become the negotiating bank as well.

The negotiating bank will make sure of both the assurance of the payment from the buyer and of the refund by the seller prior to deciding on negotiation (purchase). However, in practice, it is thoroughly dependent upon the seller's creditworthiness whether or not the negotiating bank will negotiate the draft, because negotiation is the purchase of the draft with recourse and the negotiating bank thus treats negotiation as a contingent liability of the seller.

The collecting bank acts as per the instruction by the remitting bank, and acts as an agent of the remitting bank. On receipt of the collection instruction and the documents from the remitting bank, the collecting bank will firstly examine what has been received. The collecting bank will check the collection instruction form and make sure that the documents attached are as described in the collection instruction form. The collecting bank is chosen by the buyer, and may well have a banking relationship with the buyer. However, the collecting bank is acting as an agent for the remitting bank, not for the buyer nor for the seller. The collecting bank, therefore, owes the remitting bank the duty of an agent, and this duty overrides any duty to the buyer (collecting bank's customer).

The remitting bank or the collecting bank must look to the collection instruction form for instructions only, not to the documents themselves (URC 522 Article 4a ii). In principle, banks participating in a documentary collection are not responsible for the genuineness or validity of the documents. Once the collecting bank receives the documents with the collection instruction, they will then contact the buyer and inform the buyer of the arrival of the documents. What happens next depends upon the types of documentary collection (i.e. documents against payment and documents against acceptance).

In a documents against payment that is accompanied by a sight bill (sight draft), the documents will be exchanged for payment of the draft by the buyer. However, in a documents against acceptance that is accompanied by a time bill (time draft), the documents will be exchanged for acceptance of a draft by the buyer. In either case, the buyer is allowed to examine the documents at the bank, and will pay or accept a draft where the documents conform to the sales contract.

Once a draft is accepted, the collecting bank must inform the remitting bank of the acceptance. And once payment is received from the buyer, the collecting bank will transfer the money less any charges to the remitting bank or as per the instruction.

7.2.3 Documents Against Payment

In a documents against payment (D/P) (see Fig. 7.1), the seller entrusts the collection of the payment to the remitting bank by providing the documents (e.g. transport document, commercial invoice, packing list, bill of exchange) and together with a collection/negotiation instruction, and the remitting bank also forwards the documents to the collecting bank together with a collection instruction to release the documents to the buyer against payment of the bill of exchange (documentary draft).[3]

When the collecting bank receives the documents and the collection instruction, they will notify the buyer of the arrival of the documents and request the buyer pay the amount as instructed by the remitting bank. A document against payment collection is also referred to as a "sight draft", as a sight draft is involved.

The documents will be released only after the buyer pays the draft. The documents will be exchanged for payment. The documents will not be released unless payment is made. The seller will not lose the goods unless the payment is made. Therefore, a documents against payment is normally used when the seller wishes to retain title to the goods until payment has been made.

A documents against payment could be considered as concurrent payment (or simultaneous payment) because the documents (including transport document, title

---

[3]US Commercial Services (2015), p. 161.

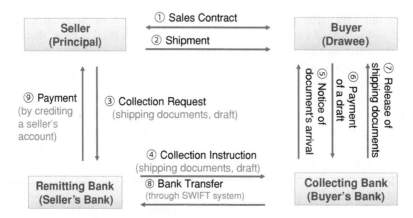

① The seller and buyer enter into a sale contract under which the payment terms is a documents against payment.

②The seller prepares the goods by manufacturing, or by procuring in a domestic market, or by using the goods in stock. The seller ships the goods according to the shipment terms in the sale contract, and obtains transport documents from the shipping company.

③ The seller prepares all the documents required under the sale contract, including sight drafts, and obtains the collection/negotiation instruction form from the remitting bank. The seller entrusts the collection of the payment to the remitting bank by providing the documents, including sight drafts and the collection/negotiation instruction form filled out. The remitting bank checks the documents and the collection/negotiation instruction form to make sure that the documents conform to the collection instruction.

④ The remitting bank sends the documents and, together with the collection instruction (the collecting bank's collection instruction form filled out by the remitting bank), to the collecting bank to entrust the collection of the payment.

⑤ The collecting bank (the collecting bank that makes such a presentation is called the "presenting bank") notifies the buyer of the arrival of the documents and requests payment of the draft.

⑥The buyer (the drawee) checks the documents and makes payment (pays the draft) if the documents conform to the sale contract.

⑦ The collecting bank releases the documents in exchange for the payment from the buyer.

⑧The collecting bank transfers the payment to the remitting bank as per the instruction.

⑨The remitting bank transfers the payment to the seller, normally by crediting the amount of payment to the seller's account.

Fig. 7.1 Documents against payment

to the goods) are exchanged for payment simultaneously. However, there is still some risk to a documents against payment. For example, the buyer's ability or willingness to pay might change between the time of shipment and the time of presentation of the documents for payment. In that case, the seller has to ship the goods back to their country at their cost or to dispose of the goods at a lower price. Moreover, the buyer's payment obligation is not backed up by any security such as a bank guarantee.

The buyer will take delivery of the goods by using the transport documents that are obtained in exchange for payment. Therefore, the bill of lading must be properly endorsed to the buyer by the seller or consigned to the buyer.

7.2.4 Documents Against Acceptance

In a document against acceptance (D/A) (see Fig. 7.2), the seller entrusts the collection of the payment to the remitting bank by providing the documents (e.g. transport document, commercial invoice, packing list, bill of exchange) and, together with a collection/negotiation instruction, and the remitting bank also forwards the documents to the collecting bank together with the collection instruction to release the documents to the buyer against acceptance of the bill of exchange (documentary draft) and to collect payment at maturity.

When the collecting bank receives the documents and the collection instruction, they will notify the buyer of the arrival of the documents, and request the buyer accept a time bill (time draft) and to pay the time bill at maturity. A document against acceptance collection is also referred to as a "time draft" (or time bill, term draft), as a time draft (or time bill, term draft) is involved.

The shipping documents will be released only after the buyer accepts the time bill, not when the buyer pays the bill. The shipping documents will be released to the buyer without payment. Therefore, a documents against acceptance is normally used when the seller extends credit to the buyer and the buyer wishes to take delivery of the goods without making payment at the time of delivery. Therefore, it is probable that the seller will lose the goods without payment if the buyer fails to make payment at maturity.

The seller's risk worsens by handing over the documents against acceptance of a draft instead of payment, and the seller is dependent upon the buyer's ability to pay the draft at a later stage. A documents against acceptance brings more risk to the seller than a documents against payment. Like a documents against payment, the buyer's payment obligation is not backed up by any security such as a bank guarantee.

The buyer will take delivery of the goods by using the transport documents that are obtained in exchanged for acceptance of the draft. Therefore, the bill of lading must be properly endorsed to the buyer by the seller or consigned to the buyer. The collecting bank keeps the accepted draft until maturity, and present the draft to the buyer for collection of payment at maturity. The buyer will make payment with the funds they earned from the sale of the imported goods in the importing country.

82   7 Documentary Collection

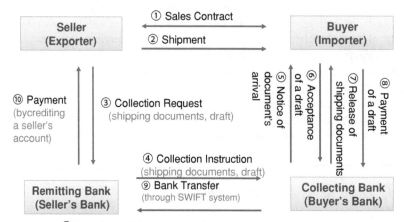

① The seller and the buyer enter into a sale contract under which the payment terms is a documents against acceptance.

② The seller prepares the goods by manufacturing, or procuring in the domestic market, or using the goods in stock. The seller ships the goods according to the shipment terms in the sale contract, and obtains transport documents from the shipping company.

③ The seller prepares all the documents required under the sale contract including the time draft, and obtains the collection/negotiation instruction form from the remitting bank. The seller entrusts the collection of the payment to the remitting bank by providing the documents including time drafts and the collection/negotiation instruction. The remitting bank checks the shipping documents and the collection/negotiation instruction form to make sure that the documents conform to the instruction.

④ The remitting bank sends the documents, together with the collection instruction, to the collecting bank to entrust the collection of the payment to the collecting bank.

⑤ The collecting bank (the collecting bank that makes such presentation is called the "presenting bank") notifies the buyer of the arrival of the documents and requests acceptance of the drafts. The buyer is also advised about the collection.

⑥ The buyer (the drawee) checks the documents and accepts the draft if the documents conform to the sale contract.

⑦ The collecting bank releases the documents in exchange for the acceptance of the draft by the buyer.

⑧ The collecting bank keeps the accepted drafts until maturity and presents the drafts for payment at maturity, and the buyer pays the draft.

⑨ The collecting bank transfers the payment to the remitting bank as per the instruction.

⑩ The remitting bank transfers the payment to the seller, normally by crediting the amount of payment to the seller's account.

Fig. 7.2 Documents against acceptance

The buyer is not obliged to pay the draft unless they sign and write "accepted" on the draft. The formal process of signing and writing "accepted" on the draft is called "acceptance" in the draft. A drawee will become an acceptor right after "acceptance" of the draft. The buyer is obliged to pay the draft once they accept it.

7.2.5 Collection Instruction

The seller submits to their bank a collection instruction form that will form the collection instruction. Every bank has their own collection instruction form, and most banks provide one form for collection as well as for negotiation. Therefore, the formal title of this form would include the expression "collection/negotiation instruction". A collection instruction form may be used for a documentary credit (letter of credit) transaction as well. The seller will obtain a collection/negotiation instruction form from their bank and will fill in the form to entrust the collection of payment.

Although every bank's collection/negotiation instruction form will differ, a collection instruction should contain the following items of information, as appropriate (URC 522 Article 4(b)):

- Details of the bank from which the collection was received including full name, postal and SWIFT addresses, telex, telephone, facsimile numbers, and reference.
- Details of the principal including full name, postal address and, if applicable, telex, telephone, and facsimile numbers.
- Details of the drawee including full name, postal address, or the domicile at which presentation is to be made and, if applicable, telex, telephone, and facsimile numbers.
- Details of the presenting bank, if any, including full name, postal address and, if applicable, telex, telephone and facsimile numbers.
- Amount(s) and currency(ies) to be collected.
- List of documents enclosed and the numerical count of each document.
- (1) Terms and conditions upon which payment and/or acceptance is to be obtained.
- (2) Terms of delivery of documents against:

  (a) payment and/or acceptance;
  (b) other terms and conditions.

The seller sends the completed collection instruction form together with the documents to the remitting bank. The remitting bank must then send the collection instructions on the collecting bank's form together with the documents to a collecting bank.

7.3   Features and Advantages/Disadvantages

7.3.1   Features

In a documentary collection, the seller entrusts the collection of the payment to the remitting bank, and the remitting bank will again entrust the collection of the payment to the collecting bank. The seller sends the shipping documents to the buyer through the banking system (through the remitting bank and the collecting bank), and the bills of exchange (drafts) are also sent to the buyer with the shipping documents. When the collecting bank receives payment from the buyer, they will transfer the payment to the remitting bank or the seller as per the instruction by the remitting bank.

In a documentary collection, the buyer pays or accepts the draft against the collection documents required under the sale contract. Therefore, the documents required under the documentary collection must be clearly specified in the contract in order to avoid disputes between the parties. The dispute will only delay the collection procedure. The collection documents normally include:

- draft (bill of exchange);
- commercial invoices;
- packing lists;
- transport documents: bill of lading, or air waybill;
- inspection certificates.

   Sometimes the collection documents also include:

- insurance documents; and
- certificates of origin.

   Although the banks control the flow of documents, they neither verify the documents nor take any risks. They can, however, influence the mutually satisfactory settlement of the documentary collection transaction. We can better understand the features of the documentary collection by a comparison of the open account and the documentary credit respectively.

   In a documentary collection, the seller sends the shipping documents via the banking system (with the assistance of the remitting bank, the collecting bank, and the presenting bank) to the buyer, while in an open account the seller sends the shipping documents directly to the buyer. Bills of exchange (documentary drafts) are used in the documentary collection, while they are not used in the open account. The role of the banks, in the open account, is very limited to transferring money by telegraphic transfer to the seller, while the role of the banks, in the documentary collection includes presenting the shipping documents to and collecting payment from the buyer. Therefore, a documentary collection costs more than an open account.

It is time to compare a documentary collection and a documentary credit (letter of credit). Although banks play a greater role in documentary collection than in an open account, banks do not undertake to pay or guarantee that the buyer pays or accepts the drafts. However, the issuing bank (and/or the confirming bank if any) undertakes to pay the complying presentation in the documentary credit, and the documentary credit is regarded as the conditional payment guarantee by an issuing bank (and/or the confirming bank if any).

7.3.2 Advantage/Disadvantage

The safest payment method for the seller would be the payment in advance, but this would be the least secure method for the buyer. The safest payment method for the buyer would be an open account, but this would be the least secured method for the seller. The documentary credit is very favorable for the seller and would be acceptable for the buyer, but this would cost much and reduce the buyer's credit limit. Therefore, compromise is required between the seller and the buyer as to payment terms.

In order to make better comparison, an understanding is required of the advantages and disadvantages in a documentary collection. The advantages for the seller would be:

- A documentary collection can increase the certainty of payment.
- A documentary collection includes drafts, and the drafts can help the seller to negotiate the documents and the drafts to the bank. In the negotiation, the negotiating bank will agree to pay the seller immediately the value of the draft. But, negotiation would be with recourse to the seller, meaning that if the bank was unable to obtain the payment from the buyer, then it would retrieve the money from the seller.
- The seller takes the benefit of the draft such as: (1) the seller can negotiate (sell) the draft to the bank, as the draft is a negotiable instrument; (2) the payment obligation under the draft is independent of the sale contract. Regardless of the dispute arising out of the sale contract, the drawee (mostly the buyer) should pay the holder in due course of the draft; (3) the litigation procedure is very favorable for the draft holder.

The advantages for the buyer would be:

- The documentary collection can provide some assurance to the buyer that the goods paid for or accepted for will arrive;
- The documentary collection can provide an opportunity to sell goods before payment has to be made.
- The documentary collection can improve cash flow to the buyer.

But there are also disadvantages to a documentary collection. The disadvantages for the seller would be:

- The security of payment is inferior to the payment in advance or the documentary credit.
- The buyer may try to bargain down the price once they take the goods, claiming some defect.
- Teh seller does not have the benefit of the bank guarantee of payment provided by the documentary credit and relies only upon the credit standing of the buyer.
- Should the buyer not pay or accept the drafts, the costs of reselling or shipping back the goods would be high.

The disadvantages for the buyer would be:

- The buyer may receive defective goods after they make payment or accept documents.
- A documentary collection costs more than an open account.

7.4   The Uniform Rules for Collections

The International Chamber of Commerce (ICC) in 1956 published the Uniform Rules for the Collections of Commercial Paper, and in 1967 the Uniform Rules for Collections (URC 322). In 1978 the ICC revised the Uniform Rules for Collections (URC 422), and in 1995 lastly revised them (URC 522). The ICC Uniform Rules for Collections are a practical set of Rules to aid bankers, buyers, and sellers in the collections process. The Rules have been prepared to resolve problems that practitioners have experienced in their everyday operations.

URC 522 applies to all collections where URC 522 is incorporated into the text of the collection instruction (Article 1). Banks have no obligation to handle either a collection or a collection instruction or subsequent related instructions. However, should the banks decide not to handle a collection instruction or any related instruction received, they must advise the party from whom they received the collection or instruction without delay (Article 1).

Article 4 covers the form and structure of collections. All documents sent for collection must be accompanied by a collection instruction indicating that the collection is subject to URC 522 and giving complete and precise instructions. Banks are only permitted to act upon the instructions given in such collection instruction, and in accordance with URC 522. A collection instruction should contain the following information, as appropriate:

- details of the bank from which the collection was received;
- details of the principal;
- details of the drawee;
- details of the presenting bank (if any);
- amount(s) and currency(ies) to be collected;

- list of documents enclosed and the numerical count of each document.
- (1) Terms and conditions upon which payment and/or acceptance is to be obtained
- (2) Terms of delivery of documents against (a) payment and/or acceptance (b) other terms and conditions;
- list of documents enclosed and the numerical count of each document;
- charges to be collected;
- interest to be collected;
- method of payment and form of payment advice;
- instructions in case of non-payment, non-acceptance and/or non-compliance with other instructions.

Articles 5 and 6 give details on the procedures relating to the form of presentation. Article 7 gives details on the release of commercial documents.

Article 9 provides that banks will act in good faith and exercise reasonable care. Article 11 provides a disclaimer for acts of an instructed party. Article 12 provides that the receiving party must check all of the documents listed on the collection instruction. Articles 13 and 14 disclaim banks from the accuracy of documentation and against any delays or loss of documentation.

Article 15 provides that banks assume no liability or responsibility for consequences arising out of the interruption of their business by force majeure. Articles 16–19 provide for definitions and explanations about payments procedures. Articles 20 and 21 provides for interest, charges and expenses and, in particular, the action that should be taken by the bank where these have been refused by the drawee.

Article 23 provides that the presenting bank is not responsible for the genuineness of any signature or for the authority of any signatory to sign a promissory note, receipt, or other instruments. Article 24 covers "protest" and provides that the collection instruction should give specific instructions regarding protest (or other legal process in lieu thereof), in the event of non-payment or non-acceptance.

Article 26 provides that it is the collecting bank's responsibility and duty to advise the fate of the collection to the bank from which the collection was received. The collecting bank must send without delay advice of payment to the remitting bank detailing the amount or amounts collected, charges and/or disbursements, and/or expenses deducted. The collecting bank must send without delay advice of acceptance to the remitting bank. The presenting bank must send without delay advice of non-payment and/or advice of non-acceptance to the bank from which it received the collection instruction.

Example of a simple D/A contract

D/A CONTRACT

WE AS SELLER HEREBY CONFIRM SALES OF THE FOLLOWING

1. CONTRACT NO: DEC-190822
2. CONTRACT DATE: AUG. 22, 2019
3. SELLER'S NAME & ADDRESS:

   SXXXX CLEANER CO., LTD

   XXXX, SEOUL, KOREA
4. BUYER'S NAME & ADDRESS:

   DXXXX S.A.S

   XXXX, PARIS, FRANCE
5. NOTIFY PARTY: LAURENT DRUGY (TEL:)
6. PORT OF LOADING: BUASN, KOREA
7. PORT OF DISCHARGE: ANTWERPEN, BELGIUM
8. PAYMENT CONDITIONS: D/A 60 DAYS FROM B/L DATE
9. DELIVERY TERMS: CIF ANTWERPEN, BELGIUM
10. CONTRACT PRICE: EUR 500,000
11. SHIPPING DATE: SEP. 21, 2019
12. PACKING: EXPORT STANDARD PACKING
13. ORIGIN: REPUBLIC OF KOREA
14. DESCRIPTION: MICRO FIBER GOODS
15. QUANTITY: 50,000 PCS
16. DOCUMENTS REQUIRED:

    (1) FULL SET OF CLEAN ON BOARD BILLS OF LADING

    (2) SIGNED COMMERCIAL INVOICE IN 3 ORIGINALS

    (3) PACKING LIST IN 3 ORIGINALS

    (4) ONE INSPECTION CERTIFICATE
17. FINAL DESTINATION : ANTWERPEN, BELGIUM
18. RESOLUTION IN DISPUTE:

    ANY DISPUTE ARISING OUT OF OR IN CONNECTION WITH THIS
    CONTRACT SHALL BE FINALLY SETTLED BY ARBITRATION IN

SEOUL IN ACCORDANCE WITH THE INTERNATIONAL ARBITRATION
RULES OF THE KOREAN COMMERCIAL ARBITRATION BOARD. THE
AWARD RENDERED BY THE ARBITRATOR(S) SHALL BE FINAL AND
BINDING UPON BOTH PARTIES CONCERNED.

19. GOVERNING LAW:

   THIS CONTRACT SHALL BE GOVERNED BY THE LAWS OF KOREA

20. REMARKS:

   (1) THIS CONTRACT SHALL BE EFFECTIVE AND VALID WHEN
   BOTH PARTIES SIGN HEREUNDER.
   (2) ALL CHARGE AND INTERESTS OUTSIDE KOREA ARE FOR THE
   ACCOUNT OF THE DRAWEE

(BUYER)   (SELLER)

(SIGNATURE)   *(SIGNATURE)*

References

Anders, G. (2014). *The Handbook of International Trade and Finance* (3rd ed., p. 47). London, U.K.: Kogan Page.
Bishop, E. (2006). *Finance of International Trade* (p. 17). Oxford, U.K.: Elsevier.
US Commercial Services. (2015). *A Basic Guide to Exporting* (11th ed., p. 161). US Commercial Services: Washington D.C., USA.

Chapter 8
Documentary Credit

8.1 Introduction

8.1.1 The Background

Unlike most domestic sales transactions, in a sale of goods across national borders, the seller and the foreign buyer may have no prior business transactions with one another; or the seller and the foreign buyer may know nothing about the other party.

The seller may not be aware of:

- whether the buyer is creditworthy (or trustworthy);
- whether information received from the buyer's associates is reliable;
- whether foreign exchange controls will hinder the transfer of the payment;
- the legal systems of another country;
- whether the courts will render unbiased (fair) judgement.

And the buyer too may not be aware of:

- whether the seller will ship the goods if the buyer prepays;
- whether the goods shipped will conform to the contract;
- whether the goods will be shipped by an appropriate carrier;
- whether the goods will be properly insured;
- whether the seller will provide the documents required.

Where the parties are strangers, these risks are very high. Since they run business at a distance from each other, the seller and the buyer are not able to concurrently exchange the goods for the payment without the help of third parties. Therefore, the present sale[1] is, in reality, not realistic in international trade. A documentary credit transaction illustrates how these potentially large risks can be allocated to the third

---

[1] "Present sale" means a sale accomplished by the making of a contract (i.e. exchanging the goods and payment at the time of a contract).

S. M. Kim, *Payment Methods and Finance for International Trade*, https://doi.org/10.1007/978-981-15-7039-1_8

parties that have special knowledge, can properly evaluate each risk assumed, and thereby can reduce the transaction risks. A documentary credit is one of the most common methods of payment in international trade,[2] and has been described as "the lifeblood of international commerce".[3]

A letter of credit comes in two types—a documentary letter of credit (or a documentary credit) and a non-documentary letter of credit (or a clean credit). A clean credit requires no commercial documents (e.g. bill of lading (or air waybill), commercial invoices, packing list, etc.), while a documentary credit requires commercial documents.[4]

8.1.2 History

Some believe that the origins of letters of credit date back to ancient Babylon in the year 3000 BC.[5] Probably the term "letter of credit" was first used in connection with traveler's letters of credit, which were widely used in the eighteenth century.[6] Traveler's letters of credit were issued by banks to provide their clients with the means of obtaining cash from overseas banks during foreign travel.[7] Clients were able to reduce the risks of carrying large amount of cash by using traveler's letters of credit.

A formal "letter of introduction" was addressed to the issuing bank's correspondent bank (or agent bank) located in a foreign country. The letter of introduction indicated that the client was a valued customer, and requested that the correspondent bank (or agent bank) provide any assistance possible. Copies of the letter of introduction were often sent to the correspondent bank (or agent bank) prior to the client's scheduled visit.

The traveler's letter of credit indicated that, in consideration of the correspondent bank paying cash to the named client, the issuing bank would honor bills of exchange drawn by the correspondent bank on the issuing bank for amount paid plus charges incurred by the correspondent bank.

---

[2]Murray et al. (2010).

[3]Gao (2007), Murray et al., *R.D. Harbollte (Mercantile) Ltd. v. National Westminster Bank Ltd.* [1978] Q.B. 146, at p. 155.

[4]Folsom et al. (2012).

[5]Hennah (2013).

[6]Collyer (2007).

[7]Ibid.

8.1.3 Concept

A documentary credit (or letter of credit) is a definite undertaking of the issuing bank to pay a complying presentation (presentation of documents). An issuing bank will pay a beneficiary (normally the seller), if the documents presented complies with the terms and conditions of the credit. A documentary credit can be thus said to be a conditional payment guarantee, not an unconditional payment guarantee.

The Uniform Customs and Practice for Documentary Credits (the sixth revision of 2007, UCP 600) Article 2 defines a documentary credit ("credit"):

> Credit means any arrangement, however named or described, that is irrevocable and thereby constitutes a definite undertaking of the issuing bank to honour a complying presentation.

UCP 600

The ICC (International Chamber of Commerce) developed and published the Uniform Customs and Practice for Documentary Credits (UCP) in 1933 firstly, and revised it six times. The latest version, the sixth revision of 2007, is called UCP 600.

A documentary credit is basically a transaction between an issuing bank and a beneficiary. A documentary credit is a separate transaction from the underlying contract under which it is issued, and is independent of the underlying contract. The issuing bank's obligations under the documentary credit are independent of the buyer's obligations under the underlying contract. This characteristic of a documentary credit is called the "independence principle"[8] or the "autonomy principle".[9]

The issuing bank's payment obligation is decided by the documents presented only, not the goods delivered or the services performed. The issuing bank examines the documents (not the goods) to determine whether to pay or not. A documentary credit transaction is thus called a paper transaction,[10] and this characteristic of a documentary credit is called "abstractness".

A documentary credit (or a letter of credit) is very useful for trade finance for both an exporter and importer. A documentary credit (or a letter of credit) is one of the basic payment methods in intrantaional trade. With a documentary credit, an exporter can obtain pre-shipment finance by providing a local supplier with a local letter of credit issued against a documentary credit. A documentary credit also enables an exporter to obtain other pre-shipment finance loan. A documentary credit (export letter of credit) also enables an exporter to obtain post-shipment finance such as negotiation, factoring, forfaiting, etc. A documentary credit can increase the export

---

[8]Folsom et al. (2012), Seyoum (2009), Chow and Schoenbaum (2010).

[9]Davidson (2003), Meral (2012). The autonomy principle is also called the "autonomy of the credit" or the "principle of autonomy": see Murray et al. (2010).

[10]Murray et al. (2010).

credit insurance (or export credit guarantee) limit for an exporter, and therefore enable an exporter to increase the export volume. By providing a documentary credit (or a letter of credit), an importer can request long credit payment terms to an exporter and pay with the funds from the sale of the imported goods.

8.2   Operation of a Documentary Credit

8.2.1   Flow of a Documentary Credit Transaction

In an international trade with a documentary credit, the exporter and importer enter into a contract for which the method of payment is a documentary credit. The third party intermediaries for documentary credit transactions are banks (banks in an importing country and banks in an exporting country). Thus, the parties involved in a documentary credit transaction are (1) the exporter (beneficiary under a documentary credit), (2) the importer (applicant under a documentary credit), (3) the importer's bank (issuing bank of a documentary credit), and (4) the exporter's bank (advising bank, nominated bank of a documentary credit). These parties divide the risks into several small and calculable risks, each of which is easily borne by the respective parties.

How does a documentary credit transaction work? The first step will be agreeing on the terms of payment as a documentary credit in an international trade transaction, and then the exporter and importer conclude a contract. Once the contract is concluded, the importer applies to its bank to issue a documentary credit in favor of the exporter.

Figure 8.1 illustrates the flow of a documentary credit transaction.

8.2.2   Application and Issuance of a Documentary Credit

The issuing bank (the buyer's bank) will be well aware of the buyer's creditworthiness, and will make "appropriate arrangements"[11] to receive the funds from the buyer (through either immediate payment or future repayment of the loan). Once a documentary credit is issued, the issuing bank is bound to the documentary credit. Thus, these arrangements will be made before the documentary credit is issued.

The issuing bank may have already established or will have to establish a documentary credit limit for the buyer. As a documentary credit is a binding undertaking to guarantee payment, the issuing bank marks the credit as a contingent liability of the applicant (the importer). The issuing bank may also wish to take security to protect itself against any loss. This may take the form of:

• security over the importer's assets;

---

[11] A foreign exchange transaction agreement.

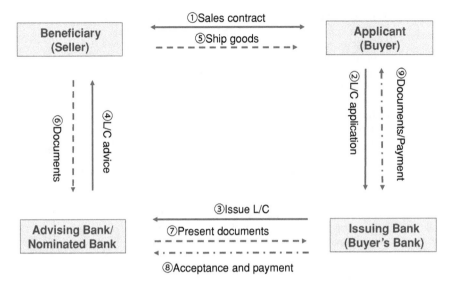

Fig. 8.1 Process flow of documentary credit transaction

①The seller (exporter) and the buyer (importer) enter into a contract for sale for which the terms of payment is a documentary credit.

②The importer (an applicant) applies to the issuing bank (the importer's bank) to issue a documentary credit in favor of the exporter by submitting a letter of credit issuing application form.

③The issuing bank processes a formal credit approval of the application and establishes credit limit for the importer. (If the credit limit for the importer is already established, this process will be omitted.) The issuing bank issues a documentary credit in favor of the exporter (the beneficiary) within the remaining credit limit of the importer. A documentary credit is normally sent to an advising bank through the SWIFT system.

④Once the advising bank receives the documentary credit, they check authenticity of the documentary credit and print it out to give to the exporter. The advising bank is usually located in the exporter's country, and its role is to take reasonable care to check the authenticity of the documentary credit and to advise it to the exporter according to its instructions. However, the advising bank bears no obligation to pay, unless it is a confirming bank.

⑤Once the exporter receives the documentary credit, they will check and compare it against the contract for sale. If anything is not complying with the contract for sale, the exporter must immediately communicate with the importer for necessary amendment. If all the details conform to the contract for sale, then the exporter prepares and ship the goods, and receives the transport documents from the carrier (or the freight forwarder).

⑥ The beneficiary (exporter) prepares all the documents (normally bill of lading, commercial invoice, packing list, inspection certificate) required under the documentary credit, and forwards them to the nominated bank (normally the advising bank). In many cases, the nominated bank negotiates (purchases, or discounts) the documents and pays the exporter, and then the nominated bank becomes the negotiating bank.

⑦ The nominated bank despatches the documents to the issuing bank.

⑧ Upon receiving the documents, the issuing bank will examine the documents. (In practice, the issuing bank requests the importer to check the documents and to decide whether or not to accept the documents.) If the documents comply with the documentary credit, the issuing bank sends "acceptance advice" (A/A) to the nominated bank, and will make payment at maturity.

⑨ The issuing bank releases the documents to the importer once the importer decides to accept the documents. Once the issuing bank pays the complying presentation of documents, the importer must repay (reimburse) the issuing bank.

Fig. 8.1   (continued)

- guarantees of the importer's parent company;
- security provided through documents such as:
  - blank endorsed original bills of lading, giving the bank the right to possession of the goods (or bills of lading issued to the order of the issuing bank);
  - the bank may be satisfied with non-negotiable transport documents that consign the goods to the bank, giving the bank control over them.

Assuming that the issuing bank is agreeable to issue a documentary credit, the buyer (the importer) will need to complete the bank's application form giving exact details of what is required. A "documentary credit application form" will require the buyer to provide information on the following:

- full details of the buyer as applicant;
- full details of the seller as beneficiary;
- details of the seller's bank through which the documentary credit will be advised and will add the confirmation if required. (If this not known to the buyer then the issuing bank would advise the documentary credit through one of its group offices or correspondent banks.);
- the nature of the documentary credit required: irrevocable, confirmed, transferable;
- the payment terms: at sight, acceptance, negotiation or deferred payment;
- the currency;
- Incoterms rules used and the associated responsibilities for each party;
- the validity of the documentary credit (expiry date);
- when shipment must be effected and documents presented;
- other shipment issues: partial shipments, transhipment, the nature of the transport documents;

- the description of the goods;
- the insurance requirements;
- if goods are to be inspected prior to shipment;
- the other documentary requirements;
- which party is responsible for bank charges.

When the issuing bank issues the documentary credit, they will use their standard format; if issued by SWIFT, then all banks use the same format. The issued documentary credit will include the following details:

- issuing bank details;
- the letter of credit reference number;
- date of issue;
- type of letter of credit: whether transferable, irrevocable etc.;
- applicant and beneficiary details;
- expiry date and place;
- availability of the credit;
- amount and currency of the letter of credit;
- details of draft if requested, e.g. tenor, drawee etc.;
- latest date for shipment;
- details of where goods are to be shipped from and to;
- whether partial shipment is allowed/not allowed;
- whether transshipment is allowed/not allowed;
- description of the goods;
- details of the documents required;
- details of any additional conditions attached to the credit;
- whether the letter of credit is to be advised with or without confirmation;
- details of charges;
- details on presentation period;
- reimbursement instructions.

8.2.3 *Responsibilities of the Advising Bank*

In its role as the advising bank, it must first check whether the credit received is genuine (or authentic). With a secure SWIFT message, no further checks are necessary, but if the documentary credit is sent in paper form, the advising bank will have to check the signatures against those specimens (signature card) held. The advising bank does not have to check a documentary credit against the sale contract. The advising bank bears no obligation to pay, unless it is the confirming bank.

If the advising bank has been asked to add their confirmation and it is not willing to do so, it must advise the issuing bank immediately. If an advising bank is willing to confirm the credit, it will advise the beneficiary of the details of the credit and its confirmation.

Once the seller is in receipt of the documentary credit, they will check that the documentary credit conforms to the sale contract and that they are able to meet the requirements of the credit. If the seller is not satisfied, they should immediately request to the buyer for a necessary amendment of the documentary credit.

8.2.4 Presentation of Documents

8.2.4.1 Required Documents

A documentary credit requires some specific documents for payment, and the documents normally include:

- negotiable bill of lading (showing shipping company's receipt and shipment of the goods, and obligation to deliver them only to the holder of the bill of lading);
- commercial invoice that sets out the description of the goods such as number of goods, unit price, etc.;
- certificate of inspection issued by a commercial inspection firm;
- insurance policy under CIF or CIP;
- certificate of origin;
- bill of exchange (documentary draft).

8.2.4.2 Complying Presentation

The issuing bank does not see the goods, only the documents presented. Therefore, the bank examines the documents thoroughly to determine that they comply exactly with the terms and conditions of the documentary credit as the documents are its only protection.

If the seller ships goods conforming to the sale contract and presents documents complying with the documentary credit, it obtains independent promises of payment from both the buyer and the issuing bank. The issuing bank's promise is enforceable despite assertions of non-conformity of the goods, so long as the documents conform to the documentary credit.

The issuing bank is at risk only if the buyer fails or refuses to reimburse the payment to them. The issuing bank had an opportunity to evaluate such risk before issuing the documentary credit, and for which it could adjust the credit issuance fee. Where the buyer's credit rating is low, the issuing bank will charge high rate of issuance fee.

On the other hand, for its reimbursement of the payment, the buyer obtains the transport documents entitling the right of taking the goods, an insurance policy protecting the buyer against loss or damage to the goods, and perhaps an inspection certificate proving the quality of the goods.

8.2.4.3 Presentation of Documents for Sight Letter of Credit

If a documentary credit is payable at sight and calls for sight drafts then, as soon as shipment has taken place, the seller can assemble the required documents and present them to their bank (along with the sight draft). Normally the seller's bank purchases the documents and advances funds to the seller with recourse prior to acceptance advice. This is called "negotiation" or "discount of bills".

The seller's bank (the nominated bank, advising bank) will forward the documents to the issuing bank. On receipt of the documents, the issuing bank will check them for conforming to the letter of credit.

The issuing bank has a maximum of five banking days to determine whether the presentation is complying (UCP 600 Article 14(b)). If the issuing bank determines that the presentation is complying with the documentary credit, it will send acceptance advice (A/A) to the seller's bank.

In practice, the issuing bank requests the buyer to examine the documents and to sign an acceptance form, and then debits the buyer's account.[12] Then the documents will be released to the buyer.

8.2.4.4 Presentation of Documents for an Acceptance Credit

If the documentary credit is payable by acceptance, then as soon as shipment has taken place, the seller will assemble the required documents and present them to their bank, along with the time draft.

Normally the seller's bank purchases the documents and drafts, and advances funds to the seller with recourse prior to acceptance advice from the issuing bank. This is called "negotiation" or "discount of bills".

The seller's bank will forward the documents to the issuing bank. On receipt of the documents, the issuing bank will check them for discrepancies. The issuing bank has a maximum of five banking days to determine whether the presentation is complying. If the issuing bank determines that the presentation is complying, it will accept the documents/draft and send acceptance advice (A/A) to the seller's bank. In practice, the issuing bank requests the buyer to examine the documents and to sign on an acceptance form. Then the documents will be released to the buyer. On the due date, the issuing bank will debit the buyer's account and will pay the time draft.

Under a "forfaiting", if any, the seller's bank advances funds to the seller without recourse when the documents are accepted by the issuing bank. On the due date, the issuing bank will debit the buyer's account and will pay the time draft.

---

[12]"Debits the buyer's account" means "withdraws (deducts) money from the buyer's account".

8.2.4.5   Presentation of Documents for a Deferred Payment Credit

This is similar to an acceptance credit except that no draft is used. Payment will be made at a future due date.

8.2.5   Advantages/Disadvantages

A documentary credit (letter of credit) offers various advantages for an exporter. Payment is guaranteed, and therefore there are fewer concerns about the importer's ability to pay, or about other restrictions or difficulties that may exist in the importing country. Only if an exporter can meet all the terms and conditions stipulated in the documentary credit (letter of credit) will it get paid. However, the documentary credit (letter of credit) brings some disadvantages to an exporter.

A documentary credit (letter of credit) also offers various advantages for the importer. While a documentary credit (letter of credit) is considerably more expensive than other forms of payment, the importer will be assured that the exporter will not be paid unless the exporter performs the contract and the documents presented conform to the terms of the letter of credit. A documentary credit (letter of credit) brings some disadvantages to the importer.

8.2.5.1   Advantages for the Exporter

The advantages for the exporter are as follows:

- payment is more secured: the issuing bank must accept and pay the complying presentation;
- the payment risk is transferred from the buyer's credit rating to the issuing bank's credit rating;
- post-shipment financing may be available such as negotiation, factoring, and forfaiting;
- pre-shipment finance may be available;
- the transport documents and the draft may be negotiated more easily.

8.2.5.2   Disadvantages for the Exporter

The disadvantages for the exporter are as follows:

- the exporter must present complying documents within the letter of credit expiry date;
- the importer may requests a price discount in return for a documentary credit;
- the exporter usually pays the cost incurred in their country.

8.2.5.3   Advantages for an Importer

The advantages for the importer are as follows:

- the importer will obtain transport documents prior to payment. The importer needs not pay out funds before the documents have arrived;
- the importer may be able to obtain a price discount in return for a documentary credit;
- the importer may be able to obtain favorable payment terms such as usance documentary credit, deferred payment documentary credit.

8.2.5.4   Disadvantages for an Importer

The disadvantages for the importer are as follows:

- the amount of the documentary credit is treated as the importer's contingent liability;
- the amount of the documentary credit will reduce the credit limit of the importer. The documentary credit will reduce the borrowing line of credit of the importer;
- the importer should pay documentary credit issuance cost;
- the importer's account will be debited on receipt of compliant documents;
- the importer may receive defective goods even after payment.

8.3   Various Types of Credits

8.3.1   Basic Types of Credit Under UCP

Article 6(b)[13] of the UCP 600 and Article 10(a)[14] of the UCP 500 state the manner in which a documentary credit may be made available, and thus for four basic types of credit by the method of availability. According to Article 6(b) of the UCP 600 and Article 10(a) of the UCP 500, a documentary credit may be available by sight payment, deferred payment, acceptance, or negotiation.

The title ("Types of Credit") of Article 10 of the UCP 500 more clearly implies that Article 10 provides four types of documentary credit[15] (i.e. sight payment credit, deferred payment credit, acceptance credit, and negotiation credit).

---

[13] Article 6 Availability, Expiry Date and Place for Presentation:
    b. A credit must state whether it is available by sight payment, deferred payment, acceptance or negotiation.

[14] Article 10 Types of Credit: a. All Credits must clearly indicate whether they are available by sight payment, by deferred payment, by acceptance or by negotiation.

[15] Adodo (2009, 2014).

8.3.1.1   Sight Credit

Sight credit (or sight letter of credit) means a credit that is available by sight payment. Sight payment means that payment should be made on presentation or on demand. In a sight credit, the issuing bank or the nominated bank pays at sight. In a sight credit, a draft may or may not be used.

8.3.1.2   Deferred Payment Credit

Deferred payment credit (or deferred payment letter of credit) means a credit that is available by deferred payment. In a deferred payment credit, the issuing bank or the nominated bank accepts a complying presentation, and pays at a future due date. In a deferred payment credit, a draft is not used.

8.3.1.3   Acceptance Credit

Acceptance credit (or acceptance letter of credit) means a credit that is available by acceptance. In an acceptance credit, an issuing bank or a nominated bank accepts drafts and/or documents complying with the credit and pay at a future due date. In an acceptance credit, time drafts are used.[16]

8.3.1.4   Negotiation Credit

Negotiation credit (or negotiation letter of credit) means a credit that is available by negotiation/acceptance. In a negotiation credit, the nominated bank is authorized to negotiate the complying presentation but is not obligated to do so. A draft may or may not be used in a negotiation credit.[17] A negotiation credit may be payable at sight or at a future date. In a negotiation credit, a draft, if any, must be drawn on a bank other than a negotiating bank.

8.3.2   Other Forms of Credit

8.3.2.1   Transferable Credit

"Transferable credit" means a credit that can be transferred to a second beneficiary by a first beneficiary. Article 38 of UCP 600 defines that a transferable credit is a credit that specifically states it is "transferable". A transferable credit may be made

---

[16] Adodo (2014).
[17] Collyer (2007).

available in whole or in part to another beneficiary ("second beneficiary") at the request of the beneficiary ("first beneficiary"). The seller and the buyer agree on the issue of transferable letter of credit, and then the buyer (the applicant) can instruct the issuing bank to issue a credit in transferable form.

The following points need to be understood (UCP 600 Article. 38):
- Transfers can be and usually are for less than the full letter of credit amount.
- There can be more than one second beneficiary provided the letter of credit allows for partial drawings or shipments.
- But onward transfers from second beneficiaries to third beneficiaries are not allowed for in UCP 600.
- The final supplier(s) benefits from the security of the letter of credit and may present compliant documents directly to the advising/transferring bank for payment.
- There is, however, an additional risk for the applicant: the applicant will know nothing of the credit standing or reliability of the supplier.

8.3.2.2 Back-to-Back Credit

Back-to-back credit is a credit that serves as the collateral for another credit. The advising bank of the first letter of credit ("back-to-back credit") becomes the issuing bank of the second letter of credit (normally "local letter of credit"). In contrast to a transferable letter of credit, the permission of the importer (the applicant of the original letter of credit) or the issuing bank is not required in a back-to-back letter of credit. Back-to-back credit is also called "counter credit" or "reciprocal letter of credit".

On receipt of a documentary credit advice in favor of the exporter as beneficiary, the exporter will apply for a new credit in favor of the local supplier. The two documentary credits operate separately but the seller (an applicant in new credit) will have to structure the new credit in such a way that when compliant documents are presented by the beneficiary of this second documentary credit, the seller can use those documents—such as bills of lading, together with any added or substituted by the seller, such as invoices—in time to make a complying presentation under the original credit in the seller's favor.

8.3.2.3 Red Clause Credit

Red clause credit is the credit that includes a clause (traditionally written or typed in red ink) that allows the advising bank to make advances to the beneficiary in advance of the shipment or before presenting the prescribed documents. Red clause credit is sometimes called as "packing" credit. Red clause credit authorizes the nominated bank to pay the beneficiary against written commitment by the beneficiary to present the shipping documents upon shipment.

The issuing bank and the applicant are liable to reimburse the advising bank for any advances made and not repaid from the proceeds of compliant documents. Therefore, it is normally used only where the buyer and seller have a close working relationship because, in effect, the buyer is extending an unsecured loan to the seller (and bears the financial risk and the currency risk). Red clause credits were once popular, for example with those involved in the wool trade with Australia.

8.3.2.4 Revolving Credit

Revolving credit can be used to avoid the need for repetition of issuing and advising credits, and thus is used for regular shipments. The credit stipulates that it is revolving whether automatically or under specified conditions.

8.3.2.5 Standby Letters of Credit

A standby letter of credit is similar to documentary credit (letter of credit) but is used as a guarantee that contractual undertakings are fulfilled. In a standby letter of credit, transport documents are not required for payment and, therefore, a standby letter of credit is called a non-documentary credit.

8.3.2.6 Confirmed Credit

A confirmed credit is used when the seller wishes to have a documentary credit issued by a foreign bank to be confirmed by a bank in an exporting country. The seller requires a confirmed credit where they are not familiar with the foreign issuing bank or are concerned about the political or economic risk in the issuing bank's country.

In a confirmed credit, the advising bank will become the confirming bank. By merely indicating "We hereby add our confirmation to this credit", the advising bank makes a direct promise to the seller that it will pay a complying presentation to the seller. The liability of the confirming bank is separate and independent of the liability of the issuing bank.

If confirmation of a credit is requested by the applicant (the buyer), the issuing bank will issue a credit with "confirmation request" or "confirmation authorization".

8.4 Independence Principle and the Fraud Exception

8.4.1 Independence Principle

A documentary credit is basically a transaction between an issuing bank and a beneficiary. A documentary credit is a separate transaction from the sale contract under which it is issued, and is thus independent from the sale contract. The issuing bank's obligations under the documentary credit are independent of the buyer's obligations under the sale contract (UCP 600 Article 4). This characteristic of a documentary credit is called the "independence principle"[18] or the "autonomy principle".[19] The promise of the issuing bank is not subject to claims or defenses by the applicant that the beneficiary has not performed its obligations under the sales contract (UCP 600 Article 4(a)).

8.4.2 Complying Presentation and Strict Compliance

Banks examine the documents thoroughly to determine that they comply exactly with the terms and conditions of the documentary credit, since banks do not see the goods, but only the documents presented. Where the seller (the exporter) ships goods conforming to the sale contract and presents documents complying with the documentary credit, it obtains independent promises of payment from both the buyer (the importer) and the issuing bank. The issuing bank's promise is enforceable despite assertions of non-conformity of the goods, so long as the documents conform to the documentary credit.

The issuing bank is at risk only if the buyer (the applicant) fails or refuses to reimburse the payment to the issuing bank. The issuing bank had an opportunity to evaluate such risk prior to issuing the documentary credit, and for which it could adjust the letter of credit issuance fee. Where the buyer's credit rating is low, the issuing bank will charge high rate of issuance fee.

Since the bank (the issuing bank, confirming bank, nominated bank) pays the beneficiary (the seller) against the documents and does not see the goods, banks insist on "strict compliance" with all documentary conditions. Under the doctrine of strict compliance, banks do not honor documents that are not in strict conformity with the terms of the credit. The harshness of the doctrine of strict compliance is eased by the UCP.[20] For instance, UCP 600 Article 14(e) provides: "In documents other than the commercial invoice, the description of the goods, services or performance, if stated, may be in general terms not conflicting with their description in the credit."

---

[18]Folsom et al. (2012), Seyoum (2009), Chow and Schoenbaum (2010).

[19]Davidson (2003), Meral (2012). The autonomy principle is also called the "autonomy of the credit" or the "principle of autonomy": see Murray et al. (2010).

[20]Carr (2010).

The commercial invoice submitted should describe the goods in exactly the same terms as the credit. Other documents can describe the goods in general terms, but not in ways that conflict with the invoice, other documents or the credit. The primary document for describing the goods in a documentary credit transaction is the commercial invoice. The description in the commercial invoice must be specific and must "correspond with the description in the documentary credit". But descriptions in all other documents can be general and need only be "consistent" with the description in the documentary credit.

Although it is the "commercial invoice" that must "strictly conform" to the documentary credit, the most important of the documents required by a documentary credit is the "transportation document".

A high percentage of documents presented (estimated to exceed 50%[21] and perhaps more) are found to be discrepant: they do not conform to the terms of the credit. This is why the theoretical benefit to a seller of a documentary credit is less than perfect in practice.

When the officer of the bank examining documents notices discrepancies, they will, in the first place, give the beneficiary time to correct the documents or, where that is not possible, to contact the applicant to arrange for an amendment or to get the applicant's agreement to accept documents as presented.

8.4.3   Fraud Exception

The "independence principle" promotes the utility of the documentary credit transaction, by providing certainty of payment to the beneficiary. In the event the documents are forged, or there is fraud or forgery in the transaction, however, the "independence principle" is not applied.

Where there is fraud or forgery, rather than a "mere" breach of the sales contract, a counter principle comes into play. The issuing bank does not have to honor a complying presentation when there is fraud in the transaction. This is called the "fraud exception" or the "fraud rule". There is as much public interest in discouraging fraud as in encouraging the use of documentary credits.

The fraud exception (or the fraud rule) was first acknowledged in 1941 in *Sztejn v. J. Henry Schroder Banking Corporation.*[22] The court held:

> It is well established that a letter of credit is independent of the primary contract of sale between the buyer and the seller. The issuing bank agrees to pay upon presentation of documents, not goods. This rule is necessary to preserve the efficiency of the letter of credit as an instrument for the financing of trade.
>
> This is not a controversy between the buyer and seller concerning a mere breach of warranty regarding the quality of the merchandise; on the present motion, it must be assumed that the seller has *intentionally failed* to ship any goods ordered by the buyer. In such a situation,

---

[21] Folsom et al. (2009).

[22] *Sztejn v. J. Henry Schroder Banking Corp.*, 31 N.Y.S.2d 631 (N.Y.Sup. 1941).

Where the seller's fraud has been called to the bank's attention before the drafts and documents have been presented for payment, the principle of "the independence of the bank's obligation under the letter of credit" should not be extended to protect the unscrupulous seller. It is true that even though the documents are forged or fraudulent, if the issuing bank has already paid the draft before receiving notice of the seller's fraud, it will be protected if it exercised reasonable diligence before making such payment. (emphasis added)

Thereafter, in 1957 the USA enacted the fraud exception in UCC 5–114(2), thereby codifying *Sztejn v. J. Henry Schroder Banking Corp.* case.[23] The fraud rule has been acknowledged in many jurisdictions. The fraud exception has expanded enormously since 1952, but it is still a matter of controversy how broad and extensive the fraud exception should be. Although the UCP has no specific provisions on the fraud exception, the fraud exception is generally recognized in many jurisdictions. Since the UCP is silent, courts have generally held that the governing laws will govern as a "gap-filling provision". Therefore, the fraud exception is subject to the national law of any one country.[24] The courts will not allow a dishonest beneficiary to make use of the "independence principle".

The traditional difference between fraud doctrines and breach of contract concepts was that the former considered the state of mind of the seller, while breach of contract concerns only whether the goods lived up to the particular objective standard set by their description. The modern fraud doctrines often do not require any "evil" intent, but only that seller knows that a particular fact is not true or, that he does not know whether a particular fact is true or not when he states it or, that he believes that a fact is true when it is not, and a court decides that he should have made a more thorough investigation before speaking.

8.5 Issuing a Documentary Credit Through SWIFT

SWIFT is a secure message platform for financial institutions mainly for banks. SWIFT is headquartered in Belgium, and SWIFT's international governance and oversight reinforces the neutral, global character of its cooperative structure.

Nowadays, most documentary credits are issued and transmitted through the MT 700 SWIFT system. MT 700 is a type of message that is used by issuing banks when issuing a documentary credit. This message is sent by the issuing bank to the advising bank. It is used to indicate the terms and conditions of a documentary credit that has been originated by the sender (the issuing bank).[25]

The advising bank must advise a documentary credit, including all its details, in a way that is clear and unambiguous to the beneficiary. To avoid misunderstandings, where possible, banks are to use bank identifier codes (BICs) rather than expressions

---

[23]The UCC of 1957 added and provided that the court may enjoin such honor where a required document is forged or fraudulent or there is fraud in the transaction: Folsom et al. (2012).

[24]Gao (2002).

[25]*SWIFT User Handbook.*

such as "ourselves", "yourselves", "us", or "you". Meanwhile, non-documentary credits (i.e. standby letters of credit) and bank guarantees are issued through the MT 760 SWIFT system.

Table 8.1 Field name in MT 700 issue of a documentary credit

Status	Tag	Field name
M	27	Sequence of Total
M	40A	Form of Documentary Credit
M	20	Documentary Credit Number
O	23	Reference to Pre-Advice
O	31C	Date of Issue
M	40E	Applicable Rules
M	31D	Date and Place of Expiry
O	51a	Applicant Bank
M	50	Applicant
M	59	Beneficiary
M	32B	Currency Code, Amount
O	39A	Percentage Credit Amount Tolerance
O	39B	Maximum Credit Amount
O	39C	Additional Amounts Covered
M	41a	Available With … By …
O	42C	Drafts at …
O	42a	Drawee
O	42M	Mixed Payment Details
O	42P	Deferred Payment Details
O	43P	Partial Shipments
O	43T	Transshipment
O	44A	Place of Taking in Charge/Dispatch from …/Place of Receipt
O	44E	Port of Loading/Airport of Departure
O	44F	Port of Discharge/Airport of Destination
O	44B	Place of Final Destination/For Transportation to…/Place of Delivery
O	44C	Latest Date of Shipment
O	44D	Shipment Period
O	45A	Description of Goods and/or Services

(continued)

Table 8.1 (continued)

Status	Tag	Field name
O	46A	Documents Required
O	47A	Additional Conditions
O	71B	Charges
O	48	Period for Presentation
M	49	Confirmation Instructions
O	53a	Reimbursing Bank
O	78	Instructions to the Paying/Accepting/Negotiating Bank
O	57a	"Advise Through" Bank
O	72	Sender to Receiver Information

O: Optional M: Mandatory

SWIFT User Handbook

References

Adodo, E. (2009). Establishing purchase of documents under a negotiation letter of credit. *Singapore Journal of Legal Studies*, 618.

Adodo, E. (2014). *Letters of credit: The law and practice of compliance* (p. 99). Oxford, UK: Oxford University Press.

Carr, I (2010). *International trade law* (4th ed., p. 480). Abingdon, UK: Routledge-Cavendish.

Chow, D. C. K., & Schoenbaum, T. J. (2010). *International business transactions: Problems, cases, and materials* (2nd ed., p. 242). USA: Wolters Kluwer, New York.

Collyer, G. (2007), *The guide to documentary credits* (3rd ed., p. 2). ifs School of Finance, Cantebury, UK.

Davidson, A. (2003). Fraud; the prime exception to the autonomy principle in letters of credit. *International Trade & Business Law Annual, 23*, 24.

Folsom, R. H., et al. (2009). *International business transactions in a nutshell* (9th ed., p. 138). USA: Thomson Reuters, St. Paul.

Folsom, R. H., et al. (2012). *International business transactions: A problem-oriented coursebook* (11th ed., p. 225). Thomson Reuters, St. Paul: SUA.

Gao, X. (2002). *The fraud rule in the law of letters of credit* (p. 56). Netherlands: Kluwer Law International, Hague.

Gao, X. (2007). The fraud rule in law of letters of credit in the P.R.C. *The International Lawyar, 41*(4), 1067.

Hennah, D. J. (2013). *The ICC guide to the uniform rules for bank payment obligations*, ICC Publication No. 751E, Paris, France, p. 8.

Meral, N. (2012). The fraud exception in documentary credits: A global analysis. *Ankara Bar Review, 12*, 44.

Murray, C., et al. (2010). *Schmitthoff's export trade: The law and practice of international trade* (11th ed., p. 189). Thomson Reuters: London, U.K.

Seyoum, B. (2009). *Export-import theory, practices, and procedures* (2nd ed., p. 254). USA: Routledge, New York.

Chapter 9
UCP and Letter of Credit Examples

9.1 UCP

9.1.1 History of the UCP

The law relating to documentary credits developed before the First World War principally in England, and thereafter by courts in the USA. In the USA, the governing law is usually the applicable state's version of Revised Article 5 of the Uniform Commercial Code (UCC).[1] However, most provisions of the UCC Article 5 is not mandatory law, and thus the terms and conditions in a documentary credit prevails over UCC Article 5.

The ICC developed and first published the Uniform Customs and Practice for Documentary Credits (UCP) in 1933, and revised the UCP six times. The latest version, the sixth revision of 2007, is called UCP 600.

The origins of the UCP can be traced back to the publication of the Regulations Affecting Export Commercial Credits, adopted in 1920 at the New York Bankers Commercial Credit Conference.[2] In 1929, the ICC national committees discussed a draft document, the Uniform Regulations for Commercial Documentary Credits, which became the forerunner for the development of the first UCP. (See Table 9.1 for the development and revision history of the UCP.)[3]

---

[1] The Revised Article 5 of the UCC was adopted by the Uniform Commissioners and the American Law Institute in 1995, and has been enacted by 48 state legislatures.

[2] Collyer (2017).

[3] Ibid.

Table 9.1 The revision history of UCP

No. of revision	Year	Effective date	ICC publication no.
Enactment	1933	June 3, 1933	Brochure No. 82
1st Amendment	1951	January 1, 1952	Brochure No. 151
2nd Amendment	1962	July 1, 1963	Brochure No. 222
3rd Amendment	1974	October 1, 1975	Publication No. 290
4th Amendment	1983	October 1, 1984	Publication No. 400
5th Amendment	1993	January 1, 1994	Publication No. 500
6th Amendment	2007	July 1, 2007	Publication No. 600

The UCP constitutes a rather detailed manual of operations for banks. The UCP does not purport to be law, but it is a restatement of "custom" in the industry. The UCP is incorporated as an express statement of contract terms and banking trade usage, and the UCP contract terms furnish the rules that usually determine the actions of the parties. While the UCP requires express indication that a documentary credit is subject to the UCP (see Article 1 of the UCP 600), the UCP may be applied to a documentary credit as a description of the custom applicable to documentary credits even if there is no express indication in a documentary credit.[4]

Although the ICC published the International Standby Practices (ISP98), which are intended to be applied to standby letters of credit,[5] the UCP may be applicable to standby letters of credit. Thus, during the course of the revision of UCP 600, the reference to standby letters of credit was suggested to be deleted. However, it could not be deleted since many standby letters of credit are issued to be subject to the UCP.[6]

9.1.2   Basic Concepts

The UCP mainly provides for the actions of the parties to a documentary credit. The UCP is normally incorporated into a documentary credit by express reference in the documentary credit. In case of a conflict between the governing law (e.g. UCC Article 5 in the USA) and the UCP, the UCP takes precedence.[7]

The UCP is not statutory law, but standard terms and rules for a documentary credit.[8] The UCP thus applies to a documentary credit (or any letter of credit) only

---

[4]ICC (2007).

[5]Byrne (2000).

[6]ICC (2007).

[7]Except to the extent of conflict with the mandatory provisions or the non-variable provisions of the governing law: Adodo (2014).

[8]Ibid. p. 14.

to the extent to which it is incorporated in the documentary credit.[9] The UCP may also be applied as the custom applicable to a documentary credit.[10]

The UCP establishes four categories of banks in a documentary credit transaction: an issuing bank, an advising bank, a confirming bank, and a nominated bank.

An issuing bank means the bank that issues the documentary credit at the request of the applicant or on its own behalf. Normally, the issuing bank issues a documentary credit at "the request of an applicant". However, when the issuing bank is the buyer itself in a sale contract and a documentary credit is required under the sale contract, it can issue a documentary credit on its own behalf. The issuing bank promises to honor a presentation on itself, if the documents stated in the documentary credit (conforming documents) are presented to it.

An advising bank means the bank that advises the credit at the request of the issuing bank. An advising bank advises the beneficiary (usually the seller) of issuance of a documentary credit, but makes no promise to pay against presentation of documents. An advising bank should take "reasonable care" to check the authenticity of a documentary credit before advising it.

A confirming bank means the bank that adds its confirmation to a credit upon the issuing bank's authorization or request. In most cases, the advising bank will be the bank that is requested or authorized to add its confirmation. When a bank is requested or authorized to add "confirmation" to a credit by an issuing bank and accordingly "adds its confirmation"[11] to honor a complying presentation, it becomes a confirming bank. When a bank is requested or authorized to add "confirmation" to a credit, it is under no obligation to do so. However, if a bank requested or authorized to add its confirmation decides not to add its confirmation, it should inform the issuing bank without delay.[12] The bank may still advise the documentary credit to a beneficiary without confirmation.

A nominated bank means the bank with which the credit is available or any bank in the case of a credit available with any bank. A nominated bank is normally a bank located in the seller's country. A nominated bank is requested and authorized by an issuing bank to pay or negotiate the drafts and/or the documents against a complying presentation. Although a bank may be named as the nominated bank in the documentary credit, unless a nominated bank is the confirming bank, the nominated bank is under no obligation to act on that nomination (Article 12(a) of the UCP 600). A documentary credit available with a nominated bank is also available with the issuing bank (Article 6(a) of the UCP 600).

---

[9]Ibid. p. 14.

[10]ICC (2007).

[11]See the typical expression of adding confirmation:

"As requested by the Issuing Bank, we hereby add our confirmation to the Credit in accordance with the stipulations under UCP 600 Art. 8."

[12]Collyer (2017).

9.1.3   Major Clauses of UCP 600

Article 1 outlines the application of the UCP. The UCP applies to a documentary credit when the text of the credit expressly indicates that it is subject to the UCP. If so, the UCP is binding on all parties unless expressly modified or excluded by the credit. The UCP may also be applicable to a standby letter of credit to the extent to which it may be applicable. Although ISP 98, published by the ICC in 1998, has specific rules for a standby letter of credit a significant number of standby letters of credit have incorporated the UCP.[13]

As the UCP itself is not statutory law, a documentary credit should expressly incorporate the UCP into it. If not, the UCP will not apply to the credit. Even if the UCP is not expressly incorporated into a documentary credit, it may be applied as a description of the customs applicable to a documentary credit.[14] However, such an application depends on the particular jurisdiction.

Article 2 provides definitions of some of the terminology used throughout the UCP. The definitions include "advising bank", "applicant", "banking day", "beneficiary", "complying presentation", "confirmation", "confirming bank", "credit", "honor", "negotiation", "nominated bank", and "presentation".

Article 3 provides a list of interpretations:

- A credit is irrevocable even if there is no indication to that effect.
- Branches of a bank in different countries are considered to be separate banks.
- The words "to", "until", "till", "from" and "between" when used to determine a period of shipment include the date or dates mentioned, and the words "before" and "after" exclude the date mentioned.
- The words "from" and "after" when used to determine a maturity date exclude the date mentioned.

Article 4 makes the distinction between credits and contracts. A credit is a separate transaction from the underlying contract. Banks are in no way concerned with or bound by the underlying contract.

Article 5 makes the distinction between documents and goods, services or performance. "Banks deal with documents and not with goods, services or performance to which the documents may relate."

Article 6 explains "availability", "expiry date", and "place for presentation":

- A credit must state the bank with which it is available or whether it is available with any bank. A credit available with a nominated bank is also available with the issuing bank.
- A credit must state whether it is available by sight payment, deferred payment, acceptance or negotiation.
- A credit must not be issued available by a draft drawn on the applicant.

---

[13]ICC (2007).
[14]ICC (2007).

Article 7 covers the issuing bank's undertaking. The issuing bank must honor a complying presentation. An issuing bank undertakes to reimburse a nominated bank that has honored or negotiated a complying presentation and forwarded the documents to the issuing bank.

Article 8 covers the confirming bank's undertaking. A confirming bank is irrevocably bound to honor or negotiate as of the time it adds its confirmation to the credit.

Article 9 gives details on the advising of credits and any subsequent amendments. An advising bank that is not a confirming bank advises the credit and any amendment without any undertaking to honor or negotiate.

Article 10 covers amendment of a credit. A credit can neither be amended nor cancelled without the agreement of the issuing bank (the confirming bank, if any) and the beneficiary.

Article 12 provides that, unless a nominated bank is the confirming bank, an authorization to honor or negotiate does not impose any obligation on that nominated bank to honor or negotiate, except when expressly agreed to by that nominated bank and so communicated to the beneficiary.

Article 13 stipulates bank-to-bank reimbursements arrangements.

Article 14 provides standards for the examination of documents. A nominated bank, a confirming bank, and the issuing bank must examine the presentation, on the basis of the documents alone. A nominated bank, a confirming bank, and the issuing bank each have a maximum of five banking days following the day of presentation to determine if a presentation is complying.

Article 15 provides what banks must do with complying presentation. When an issuing bank determines that a presentation is complying, it must honor. When a confirming bank determines that a presentation is complying, it must honor or negotiate and forward the documents to the issuing bank. When a nominated bank determines that a presentation is complying and honors or negotiates, it must forward the documents to the confirming bank or issuing bank.

Article 16 provides what banks should do with discrepant documents. When a nominated bank acting on its nomination, a confirming bank, if any, or the issuing bank determines that a presentation does not comply, it may refuse to honor or negotiate. When an issuing bank determines that a presentation does not comply, it may in its sole judgement approach the applicant for a waiver of the discrepancies. When a nominated bank acting on its nomination, a confirming bank, if any, or the issuing bank decides to refuse to honor or negotiate, it must give a single notice to that effect to the presenter

Article 17 states that at least one original of each document must be presented. If a credit requires presentation of copies of documents, presentation of either originals or copies is permitted.

Article 18 covers commercial invoices. A commercial invoice (1) must appear to have been issued by the beneficiary (except as provided in Article 38), (2) must be made out in the name of the applicant (except as provided in sub-Article 38 (g)), (3) must be made out in the same currency as the credit, and (4) need not be signed. The description of the goods, services or performance in a commercial invoice must correspond with that appearing in the credit.

Article 19 establishes the procedure when a transport document covers at least two different modes of transport.

Article 20 states how a bill of lading must appear.

Article 21 covers non-negotiable sea waybills.

Article 22 covers charter party bills of lading.

Article 23 states how air transport documents must appear.

Article 27 covers clean transport documents. A bank will only accept a clean transport document. A clean transport document is one bearing no clause or notation expressly declaring a defective condition of the goods or their packaging.

Article 28 covers insurance documents and coverage. The insurance document must indicate the amount of insurance coverage and be in the same currency as the credit. If there is no indication in the credit of the insurance coverage required, the amount of insurance coverage must be at least 110% of the CIF or CIP value of the goods.

Article 30 covers tolerance in credit amount, quantity and unit prices. When the words "about" or "approximately" are used in the credit in connection with the amount or quantity, this can be construed as allowing a tolerance of not more than 10% either more or less. Where the goods are described by weight or volume, then a 5% tolerance in the amounts actually shipped is permissible provided the claims do not exceed the amount of the credit.

Article 31 provides that partial drawings or shipments are allowed unless the credit states otherwise.

Article 36 covers force majeure. The bank assumes no liability or responsibility for consequences arising out of the interruption of its business by acts of god, riots, civil commotions, insurrections, wars, acts of terrorism, or by any strikes or lockouts, or any other causes beyond its control.

Article 38 covers transferable credit. A bank is under no obligation to transfer a credit except to the extent and in the manner expressly consented to by that bank. Transferable credit means a credit that specifically states it is "transferable".

Article 39 covers assignment of proceeds. The fact that a credit is not stated to be transferable does not affect the right of the beneficiary to assign any proceeds to which it may be or may become entitled to under the credit, in accordance with the provisions of applicable law.

9.2 Examples of Letters of Credit

9.2.1 Example by SWIFT MT700 Codes

See Table 9.2.

Table 9.2 SWIFT MT700 codes

Swift code	Meaning	Example
20	Documentary credit number	DBXXXX
23	Issuing bank's reference	DBRE-XXX
31C	Date of issue	January 27, 2020
31D	Date and place of expiry	April 26, 2020, TOKYO, JAPAN
32B	Currency code amount	Two hundred thousand US Dollars (USD 200,000.00)
39B	Maximum credit amount	Not exceeding two hundred thousand US Dollars (USD200,000.00)
40A	Form of documentary credit	Irrevocable
40E (*)	Applicable rules	UCP latest version. *(New mandatory field)*
41D	Available with… by…	Draft(s) drawn on DXX Bank, by payment
42C	Drafts at	At sight for full invoice value
42D	Drawee – name and address	DXX Bank, XXX St, Berlin, Germany
43P	Partial shipments	Prohibited
43T	Transhipments	Permitted
44A (*)	Place of taking in charge/dispatch from place of receipt	XXX Terminal, Japan
44E (*)	Port of loading/airport of departure	Tokyo, Japan
44F (*)	Port of discharge/airport of destination	Hamburg, Germany
44B (*)	Place of final destination/for transportation to/place of delivery	Berlin, Germany
44C	Latest date of shipment	March 20, 2020
45A	Description of goods and services	100 personal computers model T-300, CIF Hamburg

(continued)

Table 9.2 (continued)

Swift code	Meaning	Example
46A	Documents required	• Signed commercial invoice in five (5) copies indicating the buyers Purchase order No. GP-520 dated January 10, 2020 • Packing list in five (5) copies • Full set 3/3 clean on board ocean bill of lading, issued to order of JXX Bank, Tokyo, Japan, notify the above accountee, marked 'freight prepaid', dated latest March 20, 2020, and showing documentary credit number • Insurance policy in duplicate for 110% CIF value covering Institute Cargo Clauses (C)
47A	Additional conditions	• All documents indicating the Import License No. IP/XXX dated January 17, 2020 • Draft(s) drawn under this credit must be marked "Drawn under documentary credit No. DBXXXX of DXX Bank, Berlin, Germany dated January 27, 2020"
48	Period of presentation	Documents must be presented for payment within 15 days after the date of shipment
49	Confirmation instructions	Add your confirmation
50	Applicant	BXXX, Berlin, Germany
50B (*)	Non-bank issuer	MXX Corp. Inc
52A	Issuing bank	DXX Bank, Berlin, Germany
57D	Advise through bank	JXX Bank, 402 CXX St, Tokyo, Japan
59	Beneficiary	KTXX Co. Ltd. Tokyo, Japan
71B	Charges	All charges outside the Import-country are on beneficiary's account

(*) Revised/new fields

9.2.2   *Example 2 Documentary Credit Advice*

> Except so far as otherwise expressly stated, this documentary credit is subject

> to the "Uniform Customs and Practice for Documentary Credits" (2007 Revision) International Chamber of Commerce (Publication No. 600)

ADV700–6695-XXXXXX

------------------〈 Message Header〉 ---------------------

Date of Advice:	2010/11/27
Advice No.:	AD1010XXXXXXX
Sender:	BKXXIRXXXXXI
	PXXXX BANK
Receiver:	HVBKKRSEXXX
	XXXX BANK SEOUL KOREA,

---------------------〈 Message Text〉 -----------------------

40A Form of Documentary Credit: IRREVOCABLE

20 Documentary Credit Number: ILC/2010/XXXXXXXX

31C Date of Issue: 2010/11/25

40E Applicable Rules: UCP LATEST VERSION

31D Date and Place of Expiry: (date) 2011/2/25

(place) SOUTH KOREA

50 Applicant: TXXX CO.

XXX, XXX, IRAN

TEL:

59 Beneficiary: SXXXX CORP.

XXX, XXX, SEOUL, KOREA

TEL: 822–2772-XXXX

32B Currency code, Amount: USD 6,000,000

39B Maximum Credit Amount: NOT EXCEEDING

41a Available With ……BY: BY DEF PAYMENT

HVBKKRSEXXX

XXXX BANK, SEOUL

*42P Deferred Payment Details: 180 DAYS FROM B/L DATE

43P Partial Shipments: ALLOWED

43T Transhipment: NOT ALLOWED

44E Port of Loading/Airport of Departure: ANY PORT OF SOUTH KOREA

44F Port of Discharge/Airport of Destination: BANDAR IMAM PERSIAN GULF OF I.R.

OF IRAN

44C Latest Date of Shipment: 2011/2/25

45A Description of Goods and/or Services: 10,000 MT OF PRIME STEEL

BULLETS

SIZE: 150mm x 150mm (+/- 5mm)

LENGTH: 12,000 mm (+/- 100 mm)

NO AND KIND OF STANDARD: EN10025

.

FOB VALUE: USD 5,600,000

FREIGHT CHARGES: USD 400,000

TOTAL CFR BANDAR ABBAS PERSIAN GULF OF I.R OF IRAN: USD

6,000,000

.

PACKIMG: IN BUNDLE IN COMPLIANCE WITH STANDARD EXPORT

PACKING

.

OTHER DETAILS AS SPECIFIED IN P/I NO. SXXXX-XX 2010/11/09

ON CFR BASIS WHICH SHOULD BE INDICATED ON ALL DOCS.

46A Documents Required:

1– FULL SET CLEAN ON BOARD OCEAN B/L ISSUED BY SHIPPING

CO. OR ITS AUTHORIZED AGENT IN 3 ORIGINALS AND 3 COPIES

TO OUR ORDER (PXXX BANK) MENTIONING APPLICANT AS

NOTIFY PARTY, INDICATING NAME AND ADDRESS OF SHIPPING

CO'S REPRESENTATIVE IN I.R.I., MARKED FREIGHT PREPAID, NOT

LATER THAN 2011/3/26 NOR PRIOR TO DATE OF THIS L/C.

2– SIGNED COMMERCIAL INVOICE ISSUED BY BENEFICIARY IN 3

ORIGINALS, 1 OF WHICH CERTIFIED BY LOCAL CHAMBER OF

COMMERCE DECLARING PRICES STATED ARE CURRENT EXPORT

MARKET PRICES FOR MERCHANDISE DESCRIBED THEREIN WITH

3 COIPIES.

3– CERTIFICATE OF ORIGIN IN 1 ORIGINAL CONFIRMING GOODS ORIGINATED IN SOUTH KOREA CERTIFIED BY LOCAL CHAMBER OF COMMERCE.

4– DETAILED PACKING LIST IN 3 ORIGINALS (STANDARD EXPORT PACKING).

5– A CERTIFICATE FROM SHIPPING CO. OR ITS AUTHORIZED AGENTS CERTIFYING SHIPMENT EFFECTED ON CLASSIFIED VESSEL PLYING IN REGULAR LINER SERVICE AS PER INSTITUTE CLASSIFICATION CLAUSE IN 3 COPIES.

6– THE ORIGINAL INSPECTION CERTIFICATE IN 1 ORIGINAL ISSUED NOT PRIOR TO B/L DATE BY S.G.S CO. OR ITS AUTHOROZED AGENTS ON S.G.S CO.

LETTERHEAD CERTIFYING GOODS SHIPPED/INSPECTED ARE IN CONFORMITY WITH QUALITY AND QUANTITY AND PACKING OF GOODS LOADED/DELIVERED ARE STRICTLY COMPLYING WITH SPECIFICATIONS OF GOODS INDICATED IN RELATIVE P/I AND TERMS OF L/C AND ALL SUBSEQUENT AMENDMENTS AS ADVISED TO BEN. SUCH INSPECTION CERTIFICATE SHALL VERIFY GOODS ARE IN CONFORMITY WITH 'EN10025 STANDARD' AND SHOULD BE ATTESTED BY LOCAL CHAMBER OF COMMERCE WHERE ISSUED. INSPECTION CHARGES TO BE BORNE BY BEN.

7– FREIGHT CHARGES INVOICE ISSUED BY SHIPPING CO. OR ITS AUTHORIZED AGENTS IN 2 ORIGINALS 1 OF WHICH SHALL BE CERTIFIED BY LOCAL CHAMBER OF COMMERCE.

47A Additional Conditions:

+ INSURANCE EFFECTED IN I.R. OF IRAN BY XXXX INSURANCE CO.

UNDER INSURANCE POLICY NO. XXXXX TO BE INDICATED ON ALL DOCS.

SHIPMENT ADVICE TO BE MADE TO SAID INSURANCE CO. VIA FAX NO. (+98) 21 XXXX

INDICATING POLICY NO. AND DETAILS OF SHIPMENT A COPY

WHICH MUST BE ACCOMPANIED BY ORIGINAL DOCS.

+ CUSTOMS TARIFF NO. 7206XXXX, CB. NO. 1133XXXX AND OUR DOCUMENTARY CREDIT NO.

ILC/2010/XXXXXXXXXX SHOULD BE INDICATED ON ALL DOCS.

+ THIS CREDIT IS SUBJECT TO UCP 600.

+ THIRD PARTY B/L IS NOT ACCEPTABLE.

+ FREIGHT CHARGES TO BE REFLECTED IN BEN.'S COMMERCIAL INVOICES SEPARATELY.

+ ALL DOCS SHOULD BE PRESENTED IN ENGLISH.

+ PLEASE FORWARD ALL DOCS IN TWO SEPARATE SETS BY REGISTERED AIRMAIL/COURIER

DIRECTLY TO PXXXX BANK(NXXX BRANCH, XXX AVE.,)

OPPOSITE MEHMANSARAYE OSTANDARI, POSTAL CODE: XXXXX, ISFAHAN, IRAN

+ PLS CONFIRM THAT TERMS OF CREDIT HAVE BEEN COMPLIED WITH AND ADVISE US ANY

DISCREPANCIES   FOR   OUR   OBTAINING   APPLICANTS ACCEPTANCE OR SEND ON APPROVAL BASIS.

+ OUR CHARGES OF ALL SWIFT/TLX MSGS IN RESPECT OF APPROVAL DOCS SHOULD BE BORNE BY BEN.

+ DOCS PREPARED PRIOR TO DATE OF THIS L/C ARE NOT ACCEPTABLE AND NEGOTIABLE.

+ FREIGHT CHARGES ARE PRORATA TO GOODS SHIPPED.

+ THIS L/C IS FULLY OPERATIVE AT THE STRENGTH OF THIS SWIFT MSG.

+ RELATED GOODS ARE NOT IN LISTED EU-REGULATION NO. 423/2007 AND 428/2009.

SHIPMENT ON DECK IS NOT ACCEPTABLE.

SINCE SHIPMENT SHOULD BE EFFFECTED VIA SEA TO SOUTH IRANIAN PORTS IN 'PERSIAN GULF'

THE NAME OF 'PERSIAN GULF' SHOULD BE MARKED ON ALL SHIPPING DOCS.

71B Charges: ALL FOREIGH BANK CHARGES ARE FOR THE ACCOUNT OF THE BENEFICIARY.

49 Confirmation Instruction: WITHOUT

53a Reimbursement Bank: HVBKKRSEXXX

 XXXXI BANK, SEOUL

78 Instructions to the Paying/Accepting/Negotiating Bank:

 + PLS DEBIT OUR AED ACC. WITH YRSELVES ON DUE DATE.

 + REIMBURSEMENT CLAIMS SUBJECT TO ICC URR725

 + NEGOTIATION OF DOCS IS RESTRICTED TO YR GOOD BANK
 ONLY.

 ON EXPIRY WITH MT754 FIVE WORKING DAYS PAYMENT OF L/C
 AMOUNT.

72 Sender to Receiver: PLS ACKNOWLEDGE RECEIPT

 Information

 RGDS.,

 NXXX BRANCH

9.2.3 Example 3 Documentary Credit Advice

-------------------------- Message Header -----------------------
Swift Output: MT 700 Issue of a Documentary Credit
Sender: DXXXXLCS
DXXX BANK
(DEPARTMENT LETTERS OF CREDIT)
DUBAI AE
Receiver: SXXXSXXXX
SXX BANK SEOUL BR KR
-------------------------- Message Text --------------------------

27: Sequence of Total
 1/1
40A: Form of Documentary Credit
 IRREVOCABLE
20: Documentary Credit Number
 AIL001-9042
31C: Date of Issue
 091008

40E: Applicable Rules
   UCP LATEST VERSION
31D: Date and Place of Expiry
   100121 SOUTH KOREA
50: Applicant
   JXXX TRADING L.L.C
P.O.BOX ○○○, DUBAI, U.A.E.
59: Beneficiary - Name & Address
   AXXX TRADING CO
P.O.BOX ○○○, SEOUL, KOREA
32B: Currency Code, Amount
   Currency: USD (US DOLLAR)
Amount: #167,734.36#
39B: Maximum Credit Amount
   NOT EXCEEDING
41A: Available With...By... – Name&Addr
   CREDIT AVAILABLE WITH ANY BANK BY DEF PAYMENT
42P: Deferred Payment Details
   90 DAYS FROM SHIPMENT DATE
43P: Partial Shipments
   ALLOWED
43T: Transhipment
   ALLOWED
44E: Port of Loading/Airport of Dep.
   ANY PORT IN KOREA
44F: Port of Discharge/Airport of Dest
   JEBEL ALI PORT, U.A.E. BY SEA
44C: Latest Date of Shipment
   100101
45A: Description of Goods &/or Services
   LITHIUM BATTERRIES.
   ALL OTHER DETAILS AS PER BENEFICIARY'S PROFORMA INVOICE
      NO:
   AJXXXX-XX RV1 DATED 04–10–2009 AND ORDER OF JXXX
      TRADING L.L.C, P.O.BOX XXX DUBAI, U.A.E.
   SHIPMENT TERMS: CFR JEBEL ALI PORT, U.A.E. (INVOICE TO
      CERTIFY THE SAME)

46A: Documents Required

    1) SIGNED COMMERCIAL INVOICES IN 3 ORIGINALS STATING THE
NAME AND ADDRESS OF MANUFACTURERS/ PROCES-
SORS, CERTIFYING ORIGIN OF GOODS AND CONTENTS TO
BE TRUE AND CORRECT.

    2) FULL SET OF CLEAN SHIPPED ON BOARD OCEAN BILLS OF
LADING ISSUED TO THE ORDER OF DXXX BANK, MARKED
FREIGHT PREPAID AND NOTIFY JXXX TRADING L.L.C., P.O.

       BOX XXX, DUBAI, U.A.E.

    3) CERTIFICATE OF ORIGIN IN 1 ORIGINAL PLUS 1 COPY SHOWING
THE NAME AND ADDRESS OF MANUFACTURERS/
PROCESSORS AND STATING THAT THE GOODS ARE OF
SOUTH KOREA ORIGIN ISSUED BY CHAMBER OF COM-
MERCE.

    4) PACKING LIST IN 3 ORIGINALS.

    5) SHIPMENT ADVICE QUOTING L/C NO. AND REFERRING TO OPEN
POLICY NO:26/XXX1/2009/00184 MUST BE SENT BY FAX
WITHIN THREE BANKING DAYS AFTER SHIPMENT TO XXX
GENERAL INSURANCE AND REINSURANCE CO, P.O.BOX
XXXX, DUBAI, U.A.E FAX:XXXX X XXXXXXX.

47A: Additional Conditions

    1) B/L MUST BE ISSUED BY THE CARRIER OR THEIR AGENT'S ON
THEIR OWN B/L AND B/L MUST EVIDENCE THE SAME.

    2) B/L SHOULD BEAR NAME, ADDRESS AND TELEPHONE NO. OF
CARRIER VESSELS' AGENT AT THE PORT OF DESTIN-
ATION.

    3) ALL REQUIRED DOCS TO BE PREPARED IN ENGLISH.

    4) B/L SHOWING COST ADDITIONAL TO FREIGHT CHARGES AS
MENTIONED IN ARTICLE 26(C) OF UCPDC 2007 REVISION
ARE NOT ACCEPTABLE.

    5) CORRECTION IN ANY DOCUMENT MUST BE PROPERLY
AUTHENTICATED AND STAMPED BY ISSUER.

    6) IN CASE OF DISCREPANCIES, WE SHALL DEDUCT OR CLAIM A
SUM OF USD:60 FOR SWIFT.

7) IF THE DOCUMENTS PRESENTED UNDER THIS CREDIT
DETERMINED TO BE DISCREPANT, WE MAY IN OUR SOLE
JUDGEMENT AND DISCRETION APPROACH THE BUYER
FOR A WAIVER OF THE DISCREPANCY(IES). IN CASE THE
WAIVER IS OBTAINED, WE MAY RELEASE THE DOCU-
MENTS AND EFFECT PAYMENT IN ACCORDANCE WITH
THE CREDIT TERMS NOTWITHSTANDING ANY PRIOR
COMMUNICATION TO THE PRESENTER THAT WE ARE
HOL- DING DOCUMENTS AT THEIR DISPOSAL, UNLESS WE
HAVE RECEIVED ANY INSTRUCTIONS TO THE CONTRARY
FROM THEM PRIOR TO OUR RELEASE OF DOCUMENTS.

71B: Charges

ALL BANK CHARGES ARE FOR BENEFICIARY'S ACCOUNT EXCEPT
ISSUING BANK'S L/C ISSUANCE CHARGES AND DEFERRED
PAYMENT CHARGES.

48: Period for Presentation

DOCUMENTS TO BE PRESENTED WITHIN 21 DAYS AFTER THE
DATE OF SHIPMENT BUT WITHIN THE VALIDITY OF THE
CREDIT

49: Confirmation Instructions

WITHOUT

78: Instr to Payg/Accptg/Negotg Bank

1) UPON RECEIPT OF CREDIT COMPLIANT DOCUMENTS AT THE
COUNTERS OF DXXX BANK, CENTRAL OPERATIONS DEPT.
FOR TRADE SERVICES, XXX BLDG., XTH FLOOR, P.O.BOX
XXXX, DEIRA, DUBAI, TEL:XXXXX X XXXXXXX WE
SHALL REMIT THE PROCEEDS AS PER YOUR
INSTRUCTIONS AT MATURITY.

2) DOCUMENTS PROCESSING BANK MUST CONFIRM ON THE DOCS
COVERING SCHEDULE THAT ALL CHARGES OF THE
ADVISING BANK HAVE BEEN PAID.

3) REIMB.IS SUBJECT TO ICC URR 725.

4) NEGOTIATING BANK'S COVERING SCHEDULE MUST CER- TIFY
THAT 'ALL AMENDMENT/S UNDER THIS CREDIT
HAS/HAVE BEEN ACCEPTED/REJECTED BY THE BENEFI-
CIARIES'.

72: Sender to Receiver Information

1) PLEASE ACKNOWLEDGE RECEIPT.

2) PLS COLLECT YOUR CHARGES IN ADVANCE ARTICLE 37(C) OF
UCP 600 NOT APPLICABLE UNDER THIS CREDIT.

------------------------- Message Trailer -----------------------

References

Adodo, Ebenezer. (2014). *Letters of Credit: The Law and Practice of Compliance* (p. 13). Oxford, U.K.: Oxford University Press.

Byrne, James E. (2000) *ISP98 & UCP 500 Compared*. Institute of International Banking Law & Practice, Montgomery, USA.

Collyer, G. (2017). *Guide to Documentary Credits* (5th ed., p. 9). U.K: London Institute of Banking & Finance, Catebury.

ICC (2007) *Commentary on UCP 600*, ICC Publication No. 680, Paris, France, p. 12.

Chapter 10
Other Payment Methods

10.1 Bank Payment Obligation

10.1.1 Introduction

The bank payment obligation (BPO) (see Fig. 10.1) is a newly introduced instrument in international trade. The BPO is an irrevocable undertaking by the obligor bank (the buyer's bank) to pay the recipient bank (the seller's bank) in case of the successful electronic matching of data.

The ICC published the Uniform Rules for Bank Payment Obligation (URBPO 750), which took effect on July 1, 2013. URBPO 750 defines that:

> A bank payment obligation (BPO) or BPO is an irrevocable and independent undertaking of an Obligor Bank to pay or incur a deferred payment obligation and pay at maturity a specified amount to a Recipient Bank following submission of all data sets required by an Established Baseline resulting in a Data Match or an acceptance of a Data Mismatch or an acceptance of a Data Mismatch pursuant to sub-article 10 (c). (URBPO 750 Article 3.)

A baseline can only be established between banks, and those banks must both be connected to the same message platform (the "Transaction Matching Application" (TMA)).[1]

---

[1] Hennah (2013a), p. 24.

© The Editor(s) (if applicable) and The Author(s), under exclusive license to Springer Nature Singapore Pte Ltd. 2021
S. M. Kim, *Payment Methods and Finance for International Trade*,
https://doi.org/10.1007/978-981-15-7039-1_10

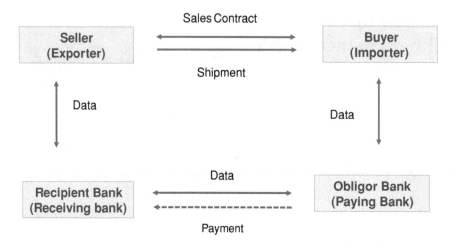

Fig. 10.1 Basic flow of bank payment obligation transaction

10.1.2   Basic Assumptions and Definitions

A BPO transaction is based on two assumptions:

- the use of minimum fields: the buyer, the seller and the respective banks agree on the payment terms and conditions and on the minimum trade information required to assess the credit risk;
- the dispatch of documents, such as the bill of lading, certificate of origin, and inspection certificate (or certificate of quality), from the seller directly to the buyer.

As the information required by the banks is limited and the document exchange is accelerated, discrepancies are expected to be low and the settlement process is expected to be expedited.

10.1.3   Some Basic BPO Definitions

According to URBPO 750 Article 3:

- "Baseline" means data in respect of an underlying trade transaction submitted to a TMA by the buyer's bank or the seller's bank.

- "Data Match" means a comparison of all required data sets with an established baseline resulting in zero mismatches as specified in the data set match report.
- "Obligor bank" means the bank that issues the BPO. The obligor bank issues the legally binding, valid, irrevocable but conditional and enforceable payment undertaking to the recipient bank. Obligor bank is an equivalent term for issuing bank under letters of credit definitions.
- "Recipient Bank" means the bank that is the beneficiary of the BPO. The recipient bank is always the seller's bank.
- "Transaction Matching Application" or "TMA" means a centralized matching and workflow application that provides the service of processing TSMT messages received from the involved banks, the automatic comparison of the data contained in such messages, and the subsequent sending of all related TSMT messages to each of the involved banks.
- TMA provides timely and accurate comparison of data taken from underlying corporate purchase agreements and related documents, such as commercial invoices, transport and insurance.
- The URBPO means the Uniform Rules for Bank Payment Obligations ICC publication No. 750. It is also referred to as ICC URBPO or ICC BPO.

10.1.4 Operation of Bank Payment Obligation

A BPO and a documentary credit have some characteristics in common. Firstly, banks play a key role in both payment methods. Secondly, banks are giving an irrevocable payment undertaking. The BPO is somewhere between a documentary and an open account. The BPO allows buyers to provide key sellers with an absolute assurance that they will be paid on time according to the payment terms of the sales contract.[2]

---

[2]Ibid., p. 29.

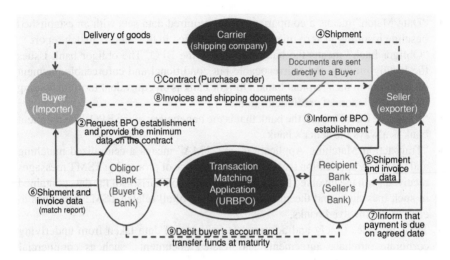

① Buyer and seller enter into a sales contract (or buyer places a purchase order) and agreed on bank payment obligation (BPO) as a payment term in the sales contract.

② Buyer requests the BPO establishment and provides the minimum data from the sales contract to the obligor bank.

③ The recipient bank informs the BPO establishment to seller, and seller confirms the data from the sales contract.

④ Seller ships the goods in accordance with the sales contract.

⑤ Seller presents shipment and invoice data to the recipient bank, which will submit them to Transaction Matching Application for matching.

⑥ Buyer receives the match report from the obligor bank.

⑦ The recipient bank informs seller about the successful data-set match and the payment due date.

⑧ Seller sends invoices and shipment documents directly to buyer, and buyer will take and clear the goods for import with these documets.

⑨ On payment due date, the obligor bank debits the fund from buyer's account, and transfers the fund to the recipient bank.

Fig. 10.2   Bank payment obligation transaction flow

10.1.5   Advantages of Bank Payment Obligation

10.1.5.1   Advantages for Exporters

The advantages of a BPO for exporters are as follows:

- The BPO is a secure payment method for exporters.
- Exporters should get their money faster from the banks under BPO transactions as documents are instantly checked by an automatic system.
- The BPO can be more secure than a documentary credit in that documents will not be checked by humans, which eliminates alleged discrepancies.
- The BPO is cheaper than a documentary credit.
- Under BPO transactions exporters have more control over the goods until they have been paid by the banks as the shipping documents will be held by the

exporters during the BPO process. Exporters do not send paper documents to the banks. Once exporters receive their money from the bank, they dispatch the documents to the importers separately.

- Exporters could reach pre-shipment and post-shipment finance in BPO transactions.
- Once the BPO is opened, it is almost impossible for the importer to cancel the order without the consent of the exporter.
- Non-payment risk shifts from importer to the importer's bank, which is called the obligor bank in BPO transactions.

10.1.5.2 Advantages for Importers

The advantages of a BPO for importers are as follows:

- The BPO is more secure than an advance payment for the importer because the BPO is a conditional payment method. Under BPO transactions, banks send the payment amount to exporters only after shipment of the goods, not before.
- Issuing a BPO may prove that the importer is a financially secure and strong company.
- The BPO is an irrevocable payment method like a documentary credit. As a result, importers can convince exporters to make shipments with BPO much more easily compared with open account or documentary collections.
- The BPO facilitates financing of the shipment for the importers.
- Importers can pay the goods amount after they receive the shipment if exporters and importers agree on a term payment due such as "60 days after match", "90 days after match", etc.
- The BPO protects buyers against non-shipments, late shipments and inferior quality of goods shipments.

10.1.6 Comparison with a Documentary Credit (Letter of Credit) and an Open Account

A documentary credit is a secure and reliable payment method in international trade but it is slow and expensive. Open account is fast and cheap but it is very risky. The BPO occupies the sweet spot between the letter of credit and the open account. BPO is fast, easy to handle, reliable, but is not as expensive as a documentary credit.

10.1.6.1 Comparison with a Documentary Credit (Letter of Credit)

- Both the BPO and a documentary credit (letter of credit) have an irrevocable structure.

- The BPO and letter of credit are governed by ICC Rules. The BPO rules are URBPO 750, and the letters of credit rules are UCP 600.
- The conditional payment guarantee is given by one bank to another bank in BPO transactions. The BPO is a bank-to-bank payment obligation. The conditional payment guarantee is given by a bank to a commercial company in letter of credit transactions. (Letters of credit can be issued as bank-to-bank transactions as well.)
- The letter of credit is paper intensive, while the BPO is an electronic payment method. Bank services are based on a paper document process in a letter of credit, while bank services are based on the electronic exchange of trade data in a BPO.[3]
- Under letter of credit transactions, documents are checked by banks' staff manually. Data match is completed by online means under BPO transactions
- Under BPO transactions shipment documents would not be sent to banks.
- The letter of credit transaction is slow and expensive, while the BPO is fast and not as expensive as letters of credit.

10.1.6.2 Comparison with Open Account

- Both the BPO and open account are fast and easy to handle.
- The open account is the riskiest payment method for exporters. Non-payment risk is stemmed from the importer and must be covered by the exporter in full under open account payments. On the contrary, the obligor bank is the entity that is giving the payment guarantee to the exporter through the recipient bank. As a result non-payment risk mitigates from the importer to the importer's bank under BPO transactions.
- No rules exist to govern open account payments. On the other hand, BPOs can be issued subject to URBPO 750.
- Under open account transactions, exporters must finance importers, whereas under BPO they can benefit from pre-shipment finance and post-shipment finance.
- Bank services are based on electronic exchange of trade data in a BPO, while bank services are limited to payment processing in an open account.[4]

---

[3]Hennah (2013b), p. 28.
[4]Ibid.

10.2 Consignment

10.2.1 Introduction

Consignment is a method of payment in which an exporter sends the goods to an importer (a consignee, distributor) on a deferred payment basis, and the importer pays for the goods after they are sold to a third party (an end customer).[5]

Consignment in an international trade transaction is a variation of an open account, and it is based on a contractual arrangement in which the importer (foreign distributor, consignee) receives, manages, and sells the goods for the exporter, who retains title to the goods until they are sold.[6] In consignment, payment is sent to the exporter only after the goods have been sold by the importer (the foreign distributor, consignee) in the importing country. Goods not sold after an agreed upon time period may be returned to the exporter at its expense.

10.2.2 Operation of Consignment

In a consignment, the title to the goods passes to the importer only after payment is made to the exporter. If the goods are not sold after an agreed-upon period, they may be returned to an exporter at his expense.[7]

A consignment is the most suitable for goods for which a proportioned stock of goods is required to meet the increasing demand in an importing country. As a sale is not completed until the goods are sold to an end customer in an importing country, any payment is not guaranteed at the time of shipment.

One of the common uses of consignment in exporting is the sale of heavy machinery and equipment, because the foreign distributor generally needs floor models and inventory for sale.

With consignment sales, exporters are able to be more competitive for the better availability and the faster delivery of goods. Selling on consignment can also help exporters reduce the direct costs of storing and managing inventory.

Consignment is very risky for an exporter as the goods are in a foreign country in the hands of an independent distributor without any security for payment. The key to success in exporting on consignment is to partner with a reputable and trustworthy foreign distributor or a third-party logistics provider. Appropriate insurance should be in place to cover consigned goods in transit or in possession of a foreign distributor as well as to mitigate the risk of non-payment.

---

[5]US Commercial Services (2015b), p. 161, Seyoum (2009), p. 239, US Department of Commerce/International Trade Administration (2012), p. 13.

[6]US Department of Commerce/International Trade Administration (2012), p. 13.

[7]US Department of Commerce/International Trade Administration (2012), p. 13.

A consignment sale may bring some problems or risks such as delays in payment, uncertainty of sales, cost of returning unsold goods, limited sales effort by an importer etc. Therefore, a consignment sale may be well used with a reliable importer, or when a reliable relationship is established with an importer.

10.3   Netting

In a netting transaction, a seller ships goods to their warehouse located in an importing country, and a buyer takes goods from the warehouse from time to time at the time the delivery of goods takes place. Payment is made after the buyer takes the goods from the seller's warehouse located in an importing country to sell in the domestic market. A netting is basically on a credit transaction, and normally the payment date is set as a future date in which the goods are sold out in an importing country.

In a netting, the delivery of goods can take place immediately whenever a buyer wants the goods, which meets the demand for immediate delivery. However, in a sales contract, an expression like "Net 30 days from acceptance" is specified. To avoid ambiguity and unnecessary dispute, "Net 30 days" should be specified as "30 days from acceptance".[8]

References

Hennah, D. J. (2013), The ICC Guide to the Uniform Rules for Bank Payment Obligations, ICC Publication No. 751E, Paris, France, p. 24.

Hennah, D. J. (2013). The ICC Guide to the Uniform Rules for Bank Payment Obligations, ICC Publication No. 751E, Paris, France, p. 28.

Seyoum, B. (2009). *Export-import theory, practices, and procedures* (2nd ed., p. 239). USA: Routledge, New York.

US Department of Commerce/International Trade Administration. (2012). *Trade finance guide: A quick reference for US Exporters*, US Department of Commerce, Washington D.C., USA, p. 13

US Commercial Services. (2015). *A basic guide to exporting*, 11th ed., US Commercial Services, Washington D.C., USA, p. 159.

US Commercial Services. (2015). *A basic guide to exporting*, 11th ed., US Commercial Services, Washington D.C., USA, p. 161

---

[8]US Commercial Services (2015a), p. 159.

Chapter 11
Independent Guarantee (Demand Guarantee)

11.1 Introduction

11.1.1 Overview

In international trade it has become increasingly common for either or both parties to demand separate undertakings covering the obligations assumed by the other party.[1] These undertakings are usually in the form of bonds, guarantees (independent bank guarantees, demand guarantees, bank guarantees), or standby letters of credit.[2]

Regardless of the obligations covered by it, such guarantee (or bond, standby letter of credit) is always a commitment to pay (wholly or partly) a sum of money, but does not guarantee the actual fulfillment of the debtor's contractual obligations that the principal obligor may have towards the beneficiary under the underlying contract. These guarantees undertake that if the principal fails to complete his contractual duties, the guarantor will pay the beneficiary a sum of money. These guarantees are usually payable upon first demand by the beneficiary and are normally unconditional.[3]

Such guarantees are often referred to as an "independent guarantee", "independent bank guarantee", "bank guarantee", "demand guarantee", "bond", "performance guarantee", or "contract bond",[4] and standby letters of credit have been widely used in the USA instead of such guarantee.[5] Regardless of the title (name), it is the wording of the written undertaking that determines the legal effects of such guarantees.

---

[1] Bertrams (2013a), p. 2.

[2] Affaki and Goode (2011), p. 1, Murray et al. (2010a), pp. 242, 245.

[3] Murray et al. (2010b), p. 243.

[4] Affaki and Goode (2011), p. 1, Murray et al. (2010c), p. 245, Bertrams (2013b), pp. 4, 13; the Uniform Rules for Demand Guarantee, 2007 Revision (URDG 758), Article 2; Carr (2010), p. 503.

[5] Bertrams (2013c), p. 7.

© The Editor(s) (if applicable) and The Author(s), under exclusive license to Springer Nature Singapore Pte Ltd. 2021
S. M. Kim, *Payment Methods and Finance for International Trade*,
https://doi.org/10.1007/978-981-15-7039-1_11

137

In practice, demand guarantees, performance bonds, performance guarantees and standby letters of credit have a similar legal character and resemble documentary credits in that they are primary in form, and generally conditional only upon presentation of a written demand for payment together with any other stipulated documents. The issuing bank is not concerned as to whether there has been any actual default by the principal.[6]

Independent guarantees (independent bank guarantees, demand guarantees, bank guarantees) are widely used in international business transactions to support performance obligations or payment obligations.[7] It could be the seller's delivery obligations that have to be secured by these guarantees, or it could be the buyer's payment obligations that have to be secured by these guarantees. These guarantees could be used for the purpose of financing trade transactions including overseas construction projects.

In certain cases, particularly with more straightforward deals or in combination with a simple service and/or performance, it is often enough that the seller, or the parent company, issues undertakings (guarantees, bonds, standby letters of credit). However, in most cases, these undertakings have to be issued by a separate party, normally in the form of a bank guarantee (issued by a bank), or an insurance bond (from an insurance company), or a standby letter of credit (issued by a bank).

Bank guarantees (bonds) or standby letters of credit are the most commonly used instruments for such undertakings in connection with ordinary transactions in international trade. There are some norms that could be applied to such guarantees (bonds) or standby letters of credit. The ICC published the Uniform Rules for Demand Guarantees in 1992 (URDG 458), and revised it in 2010 (URDG 758). The ICC also published the International Standby Practice in 1998 (ISP 98). UNCITRAL adopted the United Nations Convention on Independent Guarantees and Stand-by Letters of Credit in 1995, and the Convention entered into force in 2000.

11.1.2 Concept

An independent guarantee (or bond, demand guarantee, standby letter of credit) (see Fig. 11.1) is an irrevocable undertaking to pay a sum of money to a beneficiary (or a creditor) upon a complying demand.[8] An independent guarantee undertakes to pay the beneficiary a sum of money, if the principal (debtor) fails to complete his obligations under the underlying contract. However, an independent guarantee does not undertake the actual fulfillment of the principal's (debtor's) contractual obligations under the underlying contract. An independent guarantee is usually payable upon first demand by the beneficiary and is normally unconditional.[9]

---

[6]Murray et al. (2010c), p. 245.

[7]Bishop (2006), p. 78.

[8]Affaki and Goode (2011), p. 1, Murray et al. (2010c), p. 245, Bertrams (2013d), pp. 1, 13; Uniform Rules for Demand Guarantee, 2007 Revision (URDG 758), Article 2; Sang Man Kim (2015), p. 42.

[9]Murray et al. (2010b), p. 243.

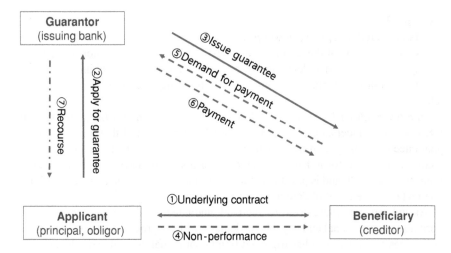

Fig. 11.1 Process flow of an independent guarantee

An independent guarantee (or a demand guarantee) is legally independent, irrevocable, and payable on demand. An independent guarantee (or a bond) is normally issued by a bank (or an insurance company) in favor of a creditor at the request of a principal (or an obligor).[10] In a conventional independent guarantee (or a demand guarantee), a guarantor (or a guarantor bank) irrevocably, absolutely, and unconditionally guarantees to pay the beneficiary (or a creditor) as primary obligor. A guarantor undertakes to pay a sum of money, but does not undertake fulfilment of the debtor's obligation under the underlying contract.[11] Most independent guarantees state that the guarantor undertakes to pay as a primary obligor or a principal obligor, not as a surety. Examples are given below of the relevant expressions used in independent guarantees issued in international transactions.

Example 1
The Guarantor hereby irrevocably and unconditionally guarantees to pay the Lender any sum up to a maximum amount of USD 24,103,518.61 to be increased by all interests, interests on late payments, and treasury costs upon receipt by the Guarantor of a first demand in writing from the Lender and the written statement of the Lender stating the amount to be paid by the Guarantor.

Example 2
The undersigned, as primary obligor and not merely as surety, hereby irrevocably, absolutely and unconditionally guarantees the full, prompt and punctual payment when due.

---

[10]Bertrams (2013e), p. 13.
[11]Sang Man Kim (2019), Grath (2014), p. 78.

Example 3

This being stated, we, [*Name of issuing bank and address*], irrespective of the validity
and the legal effects of the Contract and waiving all rights of objection and defense
arising from the principal debt, hereby irrevocably undertake to pay immediately to
you, upon your first demand, any amount up to (currency/maximum amount) (in full
letters:....................)

In *Edward Owen Engineering v. Barclays Bank International Ltd.*,[12] the leading
UK case of an independent guarantee, Lord Denning viewed that an independent
guarantee is virtually a promissory note payable on demand. Unlike a documentary
credit, n guarantee (or a demand guarantee) or a standby letter of credit serves as
security for default, and is payable in the event of non-performance of an underlying
contract or in the event of default by a principal (or an obligor).[13]

An independent guarantee (or a demand guarantee, a standby letter of credit) is
normally unconditional and payable on demand without proof. This characteristic of
an independent guarantee has triggered fraudulent demands or abusive demands. If
a principal (or an obligor) wishes to protect himself from a fraudulent demand or an
abusive demand, he can do so by imposing conditions for demand such as certificate
issued by an independent third party.[14] However, in many cases, both creditors and
guarantor banks are reluctant to such conditions. Banks in documentary credits or in
independent guarantees are reluctant to be involved in the disputes between applicants and beneficiaries; instead they wish to exercise the right of reimbursement to
applicants once paying the demand.

11.1.3 Standby Letter of Credit and Surety Bond

In some countries, standby letters of credit are often issued by banks instead of
guarantees. A standby letter of credit ("standby L/C") has the same function as
independent guarantees (bonds or demand guarantees),[15] and is just another name for
an independent guarantee.[16] A standby letter of credit and an independent guarantee
are conceptually and legally the same device.[17]

In some countries, banks are restricted by law or common practice from issuing
guarantees to third parties, so they have issued standby letters of credit as an alternative. Standby letters of credit originated in the USA because federal law was

---

[12](1978) Q.B. 159.

[13]Carr (2010), p. 503.

[14]Carr (2010), p. 503.

In *Gur Corp. v. Trust Bank of Africa Ltd.* [1987] 1 Q.B. 599, the P-bond was payable on
production of a certificate signed by a certified surveyor.

[15]Murray et al. (2010c), p. 245, Bertrams (2013f), p. 7.

[16]Goode (1995), p. 16.

[17]Bertrams (2013e), p. 13, Murray et al. (2010c), p. 245.

construed to prohibit banks from issuing guarantees, performance bonds, or insurance policies.[18] However, the power of American banks to issue guarantees was finally recognized in the final revised Interpretive Ruling 7.1016 of the Comptroller of the Currency of February 9, 1996.[19] Standby letters of credit have been widely used in the USA instead of such guarantee. But they are also used in other parts of the world.

In most countries, however, independent guarantees (bonds or demand guarantees) are the more commonly used alternatives when issuing separate bank undertakings related to normal international trade transactions. But should a standby letter of credit be asked for, it can be issued on behalf of the principal with the same wording and the same undertaking as a guarantee.

Surety bonds or ancillary guarantees undertake to fulfill the obligations of the principal obligors. The same goes in most cases, but not always, for a bond issued by an insurance company guaranteeing the obligations of a supplier of goods and services under a contract. Internationally, so-called "surety bonds" may be issued by insurance or surety companies, with the alternative obligation to fulfill or arrange for the completion of the underlying contract. A demand guarantee is in general unconditional,[20] while a surety bond is conditional.

11.2   Types of Independent Guarantees

11.2.1   A Direct Guarantee and an Indirect Guarantee

The question of who should issue the guarantee (standby letter of credit) is usually determined by the beneficiary, but could also depend on rules or local conditions in that country. There are also situations when a guarantee must be issued by a local bank in the beneficiary's country (which is the standard procedure in many Islamic and/or developing countries), particularly if a beneficiary is a local authority or similar body.

There are two types of guarantee, "direct guarantee" and "indirect guarantee". The indirect guarantee is also called the "four parties guarantee".

In a direct guarantee (see Fig. 11.2), a guarantee (or a standby letter of credit) will be sent directly to a beneficiary in a foreign country. A guarantee can also be forwarded to a beneficiary through an advising bank at the beneficiary's location, but without any responsibility for that advising bank under a guarantee. The role of the advising bank is then only to forward the guarantee to the beneficiary, verifying the authenticity of the guarantor bank (the issuing bank).

In an indirect guarantee (see Fig. 11.3), the principal's bank (the first instructing bank) issues a guarantee (a counter guarantee) to the local bank (the second issuing

---

[18]Folsom et al. (2016), p. 240.

[19]Bertrams (2013g), p. 6.

[20]Murray et al. (2010c), p. 245.

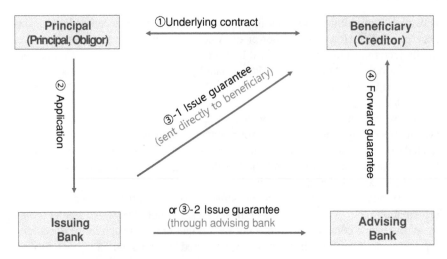

Fig. 11.2   Process flow of a direct guarantee

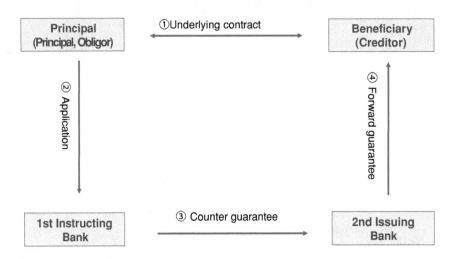

Fig. 11.3   Process flow of an indirect guarantee

bank), and the local bank (the second issuing bank) will issue a guarantee in favor of a beneficiary against a counter guarantee. An indirect guarantee, is also called a "four parties guarantee". In some countries it may even be stipulated by law that guarantees should be issued by a local bank. In these cases, the principal's bank (the instructing bank) will issue a counter guarantee as an indemnity to the local bank, which will then become the issuing bank. In these situations, the indirect guarantee is issued.

The counter guarantee would be accompanied by instructions about the wording of the guarantee to be issued—either in a specified form (if that is possible) or according to local law and practice.

11.2.2 Performance Guarantee and Payment Guarantee

11.2.2.1 Performance Guarantee

A performance guarantee (see Fig. 11.4) is a guarantee issued by a guarantor (usually banks) in favor of the buyer (the importer) on behalf of the seller (exporter), which guarantees that if the exporter fails to perform his contractual obligations, the guarantor will pay the buyer a sum of money in accordance with the guarantee.

A performance guarantee secures the performance of the contractual obligation by the seller in favor of the buyer.

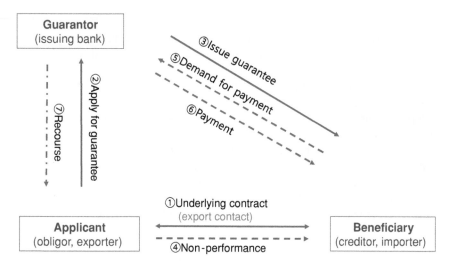

Fig. 11.4 Performance guarantee (p-bond)

11.2.2.2 Payment Guarantee

A payment guarantee (see Fig. 11.5) is a guarantee issued by a guarantor (usually banks) in favor of the seller (the exporter) on behalf of the buyer (importer), which guarantees that if the buyer fails to make payment, the guarantor will pay the seller a sum of money in accordance with the guarantee.[21] Payment guarantees are issued

---

[21] Bertrams (2013h), p. 41.

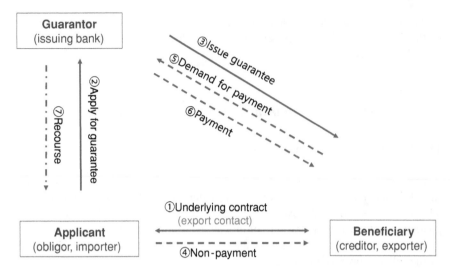

Fig. 11.5 Payment guarantee

on the instruction of the buyer in favor of the seller, to cover the buyer's payment obligations for goods or services to be delivered according to the contract. This form of guarantee is often used to cover either single or recurring deliveries under a long-term contract, with a total amount covering outstanding and anticipated deliveries.

The terms of payment used in connection with payment guarantees are often on an "open account" basis for consumer goods. The handling of delivery and documentation could then be made more flexible compared to a letter of credit, but security for the seller depends on the nature and wording of the guarantee.

A payment guarantee is similar to a documentary credit with regard to its function and structure. However, a payment guarantee does not require shipping documents, but merely a written demand for payment. Recently, there has been a growing demand for payment guarantees (or standby letters of credit) assuring payment in sales transactions.[22]

11.2.3 Various Types of Performance Guarantee (Performance Type Guarantee)

There are various stages before and during the performance of a contract at which guarantees may be required. In the export of capital goods (industrial plants or ships) or overseas construction, performance guarantees (performance type guarantees) are normally required as a security for an exporter's performance of a contract. There is a range of guarantees such as tender guarantee (or bid bond), performance guarantee,

---

[22] Bertrams (2013h), p. 41.

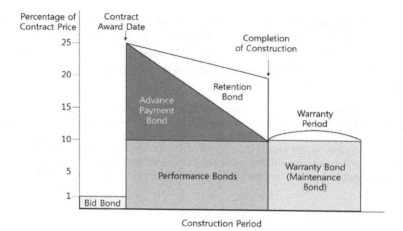

Fig. 11.6 Various types of guarantees at each stage in an overseas construction

advance payment guarantee (or refund guarantee), warranty guarantee, maintenance guarantee, etc. At the time of bidding, a tender guarantee (or a bid bond) is required. Then, at the time of conclusion of a contract, a performance guarantee (P-bond) and an advance payment guarantee (Ap-bond) are required. At the time of completion of construction (or installment of the equipment), a warranty bond (or maintenance bond) is required.

These guarantees are issued in favor of an importer by a financial institution at the request of an exporter. Normally, issuance of guarantees is set as a condition precedent to the payment of the contract price. A financial institution that issues such guarantees pays a beneficiary (normally an importer) on demand in the event an exporter fails to perform a contract or some other event of calling occurs. A financial institution will recourse to an exporter once they receive a demand for payment from a beneficiary.

11.2.3.1 Tender Guarantee or Bid Bond

When a company or government invites bidders to submit offers to complete a contract, it will be concerned to receive bids only from those genuinely capable and willing to sign a contract if their bid is selected. To protect themselves, potential buyers may ask bidders to submit a bond that can be called in the event that the bidder does not contract and/or fails to meet the other bonding requirements of the purchaser. The value of such bonds is typically a small percentage of the contract value.

A business tendering or bidding for a contract may be requested to provide a bond guaranteeing that, if successful, a contract will be established and the successful bidder may have to provide bonds covering their performance and their warranties.

A tender guarantee is to secure the payment of any loss or damage suffered or incurred by the beneficiary arising out of the failure by the principal to enter into a contract or provide a performance bond or other bond pursuant to such tender (see Article 2 of the Uniform Rules for Contract Bonds 1993 (URCB)).

The URCG 325 provides that:

"tender guarantee" means an undertaking given by a bank, insurance company or other party ("the guarantor") at the request of a tenderer("the principal") or given on the instructions of a bank, insurance company, or other party so requested by the principal ("the instructing party") to a party inviting tenders ("the beneficiary") whereby the guarantor undertakes-in the event of default by the principal in the obligations resulting from the submission of the tender-to make payment to the beneficiary within the limits of a stated sum of money.

11.2.3.2 Performance Guarantee (P-Bond)

Once a contract to supply equipment or to undertake a construction has been agreed to, the importer (employer) may require some assurance for the performance of the contract. A performance bond may therefore be required for that purpose.

A performance guarantee (or a performance bond) is a guarantee issued by a guarantor (usually banks) in favor of a buyer (or an importer, an employer) on behalf of a seller (or an exporter, a contractor), which guarantees that if a seller (or an exporter, a contractor) fails to perform his contractual obligations, the guarantor will pay the buyer (or the importer, an employer) a sum of money in accordance with the performance guarantee.

A performance guarantee (or P-bond) is to secure the performance of any contract or contractual obligation (see Article 2 of URCB). A performance guarantee secures the performance of a contractual obligation by the seller (or the exporter, the contractor) in favor of the buyer (or the importer, the employer).

The Uniform Rules for Contract Guarantees 1978 (URCG 325) provide that:

"performance guarantee" means an undertaking given by a bank, insurance company or other party ("the guarantor") at the request of a supplier of goods or services or other contractor ("the principal") or given on the instructions of a bank, insurance company, or other party so requested by the principal ("the instructing party") to a buyer or to an employer ("the beneficiary") whereby the guarantor undertakes-in the event of default by the principal in due performance of the terms of a contract between the principal and the beneficiary ("the contract") - to make payment to the beneficiary within the limits of a stated sum of money or, if the guarantee so provides, at the guarantor's option, to arrange for performance of the contract.

11.2.3.3 Advance Payment Guarantee (AP-Bond)

Should the bidder be successful, they may incorporate an advance payment into the contract to enable the bidder to purchase materials and undertake design or other preparatory work. In an export of capital goods (industrial plants or ships) or overseas construction, it is common practice that an importer (owner) pays some downpayment (advance payment) to a contractor. An importer (owner) is entitled to repayment of the downpayment (advance payment) paid in the event that an exporter is in default under the construction. Thus, as a security for such repayment, an advance payment guarantee (AP-bond) or a repayment guarantee[23] issued by a financial institution in favor of an employer is required.[24]

Advance payment guarantees (AP-bond) irrevocably and unconditionally guarantee to pay on a simple demand for payment by a beneficiary (or an importer). When an importer is entitled to repayment of advance payment under the export contract, but is not repaid, the beneficiary (importer) under an advance payment guarantee will demand payment against a guarantor.

> An advance payment guarantee (AP-bond) is issued by the guarantor in favour of the beneficiary to secure the repayment of any sum or sums advanced by the beneficiary to the principal under or for the purposes of the underlying contract, where such sum or sums is or are advanced before the carrying out of works, the performance of services or the supply or provision of any goods pursuant to such contract. (Article 2 of the URCB).

An advance payment guarantee under an overseas construction contract normally contains a "reduction clause" that the guaranteed amount will be automatically reduced as per performance of construction.[25]

The URCG 325 provides that:

> "repayment guarantee" means an undertaking given by a bank, insurance company or other party ("the guarantor") at the request of a supplier of goods or services or other contractor ("the principal") or given on the instructions of a bank, insurance company or other party so requested by the principal ("the instructing party") to a buyer or to an employer ("the beneficiary") whereby the guarantor undertakes-in the event of default by the principal to repay in accordance with the terms and conditions of a contract between the principal and the beneficiary ("the contract") any sum or sums advanced or paid by the beneficiary to the principal and not otherwise repaid-to make payment to the beneficiary within the limits of a stated sum of money.

In a typical shipbuilding contract, a shipbuilder is paid in five instalments: the first to fourth instalments are paid before delivery ("pre-delivery instalments"), and the fifth instalment is paid at the time of delivery ("delivery instalment"). The buyer (or owner) is entitled to repayment of those instalments paid where a shipbuilder is in default under a shipbuilding contract. In a shipbuilding contract, a refund guarantee (also referred to a repayment guarantee or refundment guarantee) is required as a security for repayment of the pre-delivery instalments paid to a shipbuilder.[26] A refund guarantee is to indemnify a buyer for losses resulting from a shipbuilder's default under the shipbuilding contract. A refund guarantee is one type of advance payment guarantee, but normally contains an "increase clause" in contrast with a

---

[23] The ICC Uniform Rules for Contract Guarantees (1978) refer to a "repayment guarantee" instead of an advance payment guarantee (Article 2).

[24] Murray et al. (2010d), p. 39, Curtis (2002), p. 251.

[25] Sang Man Kim (2018), p. 571.

[26] Sang Man Kim (2019).

"reduction clause" in an advance payment guarantee under an overseas construction contract.[27] This distinguishes a refund guarantee from other advance payment guarantees.

11.2.3.4 Retention Bond

A retention bond (R-bond) is used to secure the payment of any sum or sums paid or released to the principal by the beneficiary before the date for payment or release thereof contained in the underlying contract (see Article 2 of the URCB).

An overseas construction contract provides that an employer pays interim installments as the construction progresses, in which case an employer is sometimes entitled to retain a percentage of such interim installments, normally between 5% and 10%, as security for defects.[28] When a retention bond (R-bond) is offered to an employer, an employer releases the retention money to a contractor. As the retention money increases as the construction progresses, the maximum amount payable under a retention guarantee will increase accordingly. This is very similar to the increase clause in a refund guarantee under a shipbuilding contract.

11.2.3.5 Warranty Guarantee (Warranty Bond, Maintenance Bond)

Warranty bonds may be required by the importer (employer) to cover warranty once a performance bond has expired. Nowadays, performance bonds are extended to cover the warranty period.

A warranty guarantee (or maintenance bond) is used to secure contractual obligations relating to the maintenance of works or goods following physical completion pursuant to a contract (see Article 2 of the URCB). A warranty guarantee (or maintenance bond) is required to cover the defect during the warranty period once construction is completed. Nowadays, a performance guarantee is extended to cover the defect during the warranty period, and replaces a warranty bond. This is to reduce the inconvenience of issuing an additional guarantee in a single overseas construction project.

---

[27] Harwood (2006), p. 47, Sang Man Kim (2019).
[28] Bertrams (2013i), p. 40.

11.3 Independence Principle and Fraud Exception

11.3.1 The Independence Principle

An independent guarantee (demand guarantee or standby letter of credit) is basically independent of the underlying contract under which it is issued. This characteristic is called the "independence principle". The "independence" from the underlying contract is essential in an independent guarantee. Most independent guarantees expressly state the "independence principle" in them.

The UN Convention[29] provides for the "independence nature" of a guarantee (or a standby letter of credit) in Article 2(1)[30] and Article 3.[31] Even though the UN Convention is, as of August 2018, ratified by only eight states (Belarus, Ecuador, El Salvador, Gabon, Kuwait, Liberia, Panama, Tunisia) and the trade volume of those states is marginal, it could be used to supplement the operation of the rules and laws on a specific independent guarantee. The URDG 758 also provides in Article 3 for the "independence nature" of a demand guarantee:

a. A guarantee is by its nature independent of the underlying relationship and the application, and the guarantor is in no way concerned with or bound by such relationship. A reference in the guarantee to the underlying relationship for the purpose of identifying it does not change the independent nature of the guarantee. The undertaking of a guarantor to pay under the guarantee is not subject to claims or defenses arising from any relationship other than a relationship between the guarantor and the beneficiary.

b. A counter guarantee is by its nature independent of the guarantee, the underlying relationship, the application and any other counter guarantee to which it relates, and the counter guarantor is in no way concerned with or bound by such relationship. A reference in the counter guarantee to the underlying relationship for the purpose of identifying it does not change the independent nature of the counter

---

[29] United Nations Convention on Independent Guarantees and Stand-by Letters of Credit of 1995.

[30] Article 2. Undertaking: (1) For the purposes of this Convention, an undertaking is an independent commitment, known in international practice as an independent guarantee or as a stand-by letter of credit, given by a bank or other institution or person ("guarantor/issuer") to pay the beneficiary a certain or determinable amount upon simple demand or upon demand accompanied by other documents, in conformity with the terms and any documentary conditions of the undertaking, indicating, or from which it is to be inferred, that payment is due because of a default in the performance of an obligation, or because of another contingency, or for money borrowed or advanced, or on account of any mature indebtedness undertaken by the principal/applicant or another person.

[31] Article 3. Independence of undertaking:

For the purposes of this Convention, an undertaking is independent where the guarantor/issuer's obligation to the beneficiary is not: (a) Dependent upon the existence or validity of any underlying transaction, or upon any other undertaking (including stand-by letters of credit or independent guarantees to which confirmations or counter guarantees relate); or (b) Subject to any term or condition not appearing in the undertaking, or to any future, uncertain act or event except presentation of documents or another such act or event within a guarantor/issuer's sphere of operations.

guarantee. The undertaking of a counter guarantor to pay under the counter guarantee is not subject to claims or defenses arising from any relationship other than a relationship between the counter guarantor and the guarantor or other counter guarantor to whom the counter guarantee is issued.

The International Standby Practice (the "ISP98") also has provisions stipulating the "independence principle" of a guarantee (or a standby letter of credit) in Article 1.06:

a. A standby is an irrevocable, independent, documentary, and binding undertaking when issued and need not so state.
b. Because a standby is irrevocable, an issuer's obligations under a standby cannot be amended or cancelled by the issuer except as provided in the standby or as consented to by the person against whom the amendment or cancellation is asserted.
c. Because a standby is independent, the enforceability of an issuer's obligations under a standby does not depend on:

   i the issuer's right or ability to obtain reimbursement from the applicant;
   ii the beneficiary's right to obtain payment from the applicant;
   iii a reference in the standby to any reimbursement agreement or underlying transaction; or
   iv the issuer's knowledge of performance or breach of any reimbursement agreement or underlying transaction.

d. Because a standby is documentary, an issuer's obligations depend on the presentation of documents and an examination of required documents on their face.
e. Because a standby or amendment is binding when issued, it is enforceable against an issuer whether or not the applicant authorised its issuance, the issuer received a fee, or the beneficiary received or relied on the standby or the amendment.

Those provisions stipulating the "independence nature" of an independent guarantee show that the independence guarantee, including advance payment guarantees in international trades, are to be by nature "independent" of the underlying transaction. An independent guarantee is also independent of the application for issuance between an applicant and a guarantor and, therefore, the instructions by the applicant do not give effect to the payment obligation by the guarantor.

11.3.2 The Fraud Exception

The "independence principle" in an independent guarantee (demand guarantee or standby letter of credit) has contributed to securing the applicant's obligation, enhancing assurance of payment, but has triggered fraudulent demands or abusive demands. Many courts have recognized a number of exceptions to the independence principle. Although most jurisdictions admit certain exceptions to the independence principle, the ambit of the fraud exception has been debated and is controversial.

The Uniform Rules for Demand Guarantee, 2007 Revision, ICC Publication no. 758 (the "URDG 758"), the International Standby Practice of 1998 (the "ISP 98") and the Uniform Customs and Practice for Documentary Credits, 2007 Revision, ICC Publication No. 600 (the "UCP 600") do not have provisions specifying the fraud exception for fraudulent or abusive demand. The United Nations Convention on Independent Guarantees and Stand-by Letters of Credit of 1995 has a provision specifying the fraud exception for fraudulent demand (see Article 19), it is not widely used in international transactions for the small number of ratifying countries.

If a principal (or an obligor) wishes to protect himself from fraudulent demands or abusive demands, he can do so by imposing conditions for demand such as a certificate issued by an independent third party.[32]

11.4 Examples of Independent Guarantees

11.4.1 Example Tender Guarantee (Bid-Bond)

TENDER GUARANTEE No.

[Date of Issuance]

To: *[Beneficiary's name]*

We, *[XXX Bank]*, hereby open our irrevocable Letter of Guarantee No. in your favor for account of *[Bidder]* up to an aggregate amount of US$ (say US Dollars only) as a Bid Guarantee in accordance with the terms and conditions of the tender for *[Project Name]*.

This guarantee shall be payable upon your first demand accompanied by your signed statement certifying that *[Bidder]* has been awarded the tender and has failed to enter into a corresponding contract or has failed to furnish a performance guarantee within the designated period.

This guarantee will expire on *[Expiry Date]* and any claims must be received by us in writing on or before *[Expiry Date including 20 days mailing date]* after which date this guarantee shall be null and void.

Yours faithfully

(Authorized Signature)

XXX Bank

---

[32] Carr (2010), p. 503. In *Gur Corp. v. Trust Bank of Africa Ltd.* [1987] 1 Q.B. 599, the P-bond was payable on production of a certificate signed by a certified surveyor.

11.4.2   *Example Performance Guarantee (In the Form of Indirect Guarantee/Counter Guarantee Type)*

Our reference number
At the request of, please issue on our responsibility in favor of your guarantee in the following wording:

QUOTE

We have been informed that you have concluded on a contract No (hereinafter called the "Contract") with Messrs (hereinafter called the "Principal") for the supply of at a total price of According to the Contract, The Principal is required to provide you with a performance guarantee in the amount of (% of the total price).

This being stated, we, (name of issuing bank and address), irrespective of the validity and the legal effects of the Contract and waiving all rights of objection and defense arising from the principal debt, hereby irrevocably undertake to pay immediately to you, upon your first demand, any amount up to (currency/maximum amount) (in full letters:) upon receipt of your written request for payment and your written confirmation stating that The Principal is in breach of his obligation(s) under the Contract and explaining in which respect the Principal is in breach.

Our guarantee is valid until.
Consequently, any demand for payment under this guarantee must be received by us at this office on or before expiry date.
This guarantee is subject to the Uniform Rules for Demand Guarantees, ICC Publication No. 758.

UNQUOTE

In consideration of issuing your guarantee as above, we hereby give you our irrevocable counter guarantee and undertake to pay you any sum or sums not exceeding in total amount of (currency/maximum amount) (in full letters:) upon receipt by us at this office no later than of your first written demand. Such a demand shall be supported by your written statement that you have received a demand for payment under your guarantee in accordance with its terms and with Article 15 of the Uniform Rules for Demand Guarantees.

This counter guarantee is subject to the Uniform Rules for Demand Guarantees, ICC Publication No. 758.

Please confirm to us the issuance of your guarantee.

XXX BANK

(Place, date)

11.4.3   *Example Performance Guarantee (P-Bond)*

PERFORMANCE GUARANTEE

[*Date of Issue*]

To: [*Employer's (Beneficiary's) Name and Address*]

Re; Our Irrevocable Letter of Guarantee No. as Performance Bond

By an agreement dated ( ) ("the Agreement") made between yourselves and [Contractor's name] (a company incorporated under the laws of Republic of Korea and having its registered office at [Contractor's Address] ("the Contractor") the Contractor agreed, and became bound to inter alia, design, manufacture, supply, erect, assemble, deliver, commission, and warrant three units of quayside cranes and associated works.

The terms of the Agreement oblige the Contractor to provide you with a bond as security for the due performance of the Contractor's obligations under the Agreement.

In consideration of your accepting our obligations hereunder in discharge of the Contractor's obligations to provide such a bond, we, [*Guarantor Bank's Name*] hereby and irrevocably and unconditionally undertake to pay you the sum [*USD 10,000,000*] and accordingly, covenant and agree with you as follows:

1. Forthwith upon receipt of a written demand by you upon us at any time within the validity of this bond (as defined in item 7 in this bond) stating (i) that the Contractor has failed to perform its obligations under the Agreement specifying the Contractor's default and (ii) the amount of the damage suffered by you as result of the Contractor failing to perform such obligations, and notwithstanding any objection by the Contractor or any other person to set off or counterclaim, we shall forthwith pay you the amount specified in such demand not exceeding in aggregate the stipulated sum.
2. For the avoidance of doubt, it is confirmed that you may make as many separate demands hereunder as you think fit, provided that the total amount paid by us hereunder or demanded from us hereunder, at any time, shall not exceed the stipulated sum.
3. All payments hereunder shall be made free and clear of and without deduction for or an account of any present or future taxes, duties, charges, fees, deductions or withholding of any nature whatsoever and by whomsoever imposed.
4. Our obligations hereunder shall not be affected by any act, omission, matter or thing which but for this provision might operate to release or otherwise exonerate us from our obligations hereunder, in whole or in part, including, but not limited to and whether or not known to us or you;

    (a) any time or waiver granted to the Contractor or any other person; or
    (b) any taking, variation, compromise, renewal or release of or any refusal or neglect to perfect; or

(c) any limitation, disability or incapacity relating to the Contractor or any other person; or

(d) any variation of or amendment or supplement to the Agreement or the works to be performed thereunder or any other document or security so that references in this bond to the Agreement shall include each such variation, or supplement; or

(e) any unenforceability, invalidity or frustration of any obligations of the Contractor or any other person under the Agreement or any other document or security.

5. The benefit of this bond may be assigned by you at any time and references in the bond to "you" "yourselves" and the like shall include your successors and assignees.

6. This bond shall be governed by and construed in accordance with [*Governing Law*] and we hereby submit to the non-exclusive jurisdiction of the courts of [*Jurisdiction*] over any claim arising out of this bond.

7. The validity of this bond is up to the date on which you notify us in writing that the Contractor has compiled in all respects with the provisions of Clause [*Article XX*] of the Agreement.

8. This bond shall automatically become null and void, if no written demand as defined in item 1 in this bond from you is received by us within the validity of this bond, and then this bond shall be returned to us in the earliest manner.

In witness whereof this Bond has been executed on [*Date of Issue*].

11.4.4   Example Standby Letter of Credit (For an AP-Bond)

STANDBY LETTER OF CREDIT

Date: [ ]

Messrs

[*Name and Address of the Issuer*]

Since our client, [AAA] Engineering & Construction Co., Ltd. ("[AAA]") acknowledge that [Name and Address of the Issuer] ("Issuer"), has issued an Advance Payment Bond in favor of [Name and Address of the Beneficiary] ("Beneficiary") for the amount of US$ [ ] ([ ] US Dollars) for the [Name of Project], and that [AAA] has a share in this indemnity of US$ [ ] ([ ] US Dollars) representing a [ ] % of the Advance Payment Bond, we, the BBB Bank, issue in your favor this Standby Letter of Credit

According to the Article XIV, Section [ ] of the Agreement between Issuer and [AAA], we herewith irrevocably undertake to pay you on first demand, without any reservation and notwithstanding any objection by [AAA], any amount you demand up to US$ [ ] ([ ] US Dollars) upon receipt of your written request for payment duly signed confirming that the amount claimed under this Standby Letter of Credit is due because of a failure of [AAA] in the delivery of equipment and/or materials to the Construction Site in [*Name of the Country*].

Any payment made hereunder shall be made free and clear of, and without deduction for or on account of, any present or future taxes, levies, imposts, duties, charges, fees, deductions or withholdings of any nature whatsoever and by whomsoever imposed.

This Standby Letter of Credit shall remain valid and in full force and effect until [ ] or, if earlier, the date on which you notice to us that [AAA] has delivered the equipment and/or materials to Construction Site in Saudi Arabia. If the notice date is later than [ ], this Letter of Credit shall automatically be extended for successive periods of [ ] months each, thereafter until the certification Date.

This Standby Letter of Credit is issued subject to the International Standby Practices, approved on April 6, 1998, International Chamber of Commerce Publication No. 590.

For and on behalf of
[BBB Bank]

By:
Name: [ ]
Title: [ ]

11.4.5 *Example Refund Guarantee in a Shipbuilding Contract*

REFUND GUARANTEE NO.

We hereby open our irrevocable Letter of Guarantee number in favour of XXX INTERNATIONAL SHIP CO. [*Address*] (hereinafter called the "Buyer") for account of XXX HEAVY INDUSTRIES CO LTD. [*Address*] (hereinafter called the "Builder") as follows in connection with the shipbuilding contract dated December X, 20XX "The Contract" made by and between the Buyer and the Builder for the construction of One(1) about 81,140 DWT Bulk Carrier having Builder's Hull No. XXX (hereinafter called the "Vessel").

In consideration of the Buyer entering into the Shipbuilding Contract with our customer the Builder, if in connection with the terms of the Contract the Buyer shall become entitled to a refund of the advance payment made to the Builder prior to the delivery of the Vessel, we hereby irrevocably guarantee the repayment of the same to the Buyer within thirty (30) days after demand by the Buyer not exceeding US$19,500,000 (say U.S. Dollars Nineteen Million Five Hundred Thousand only) together with interest thereon at the rate of six percent (6%) per annum from the date following the date of receipt by the Builder to the date of remittance by telegraphic transfer of such refund.

The amount of this guarantee will be automatically increased upon Builder's receipt of the respective instalments under the shipbuilding contract, not more than three times, each time by the amount of each instalment plus interest thereon as provided in the Contract, but in any eventuality the amount of this guarantee shall not exceed the total sum of US$19,500,000 (say U.S. Dollars Nineteen Million Five Hundred Thousand only) plus interest thereon at the rate of six percent (6%) per annum from the date following the date of Builder's receipt of each instalment to the date of remittance by telegraphic transfer of the refund.

This Letter of Guarantee is available against Buyer's simple demand and signed statement certifying that Buyer's demand for refund has been made in conformity with Article 10 of the Contract and the Builder has failed to make the refund.

Notwithstanding the provisions hereinabove, in the event that within thirty (30) days of the date of your demand to the Builder referred to above we receive notification from you or the Builder accompanied by written confirmation to the effect that an arbitration has been initiated and that your claim to cancel the Contract or your claim for refund thereunder has been disputed and referred to arbitration in accordance with the provisions of the Contract, we shall under this Letter of Guarantee refund to you the sum due to you from the Builder pursuant to the award made under such arbitration immediately upon receipt from you of a demand for payment of the sum and a copy of the award.

This Letter of Guarantee shall become null and void upon receipt by the Buyer of the sum guaranteed hereby or upon acceptance by the Buyer of the delivery of the Vessel in accordance with the terms of the Contract and, in either case, this Letter of Guarantee shall be returned to us.

This Letter of Guarantee is assignable and valid from the date of this Letter of Guarantee until such time as the Vessel is delivered by the Builder to the Buyer in accordance with the provisions of the Contract.

This guarantee shall be governed by and construed in accordance with the laws of England and the undersigned hereby submits to the non-exclusive jurisdiction of the courts of England.

11.4.6 Example Payment Guarantee

LETTER OF GUARANTEE NO.

(October XX, 20XX)

In consideration of your delivering [*Object of Contract*] to [*Importer's Name*] having its principal place at [*Importer's Address*] ("Purchaser"), on a deferred payment basis under the purchase and sale agreement dated *[Date of Contract]* ("Agreement") entered into by and between you and Purchaser, the undersigned, as primary obligor and not merely as surety, hereby irrevocably, absolutely and unconditionally guarantees the full, prompt and punctual payment when due(whether at stated maturity, by acceleration or otherwise) by Purchaser of a series the (10) promissory notes ("Note") to be issued by Purchaser to your order pursuant to the Agreement, respectively numbered "XXX 1" to "XXX 10", inclusive, the aggregate principal amount of which is U.S. Dollars Thirty Four Million (U$34,000,000) plus pre-delivery interest capitalized in accordance with the Agreement, the first of the said Notes to be due and payable six (6) months after the Last Shipment Date of the Commodities and remaining Notes to be due and payable at intervals of six (6) months thereafter, and also guarantees the due and punctual payment by the Purchaser of interest on the principal amount of the Notes, the first such payment of interest to be due and payable six (6) months after the Last Shipment Date of the Commodities and subsequent payments to be made at intervals of six (6) months thereafter at the rate of zero point seven five (0.75) plus six (6) month London Inter-Bank Offered Rate (LIBOR) per annum until maturity (by acceleration or otherwise) and thereafter at the rate of fifteen percent (15%) per annum until full payment.

Interest on the principal amount of the Notes shall be calculated on the basis of a year of 360 days and actual number of days elapsed.

The undersigned here waives the right to interpose any set-off or counterclaim of any nature or description in any action or proceedings arising out of or in any way connected with the Notes, this Letter of Guarantee or the Agreement.

In the event that Purchaser fails to pay any amount of principal or interest on any Note on the maturity date or upon acceleration on the Notes in accordance with their terms, the undersigned will pay you or any assignees hereof the outstanding principal amount of the Notes which are then payable and interest (including default interest for the period from the due date to and including the date of actual payment of the full amount demanded by you or any such assignee) accrued thereon as aforesaid within five (5) days after receipt by us of written demand from you or any such assignee including a statement that the Purchaser is in default of payment of the amount claimed in respect of the said Notes and/or interest thereon, without requesting you to take any or further procedure or step against Purchaser or with respect to the Notes and/or interest in default; provided, however, that no demand hereunder may be made after the date which is sixty (60) days after the maturity date of the last maturing Note.

This undersigned hereby consents to any renewal, changes, extensions and partial payments of the Notes or the indebtedness for which they are given without notice to it, and consents that no such renewals, changes, extensions or partial payments shall discharge any party to the Notes or the undersigned from any liability thereon or hereon in whole or in part; provided that no amendment or extension of any of the Notes, the Notes, the effect of which would be to increase the principal amount of the Notes and the interest payable thereon or to vary the dates or payment under the

Notes shall be entered into by you with Purchaser without the written consent of the undersigned.

The undersigned hereby agrees that this Letter of Guarantee and the undertakings hereunder shall be assignable in whole or in part to and shall enure to the benefit of any holder of the Notes as if each of them were originally named herein; provided that upon each such assignment by you or by any other assignee, the assignor thereof shall give written notice to the undersigned of the name and address of any such assignee and the extent of the interest assigned to such assignee within ten (10) days of its taking place. The undersigned shall be entitled to treat any such assignee as the person entitled to the benefit of this Letter of Guarantee to the extent of his interest (as so notified to the undersigned) until the undersigned is notified of a further assignment.

Payments by the undersigned under this Letter of Guarantee shall be made in United States Dollars by telegraphic transfer to the account nominated by you in favor of you or your assignee without deduction, withholding or set-off of any kind.

In the event that any withholding or deduction is imposed on any payment to be made hereunder by law or by any taxing authority, except taxes on the income of the holder of the Notes, we agree to pay such additional amount as may be necessary in order that the actual amount received after deduction or withholding shall be equal to the amount that would have been received if such deduction or withholding were not required after allowance for any increase in taxes or charges payable by virtue of the receipt of such additional amount.

This letter of Guarantee shall come into full force and effect upon its issue and shall continue in force and effect until sixty (60) days after the maturity date of the last Note in the said series or until the full payment of the said the (10) Notes and interest thereon whichever occurs first.

Notwithstanding the other provisions of this Letter of Guarantee, the undersigned shall be fully discharged of any further liability under this Letter of Guarantee if on any due date of the Notes, upon the giving of thirty (30) days prior written notice to you(or any assignee hereof), the undersigned pays by telegraphic transfer to the account nominated by you in favor of you or any such assignee an amount in United States Dollars equal to the full outstanding unpaid principal amount of such Notes together with accrued interest thereon up to the date of payment. Any such notice by the undersigned shall identify the Note(s) in question by number, shall specify the date of payment, shall be irrevocable and shall oblige you or any assignee thereof to cancel and surrender such Note(s) against such payment by the undersigned being made in full.

The obligation of the undersigned are joint and several with any other guarantee or security and are absolute and unconditional irrespective of any legal limitation, disability, incapacity or other circumstance relation to Purchaser or any other persons, or any amendments or supplements to the Agreements, the Notes or any other documents, instruments or agreements contemplated therein or of the genuineness, legality, validity, regularity or enforceability of the Agreement, the Notes or any other documents, instruments or agreements contemplated therein.

This shall be a continuing guarantee and shall cover and secure any balance owing under the Notes, but you shall not be obliged to exhaust your recourse against Purchaser or the securities which you may hold before being entitled to payment from the undersigned of the obligation hereby guaranteed.

The undersigned hereby represents and warrants that (a) it is duly organized, validly existing and in full compliance with the laws of [*Importing Country*] and in full legal right, power and authority to execute this Letter of Guarantee and to perform its obligations hereunder, (b) it has taken all appropriate and necessary corporate action to authorize the issuance of this Letter of Guarantee and the performance by it of its obligations hereunder, (c) the execution, delivery and performance of this Letter of Guarantee and the covenants herein contained will not violate or contravene any provisions of any existing treaty, law or regulation or any judgement, order or degree of any court, or governmental agency, or violate or result in a default under any mortgage, indenture, contract or agreement to which the undersigned is a party, or by which we or our assets are bound, (d) this Letter of Guarantee constitutes the legal, valid and binding obligation of the undersigned enforceable in accordance with its terms and (e) the undersigned has obtained all necessary consents, licenses, approvals, and authorizations and registrations or declarations, with any governmental authority required in connection with the validity and enforceability or this Letter of Guarantee and the same are in full force and effect.

This Letter of Guarantee shall be governed by and construed under and in accordance with the laws of the State of New York, U.S.A. The undersigned hereby irrevocably submits to the non-exclusive jurisdiction of the courts of the State of New York, U.S.A.

The undersigned hereby consents to the service of process out of said courts by registered airmail, postage prepaid to the undersigned or in any other manner provided by law.

The undersigned represents and warrants that this Letter of Guarantee is a commercial and not a public or governmental act and the undersigned is not entitled to claim immunity from legal proceeding with respect to itself or any of its properties or assets on the grounds of sovereignty or otherwise under any law. To the extent that the undersigned or any of its property or assets has or hereafter may acquire any right to immunity from set-off, legal proceedings, attachment prior to judgement, other attachment or execution of judgement on the grounds of sovereignty or otherwise, the undersigned for itself and its properties and other assets hereby irrevocably waives such right to immunity in respect of its obligations under this Letter of Guarantee.

IN WITNESS WHEREOF, the undersigned has caused this Letter of Guarantee to be executed and delivered by its duly authorized representative as of the day and year first written above.

11.5   Comparison of and Key Distinctions Between a Documentary Credit and a Standby Letter of Credit

A performance type guarantee or a standby letter of credit (which is issued in favor of a buyer for the assurance of a seller's performance of a contractual obligations) is distinguished from a documentary credit in various aspects.

Table 11.1 Key distinctions between documentary credit and standby letter of credit

	Documentary credit	(Performance) Standby letter of credit*
Applicant	Buyer (importer)	Seller (exporter)
Beneficiary	Seller (exporter)	Buyer (importer)
Issuing bank	Buyer's bank	Seller's bank
Documents required	Bill of lading, commercial invoice, packing list, inspection certificate, draft	Simple statement
Conditions for payment	The seller carries out a contract	The seller fails to carry out a contract
Assurance for	Buyer's payment	Seller's performance
Securities for issuing bank	Shipping documents (equivalent to the title of goods) *Issuing bank makes payment in exchange for shipping documents (bill of lading, commercial invoices, etc.)	none
Applicable rules	UCP 600	ISP98, UN Convention, UCP 600
Underlying transaction	Sales of goods	Sales of goods, construction contract (all constructions require standby letter of credit (bank guarantee, bond)

*Supposition: A standby letter of credit issued in favor of a buyer for the assurance of a seller's performance of a contractual obligations

References

Affaki, G., & Goode, R. (2011). *Guide to ICC uniform rules for demand guarantees URDG 758* (p. 1). France: ICC Services Publications, Paris.

Bertrams, R. F. (2013a). *Bank guarantees in international trade* (4th ed., p. 2). Netherlands: Kluwer Law International, Hague.

Bertrams, R. F. (2013b). *Bank guarantees in international Trade* (4th ed., pp. 4, 13). Hague, Netherlands: Kluwer Law International.

Bertrams, R. F. (2013c). *Bank guarantees in international trade* (4th ed., p. 7). Netherlands: Kluwer Law International, Hague.

Bertrams, R. F. (2013d). *Bank guarantees in international trade* (4th ed., pp. 1, 13). Hague, Netherlands: Kluwer Law International.

Bertrams, R. F. (2013e). *Bank guarantees in international trade* (4th ed., p. 13). Hague, Netherlands: Kluwer Law International.

Bertrams, R. F. (2013) *Bank guarantees in international trade* (4th ed., p. 7). Hague, U.K.: Kluwer Law International.

Bertrams, R. F. (2013g). *Bank guarantees in international trade* (4th ed., p. 6). Hague, Netherlands: Kluwer Law International.

Bertrams, R. F. (2013h). *Bank guarantees in international trade* (4th ed., p. 41). Hague, Netherlands: Kluwer Law International.

Bertrams, R. F. (2013i). *Bank guarantees in international trade* (4th ed., p. 40). Hague, Netherlands: Kluwer Law International.

Bishop, E. (2006). *Finance of international trade* (p. 78). Oxford, U.K.: Elsevier.

Carr, I. (2010). *International trade law* (4th ed., p. 503). Abingdon, U.K.: Routledge-Cavendish.

Curtis, S. (2002). *The law of shipbuilding contracts* (3rd ed., p. 251). Oxfordshire, U.K.: Lloyd's Shipbuilding Law Library.

Folsom, R. H., et al. (2016). *International business transactions in a nutshell* (10th ed., p. 240). USA: West Academic, St. Paul.

Goode, R. (1995). *Guide to the ICC uniform rules for demand guarantees* (p. 16). Paris, France: ICC Publication No. 510.

Grath, A. (2014). *The handbook of international trade and finance* (3rd ed., p. 78). London, U.K.: Kogan Page.

Harwood, S. (2006). *Shipping finance* (3rd ed., p. 47). Euromoney Institutional Investor: London, U.K.

Murray, C. et al. (2010a). *Schmitthoff's export trade: the law and practice of international trade* (11th ed., pp. 242, 245). London, U.K.: Thomson Reuters.

Murray, C., et al. (2010a). *Schmitthoff's export trade: The law and practice of international trade* (11th ed., p. 243). Thomson Reuters: London, U.K.

Murray, C., et al. (2010b). *Schmitthoff's export trade: the law and practice of international trade* (11th ed., p. 245). Thomson Reuters: London, U.K.

Murray, C., et al. (2010c). *Schmitthoff's export trade: The law and practice of international trade* (11th ed., p. 39). Thomson Reuters: London, U.K.

Sang Man Kim. (2015). The Supreme Court of Korea's decisions on the fraud exception in a demand guarantee. *Journal of Korea Trade, 19*(3), 42.

Sang Man Kim. (2018). Why is a refund guarantee independent from a shipbuilding contract? *International Journal of Economic Research, 15*(3), 571.

Sang Man Kim. (2019). Reduction clause in an advance payment guarantee (AP-Bond) under an overseas construction contract. *Journal of Korea Trade, 23*(1).

Chapter 12
Trade Finance for International Sale of Goods

12.1 Introduction

12.1.1 Concept of Trade Finance

"Trade finance" means financing the funds required for the performance of an international trade transaction.[1] In an international sale of goods, both parties seek trade finance depending on the terms and conditions of a transaction.[2] For the successful completion of an international trade, depending on the payment terms and other conditions of a particular transaction, the exporter and/or the importer need access to funds. Thus, it is essential to understand trade finance mechanisms for the successful outcome of international trade.

The ability to allow longer payment terms has become a competitive factor in international trade, but long payment terms bring cash flow shortage to the exporter. Thus, the exporter needs to obtain trade finance in order to make up the cash flow shortage arising out of an international trade transaction with credit terms (or long payment terms).

Trade finance is self-liquidating as it is financed from the cash flow of the underlying international trade transaction. Trade finance is generally secured by account receivables and/or securities such as bills of exchange, promissory notes, cargo insurance policies, export credit insurances, letters of credit, payment guarantees, etc. The payment from the underlying transaction will first be used for the repayment of any outstanding trade finance loan. Trade finance, therefore, is considered more secure financing for the financing banks.

Typical trade finance lending assures the banks that the incoming payment from the overseas buyers (or issuing banks) will first be used for the repayment of any outstanding loan before being released to the exporter.

---

[1] Grath (2014a), p. 142.

[2] Bishop (2006a), p. 132.

S. M. Kim, *Payment Methods and Finance for International Trade*, https://doi.org/10.1007/978-981-15-7039-1_12

Exporters need to allow longer credit terms to meet competition, which may cause cash flow shortage. Thus exporters need to obtain trade finance in order to make up any cash flow shortage arising out of the underlying international transaction with longer credit terms. In practice, exporters consult their banks for the availability of trade finance before they conclude export contracts with credit terms.

12.1.2 Overview of Types of Trade Finance

Trade finance can be classified into:

- "pre-shipment finance" and "post-shipment finance" by the time of finance;
- "supplier credit" and "buyer credit" by who undertakes to provide the funds required for the performance of a contract; and
- "short-term trade finance" and "mid–long-term trade finance" by the loan period.

Pre-shipment finance refers to finance provided to the exporter for the purposes of purchasing raw materials, manufacturing/processing the goods, and/or purchasing the finished goods from local suppliers. Post-shipment finance refers to finance extended to the exporter after the goods have been shipped to the importer. Post-shipment finance includes negotiation (or purchase of bills of exchange), forfaiting, factoring, etc.[3]

The financing scheme for international trade transactions (in particular for the export of capital goods) comes in two types—a supplier credit and a buyer credit[4] by who undertakes to provide the funds required for the performance of a contract. A supplier credit means a financing scheme in which the supplier (or the exporter) is responsible for providing the funds, and a buyer credit means a financing scheme in which the buyer (or the importer) is responsible for providing the funds.[5] While an exporter would be a borrower under a loan agreement, if any, for the international transaction in a supplier credit, an importer would be a borrower under a loan agreement, if any, in a buyer credit.

While an importer will purchase on deferred payment terms with the credit provided by an exporter in a supplier credit,[6] an exporter will be paid on a milestone basis during the construction in a buyer credit. In a buyer credit, the funds are not usually disbursed directly to the borrower (normally the importer), but directly to the exporter or to an escrow account.

The parties to an international trade will choose either a supplier or a buyer credit depending on the cost of funding for the trade. Today, a buyer credit is more common

---

[3] Ibid., p. 138.
[4] "Buyer credit" is also referred to as "buyer's credit", and "supplier credit" is also referred to as "supplier's credit": Willsher (1995a), p. 66.
[5] Ibid., p. 66.
[6] Sang Man Kim (2010, 2017).

than a supplier credit in shipbuilding contracts, which is presumed to be due to low interest rate in the international financial market.

12.1.3 The Bank's Role in International Trade

In a traditional trade finance, an exporter and an importer make use of the integrity of the international banking system in order to ensure the safety of a particular international trade transaction.[7]

An international trade transaction may not be completed without banks' assistance. Banks play various roles in support of international trade, and providing trade finance will be the most important. A bank's key roles in international trade are:

- to transfer money for payment;
- to collect money for payment;
- to issue a letter of credit;
- to advise a letter of credit;
- to issue a demand guarantee (or a standby letter of credit);
- to loan money (advance funds);
- to negotiate drafts and shipping documents;
- to conduct credit investigation;
- to receive deposit;
- to provide trade finance.

Most banks have international divisions or departments that are specifically targeted at assisting exporters and importers in international trade activities, and overseas branches in major global markets.

12.2 Export Working Capital Financing for Pre-shipment

12.2.1 Export Working Capital Financing

"Export working capital financing" means financing the temporary working capital needs for the fulfillment of an export transaction. Export working capital financing allows exporters to purchase the goods and services for the performance of an export transaction.[8] Export working capital financing covers the cash flow related to purchasing raw materials, manufacturing the goods, and/or purchasing the goods from local suppliers.

---

[7]Palmer (1999a), p. 21.

[8]US Department of Commerce/International Trade Administration (2012a), p. 15.

The pre-shipment period (the period between the conclusion of a contract and the delivery (or shipment) of the goods) is often the most difficult part of the export transaction, particularly when trading on an open account basis. In that stage of the transaction, the seller does not have bills of exchange nor any of the shipping documents, but has only a sales contract.

In some instances, the sales contract itself can be used for creating that additional finance during the pre-shipment period. A documentary credit or a payment guarantee in favor of the seller could facilitate the pre-shipment finance requirements.

Many banks provides special "export loans" on the basis of the documentary credit up to the letter of credit amount. A documentary credit and its future proceeds (payments from an issuing bank or a nominated bank) will normally be pledged for the loan. A payment guarantee in favor of an exporter will also be used for a specific export loan. Most banks will treat documentary credits or payment guarantees as important securities for increasing the exporter's credit limit.

An advising bank normally provides an export loan by way of issuing a local letter of credit in favor of the local supplier at the request of the exporter. Once the local supplier (the beneficiary under a local letter of credit) presents the documents under a local letter of credit and the exporter presents the documents under an export letter of credit with a negotiation request form, the local letter of credit issuing bank (normally the negotiating bank under an export letter of credit) pays the local supplier with the negotiated amount of the export letter of credit. Thereafter, in the event the negotiating bank receives payment (is reimbursed by the issuing bank), it settles the negotiation transaction with the exporter.

Figure 12.1 shows in detail the process of pre-shipment finance in a transaction with an export letter of credit and a local letter of credit.

12.2.2 Export Credit Guarantee Programmes for Pre-shipment Finance

Many export credit agencies (ECAs) provide programmes for export working capital financing in the form of an export credit guarantee.[9] An export credit guarantee for pre-shipment (or a working capital loan guarantee) is offered to a lending bank as security for the pre-shipment loan needed for purchasing raw materials, manufacturing the goods, and/or purchasing the goods from local suppliers. With an export credit guarantee for pre-shipment (or a working capital guarantee), the exporter is able to increase their borrowing capacity considerably.

These programmes aim at promoting national exports by facilitating pre-shipment finance for their exporting companies. The Export-Import Bank of the United States US EXIM Bank) provides the Working Capital Loan Guarantee for respective exporters. UK Export Finance (UKEF) offers the Export Working Capital Scheme.

---

[9]Grath (2014b), p. 145.

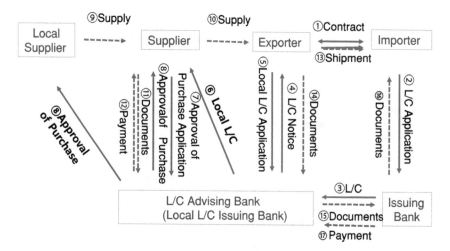

① The exporter and importer enter into an export contract with payment terms of a documentary credit (letter of credit).

② The importer (the applicant) applies to the issuing bank to issue a letter of credit ("export letter of credit") in favor of the exporter by submitting a letter of credit issuing application form.

③ The issuing bank processes a formal credit approval of the application and establishes the credit limit for the importer. (If the credit limit for the buyer is already established, this process will be omitted.)

The issuing bank issues a documentary credit in favor of the exporter (the beneficiary) within the remaining credit limit of the importer. A documentary credit is normally sent to the advising bank through the SWIFT system.

④ Once the advising bank receives the export letter of credit, they check the authenticity of the documentary credit and print it out to give to the exporter. The advising bank is usually located in the exporting country, and its role is to take reasonable care to check the authenticity of the export letter of credit and to advise it to the exporter according to its instructions. The advising bank owes no obligation to pay, unless it is a confirming bank. Once the exporter receives an export letter of credit, they will check and compare it against the export contract. If all the details conform to the export contract, then the exporter prepares and performs the export contract.

⑤ Where a bank provides pre-shipment finance by a way of issuing a local letter of credit, the exporter applies to the bank (normally the advising bank) to issue a local letter of credit in favor of the local supplier. If a local letter of credit is issued, the exporter can be supplied by the local supplier without paying in advance.

⑥ The local letter of credit issuing bank (the advising bank of an export letter of credit) issues the local letter of credit against the export letter of credit. In this case, the export letter of credit must be negotiated by the local letter of credit issuing bank (the advising bank) only, as it is used as security for the local letter of credit payment undertaking.

Fig. 12.1 Flow of pre-shipment finance with an export letter of credit and a local letter of credit

⑦ The supplier applies to the local bank to issue "approval of purchase".

⑧ The local bank issues "approval of purchase" to the supplier and the local supplier.

⑨ The local supplier supplies raw materials and/or parts to the supplier in accordance with the local supply contract.

* ⑦–⑨ will be omitted if there is no local supplier that supplies to the supplier.

⑩ The supplier supplies to the exporter in accordance with the local letter of credit, and prepares all the documents required under the local letter of credit.

⑪ The local supplier (the beneficiary under a local letter of credit) presents the local letter of credit issuing bank with the documents required under the local letter of credit.

⑫ The local letter of credit issuing bank pays the supplier if the documents presented complies with the local letter of credit.

⑬ The exporter ships the goods in accordance with the export letter of credit and prepares all the documents (normally bill of lading, commercial invoice, packing list, inspection certificate) required under the export letter of credit.

⑭ The exporter (the beneficiary under an export letter of credit) presents the documents (and the drafts if any) to the negotiating bank (the local letter of credit issuing bank) for negotiation.

⑮ The negotiating bank examines the documents with care. Once the documents are deemed to comply with the terms of the export letter of credit, the negotiating bank advances funds to the exporter. However, where the negotiating bank issued a local letter of credit, it will not advance funds to the exporter. Instead, the negotiating bank will pay the local supplier for payment of the local letter of credit. The negotiating bank will advance the remaining funds, if any, after payment of the local letter of credit.

The negotiating bank despatches and presents the documents to the issuing bank for payment.

⑯ Upon receiving the documents, the issuing bank examines the documents with care. In many instances, the issuing bank requests the applicant (or the importer) to check the documents to decide whether or not to accept the documents. The issuing bank releases the documents to the importer (the applicant) against payment at sight (or at any later date) as stipulated in the export letter of credit. The applicant repays (reimburses) the issuing bank.

⑰ If the documents comply with the export letter of credit, the issuing bank sends "acceptance advice" (A/A) to the negotiating bank and makes payment at maturity (or the issuing bank preimburses the negotiating bank at sight or at maturity).

Fig. 12.1 (continued)

The Korea Trade Insurance Corporation (K-Sure) provides Pre-shipment Export Credit Guarantee programmes.

The US EXIM Bank operates the Working Capital Loan Guarantee for pre-shipment export working capital. The Working Capital Loan Guarantee empowers exporters to unlock cash flow to fulfill sales orders and take on new business abroad, and enables exporters to borrow more funds from the banks. The Working Capital Loan Guarantee works with lenders to provide a loan guarantee that backs the exporter's borrowings. The Working Capital Loan Guarantee can be used for paying for materials, equipment, supplies, labor, and other inputs to fulfill export orders, for posting demand guarantees (or standby letters of credit) serving as bid bonds, performance bonds, or payment guarantees, and for purchasing finished products for export.[10]

The UKEF[11] operates the Export Working Capital Scheme for export working capital. The Export Working Capital Scheme assists UK exporters in gaining access to working capital finance both pre-shipment and post-shipment in respect of specific export-related contracts.[12] The Export Working Capital Scheme enables UK exporters to take export loans in circumstances where their banks are reluctant to provide the full facility amount.

In the Export Working Capital Scheme for pre-shipment finance, the UKEF issues a guarantee to a guaranteed bank at the request of a UK exporter. The guaranteed bank pays the UKEF a premium for the guarantee with the interest received from the exporter. The exporter preforms an export contract with the funds advanced by the guaranteed bank (i.e. the exporter purchases raw materials to manufacture the goods, the exporter purchases finished goods from a local supplier). The exporter gets payment from an importer after performance of the export contract. The exporter repays the loan with the payment received from the importer.

The K-Sure operates the Pre-shipment Export Credit Guarantee. The Pre-shipment Export Credit Guarantee is designed to help exporters, who can produce the guarantee as security toward securing pre-shipment finance. The Pre-shipment Export Credit Guarantee is very helpful, in particular, to small and medium-sized enterprises that have difficulty in receiving trade financing from banks. Pre-shipment Export Credit Guarantee programmes are provided for import as well as export, but the guarantee programme for import is limited to the issuance of a documentary credit for import of raw materials for export.

12.3 Negotiation (Or Purchase) of Bills of Exchange

12.3.1 Introduction

Negotiation in trade finance means the purchase of bills of exchange and/or shipping documents "with recourse" by a bank from an exporter.[13] Negotiation also refers to "discounting bills of exchange (documentary drafts) and/or documents". The bank

---

[10]US EXIM Bank website available at www.exim.gov/what-we-do/working-capital.

[11]"UK Export Finance" is the operating name of the Export Credits Guarantee Department (ECGD), the UK's export credit agency. ECGD was founded in 1919 and sits within the Department for Business, Innovation and Skills. Its purpose is to complement the private market by providing assistance to UK exporters, principally in the form of insurance and guarantees to banks. See www.eca-watch.org/ecas/uk-export-finance-ukef.

[12]UKEF website: www.gov.uk/government/organisations/uk-export-finance.

[13]Donnely (2010b), p. 26; Bishop (2006b), p. 138.

then collects the proceeds (or payment) in their own name. The finance will be for up to 100% of the bills of draft (or the invoice) amount less interest and fees.[14]

The exporter sends his documents and/or bills of exchange to his bank. Instead of signing a collection instruction form, the exporter signs a negotiation request form. The decision of negotiation would be made by the bank like any other lending decision.

Negotiation is normally available in a documentary transaction, and also available in a documentary collection transaction (documents against payment (D/P), documents against acceptance (D/A)).

12.3.2 Operation

In a negotiation, the bank (the exporter's bank) will agree to pay the exporter immediately the value of the bill of exchange (or the value of the receivables) when the exporter signs a foreign exchange transaction arrangement attached to the negotiation request form. Negotiation is normally "with recourse" to the exporter. Thus, if the negotiating bank is not paid from the importer (or the issuing bank in a letter of credit), then the bank will retrieve the negotiated amount from the exporter (or the drawer of the bill of exchange) immediately.[15]

The amount of negotiation will be calculated after taking into account the foreign exchange rate, if applicable, and credited to the exporter's account. The exporter would also agree to pay interest charged for the period between the negotiation date and the date of payment from the importer (or the issuing bank).

Once agreed to negotiate the drafts and/or the documents, the exporter's bank (the negotiating bank) immediately credits the exporter's account with the face value of the draft less interest and fees. (The exporter will receive a sum less than the face value of the draft drawn or documents presented, taking into account the exchange rate (if the documents are in a different currency) and the delayed period between the negotiating bank's payment and the receipt of funds from the importer.)

12.3.3 Negotiation in a Documentary Credit Transaction

A documentary credit (or a letter of credit) is very useful for trade finance for both the exporter and importer. A documentary credit (or a letter of credit) is one of the basic payment methods in intranational trade. With a documentary credit, the exporter can obtain pre-shipment finance by providing the local supplier with a local letter of credit issued against a documentary credit (export letter of credit). A documentary credit (export letter of credit) also enables the exporter to obtain other

---

[14]Bishop (2006c), p. 137.
[15]Ibid., p. 138.

pre-shipment finance loan and post-shipment finance such as negotiation, factoring, and forfaiting. A documentary credit (export letter of credit) can increase the export credit insurance (or export credit guarantee) limit for the exporter, and therefore the exporter can increase the export volume. By providing a documentary credit (or a letter of credit), the importer can request long credit payment terms to the exporter and pay with the funds from the sale of the imported goods.

Article 2 of the UCP 600[16] defines that:

> negotiation means the purchase by the nominated bank of drafts (drawn on a bank other than the nominated bank) and/or documents under a complying presentation, by advancing or agreeing to advance funds to the beneficiary on or before the banking day on which reimbursement is due to the nominated bank.

The term "negotiation" under the UCP 600 is not exactly the same as in international trade. In a documentary credit transaction, the negotiating bank is limited to a nominated bank. Nominated bank means "the bank with which the credit is available or any bank in the case of a credit available with any bank" (Article 2 of the UCP 600). A nominated bank is designated in the documentary credit itself.

In a documentary credit, the nominated bank (the negotiating bank) may negotiate drafts and/or documents when the presentation complies with the terms of the documentary credit. The negotiating bank is reimbursed by the issuing bank if the presentation is complying with the documentary credit. Unless the nominated bank is a confirming bank, they have no obligation to negotiate, except when expressly agreed to by that nominated bank and so communicated to a beneficiary (UCP 600 Article 12).

Negotiation by a negotiating bank is usually "with recourse" to the exporter[17]: if the issuing bank does not pay, the negotiating bank will request the negotiated amount back from the exporter. However, the confirming bank should negotiate "without recourse" (UCP 600 Article 8(e)).

In the negotiation process under a documentary credit, once the beneficiary (or the seller) performs the export contract (delivery of goods), they request the negotiating bank to negotiate the drafts and/or the documents. Once the negotiating bank decides to negotiate, they will advance funds to the beneficiary (or credit the beneficiary's account). Then, the negotiating bank presents the drafts and the documents to the issuing bank for acceptance or for payment.

Figure 12.2 shows in detail how negotiation works in a documentary credit transaction.

---

[16]UCP 600 means the Uniform Customs and Practice for Documentary Credits, 2007 Revision, ICC Publication No. 600. UCP 600 are rules that apply to a documentary credit.
[17]Bishop (2006b), p. 138.

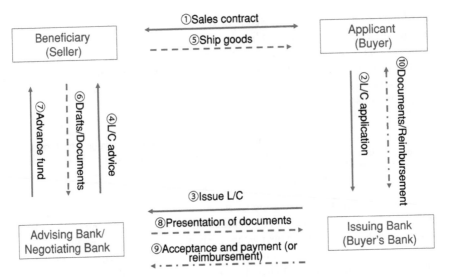

① The seller (the exporter) and the buyer (the importer) enter into an export contract with payment terms of a documentary credit. The seller and the buyer agree on the details of the documentary credit to be issued.

② The buyer (the applicant) applies to the issuing bank to issue a documentary credit in favor of the seller by submitting a documentary credit issuing application form.

③ The issuing bank processes a formal credit approval of the application and establishes the credit limit for the buyer. (If the credit limit for the buyer is already established, this process will be omitted.) The issuing bank issues a documentary credit in favor of the seller (the beneficiary) within the remaining credit limit of the buyer. The documentary credit is normally sent to the advising bank through the SWIFT system.

④ Once the advising bank receives the documentary credit, they check the authenticity of the documentary credit and print it out to give to the seller. The advising bank is usually located in the seller's country, and its role is to take reasonable care to check the authenticity of the documentary credit and to advise a documentary credit to the seller according to its instructions. The advising bank owes no obligation to pay, unless it is a confirming bank.

⑤ Once the seller receives the documentary credit, they will check and compare the documentary credit against the export contract. If anything is not complying with the export contract, the seller must immediately communicate with the buyer for the necessary amendment. If all the details conform to the export contract, then the seller prepares and performs the export contract (or ships the goods in an export contract for sale of goods), and obtains the transport documents from the carrier (or the freight forwarder).

⑥ The beneficiary (the seller) prepares all the documents (normally bill of lading, commercial invoice, packing list, inspection certificate) required under the documentary credit. The beneficiary presents the documents (and the drafts if any) to the nominated bank (normally an advising bank) for negotiation.

⑦ The nominated bank will examine the documents with care. In many instances, the nominated bank decides to negotiate the documents (and the drafts if any) to advance funds to the beneficiary; then the nominated bank is rendered a negotiating bank.

⑧ The negotiating bank dispatches and presents the documents (and the drafts if any) to the issuing bank for payment or acceptance.

Fig. 12.2   Process flow of negotiation in a documentary credit transaction

⑨ Upon receiving the documents, the issuing bank examines the documents with care. In many instances, the issuing bank requests the applicant (or the buyer) to check the documents and to decide whether or not to accept the documents.

If the documents are complying with the documentary credit, the issuing bank sends "acceptance advice" to the negotiating bank and will make payment at maturity.

⑩ The issuing bank releases the documents to the applicant against payment at sight (or at any later date) as stipulated in the documentary credit. Once the issuing bank pays the complying presentation of documents, the applicant repays (reimburses) the issuing bank.

Fig. 12.2 (continued)

12.3.4 Negotiation in a Documents Against Acceptance Transaction

In a documents against acceptance, the seller (the exporter) entrusts the collection of the payment to the remitting bank by providing the shipping documents (e.g. transport document, commercial invoice, packing list, bills of exchange), together with the collection/negotiation instruction, and the remitting bank also sends the documents including the drafts together to the collecting bank with the collection instruction to release the documents to the buyer (the importer) against acceptance of the draft and to collect payment at maturity.

When the collecting bank receives the documents and the collection instruction, they will notify the buyer of the arrival of the documents, and request the buyer to accept the term draft and to pay the draft at maturity. A document against acceptance collection is also referred to a time draft (or time bill, term draft, usance bill), as a time draft is involved.

The shipping documents will be released only after the buyer accepts the term draft, not the buyer pays the draft. The shipping documents may be released to the buyer without payment. Therefore, a documents against acceptance is normally used when the seller extends credit to the buyer and the buyer wishes to take delivery of the goods without making payment at the time of delivery. Therefore, it is probable that the seller will lose the goods without payment if the buyer fails to make payment at maturity.

Where the remitting bank negotiates the drafts with the shipping documents, it will become a negotiating bank. When the collection is paid, the collecting bank will transfer the payment to the negotiating bank. If the collection is not paid (or the drafts are dishonored), the negotiating bank will recourse the amount of negotiation to the exporter immediately.[18]

Finance can also be provided to an importer by the importer's bank by way of advance to the importer to pay (to pay advance payment, to pay a sight bill, or to pay a term bill). The importer's bank may also add "aval" to the bill of exchange accepted by the importer. "Aval" means an unconditional guarantee of the payment of a bill of exchange or promissory note by a third party (usually the drawee's bank

---

[18]Bishop (2006b), p. 138.

or the maker's bank) other than the drawee or the maker. Aval is required when the drawee's (or the maker's) credit is in itself not sufficient.

Figure 12.3 illustrates the detailed process of negotiation in a document against acceptance transaction.

12.4   Export Factoring

12.4.1   Concept

Export factoring (international factoring) means trade finance where a factor purchases the exporter's receivables without recourse (or with recourse) to the exporter, and performs the credit control of the sales or debt collection functions.[19] Export factoring is a package of financial services that meets the requirements of the exporter on short-term credit to a foreign importer. It is a legal agreement between a factor (a division of a bank or a factoring house) and an exporter whereby the exporter assigns to the factor the account receivables of an export transaction.

Factoring originated in the USA where factors, who distributed goods around the nation, would pay the suppliers prior to the payment from the end customers.[20] Export factoring combines export working capital financing, credit risk protection, booking of account receivables, and collection services.[21]

The factor's service includes the discounting of receivables, the collection of receivables, the sales ledger administration, and customer protection against bad debt. Thus, export factoring of receivables can be an alternative to an export credit insurance.[22] With factoring, the exporter is able to offer credit terms (or long payment terms) such as an open account without collection problems.[23]

The UNIDROIT Convention on International Factoring (1988) Article 2 provides:

"factoring contract" means a contract concluded between one party (the supplier) and another party (the factor) pursuant to which:

(a) the supplier may or will assign to the factor receivables arising from contracts of sale of goods made between the supplier and its customers (debtors) other than those for the sale of goods bought primarily for their personal, family or household use;

(b) the factor is to perform at least two of the following functions:

   – finance for the supplier, including loans and advance payments;
   – maintenance of accounts (ledgering) relating to the receivables;
   – collection of receivables;

[19] Jimenez (2012); US Department of Commerce/International Trade Administration (2012b), p. 21.
[20] Willsher (1995b), p. 37.
[21] US Department of Commerce/International Trade Administration (2012b), p. 21.
[22] US Department of Commerce/International Trade Administration (2012b), p. 21.
[23] Jimenez (2012), p. 142.

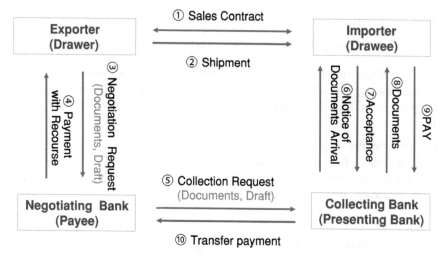

① The exporter (the seller) and the importer (the buyer) enter into a contract for sale under which the payment is on a documents against acceptance basis.

② The exporter prepares the goods by manufacturing, or procuring in the domestic market, or using the goods in stock. The exporter ships the goods according to the shipment terms in the sales contract, and obtains transport documents from the shipping company.

③ The exporter prepares all the documents required under the sales contract, including time drafts, and obtains the collection/negotiation instruction form from the remitting bank. The exporter requests negotiation of the drafts and shipping documents to the remitting bank (the negotiating bank) by providing the documents including term drafts and the collection/negotiation instruction.

④ The negotiating bank checks the shipping documents and the collection/negotiation instruction form to ensure that the documents conform to the instruction. Once the documents conform to the instruction, the negotiating bank pays the exporter the amount of the draft less exchange fee.

⑤ The negotiating bank sends the drafts and the shipping documents together with the collection instruction to a collecting bank to entrust the collection of the payment.

⑥ The collecting bank (the collecting bank that makes such presentation is called "the presenting bank") notifies the importer of the arrival of the documents and requests acceptance of drafts. The importer is also advised about the collection.

⑦ The importer (the drawee) checks the documents and accepts the drafts if the documents conform to the sales contract.

⑧ Once the importer accepts the drafts and the documents, the collecting bank releases the documents to the importer.

⑨ The collecting bank keeps the accepted drafts until maturity and presents the drafts for payment at maturity.

⑩ The collecting bank transfers the payment to the negotiating bank as per the instruction, if the importer pays the draft at maturity.

⑪ Where the drafts are not accepted on presentation, or not paid at maturity, the negotiating bank recourses to the exporter.

Fig. 12.3 Negotiation process of a time draft (in a documents against acceptance transaction)

  – protection against default in payment by debtors;

(c) notice of the assignment of the receivables is to be given to debtors.

In export factoring, the exporter will assign to the factor export account receivables arising from the export transaction, and the factor is to perform at least two of the following functions (UNIDROIT Convention on International Factoring 1988 Article 1):

- finance for the supplier, including loans and advance payments;
- maintenance of accounts relating to the receivables;
- collection of receivables;
- protection against default in payment by debtors.

12.4.2 *Operation of Export Factoring*

Factoring involves not only finance but also additional services, and is generally more complex. Therefore, factoring is often used for larger individual amounts compared with negotiation. A factor (or a factoring house) is a bank or a financial institution that performs export financing through the purchase of account receivables. The exporter enters into a factoring agreement to sell the receivables to the factor. The agreement normally includes the credit control and debt collection functions by the factor against a fee. The factor obtains the title to the invoice and the right to the payment by the importers (or the issuing bank).

There are, in principle, two basic forms of factoring: "two-factor export factoring" and "direct export factoring". In "two-factor export factoring", the seller's domestic factoring company uses a local factoring company (either an independent company or a branch) in an importing country. The use of a local factoring company has the big advantage of a local presence and knowledge of the buyers, but will bring an increase of the overall cost. In "direct export factoring", the seller's domestic factoring company does not use a foreign factoring company, and, therefore, a local factor in an importing country is not involved.

Figure 12.4 illustrates the detailed process of negotiation in an international factoring transaction.

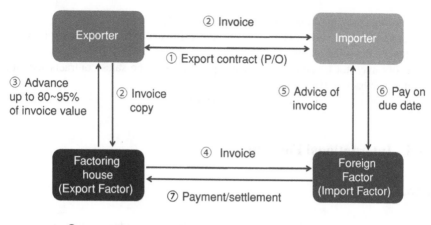

① The exporter (the seller) and the importer (the buyer) enter into a contract (or the importer issues a purchase order).

② The exporter raises an invoice on the buyer (or the importer), with a copy of the invoice to the export factor (the factoring company).

③ The export factor (the factoring house) advances to the exporter up to 70–90% of the invoice value. (Specific percentage of invoice value varies depending on an individual transaction.)

④ The export factor (the factoring house) assigns the invoice to the import factor (the foreign factor).

⑤ The import factor (the foreign factor) requests the importer to pay the invoice.

⑥ The importer pays the invoice on the due date.

⑦ The import factor (the foreign factor) transfers the payment to the export factor (the factoring house).

⑧ The factoring house pays the remaining balance of the invoice, minus fee.

Fig. 12.4 Process flow of international factoring

12.4.3 Advantages/Disadvantages of Export Factoring

Factoring could have the following advantages for the exporter[24]:

- factors are expert at collection of unpaid receivables;
- factors have excellent credit control systems, which might be expensive for the seller to provide for themselves;
- the borrowing value of the receivables could be higher than the ordinary bank loan;
- without recourse factoring eliminates the non-payment risk by the buyer;
- the factor provides additional administrative systems;
- the seller will be able to maximize cash flows.

However, factoring has some disadvantages for the exporter[25]:

---

[24]Donnelly (2010a), p. 125; US Department of Commerce/International Trade Administration (2012b), p. 21.

[25]Donnelly (2010a), p. 125.

- factoring costs more than export credit insurance;
- factors with poor services can have an adverse impact on the business relationship between the seller and the buyer;
- factors may not be able to deal with queries about the sales contracts without reference back to the seller;
- generally not available in developing countries.

12.5   International Forfaiting

12.5.1   Concept

Forfaiting means the purchase of future receivables on a "without recourse" basis.[26] "Forfaiting" can be also defined as a purchasing (or discounting) negotiable financial instrument such as a bill of exchange "without recourse". In classic forfaiting, a forfaiter purchases obligations falling due at future date, arising from delivery of goods and services in export transaction.[27] The Uniform Rules for Forfaiting (URF 800) define "forfaiting transaction" as "the sale by the seller and the purchase by the buyer[28] of the payment claim on a without recourse basis on the terms of these rules" (Article 2).

Forfaiting allows exporters to obtain cash by selling their medium and long-term foreign accounts receivable at a discount on a "without recourse" or "non-recourse" basis.[29] "Without recourse" or "non-recourse" means that the forfaiter assumes and accepts the risk of non-payment. The forfaiter offers discount terms based on "tenor of draft" (or note), "forfaiter's cost of funding", and "default risk of obligor" (or a drawee, an avaliser).

Forfaiting eliminates the risk of non-payment, once the goods have been delivered to the importer in accordance with the terms of the sale. Forfaiting is a special type of discounting of trade-related and mostly fixed-term interest bills of exchange. The forfaiter is a specialized financial institution or a department in a bank that provides non-recourse export financing through the purchase of future account receivables. In practice, forfaiting is normally used in a documentary credit (letter of credit) transaction or in a transaction with payment guarantee. A deferred payment letter of credit with no bills of exchange (or drafts) is an ideal instrument for international forfaiting.[30]

---

[26] International Trade & Forfaiting Association (ITFA).

[27] Palmer (1999b), p. 99.

[28] Here, the "buyer" means a forfaiter.

[29] US Department of Commerce/International Trade Administration (2012c), p. 23.

[30] Palmer (1999c), p. 107.

12.5.2 Operation of International Forfaiting

Unlike export factoring, forfaiting normally requires larger transactions with a minimum of at least USD100,000.[31] Prior to finalizing the transaction's structure, the exporter approaches the forfaiter. Once the forfaiter commits to the deal and sets the discount rate, the exporter can incorporate the discount into the selling price. The exporter then accepts a commitment issued by the forfaiter, signs the contract with the importer, and obtains, if required, a guarantee from the importer's bank that provides the documents required to complete the forfaiting.

The exporter delivers the goods to the foreign importer and delivers the documents to the forfaiter who verifies them and pays for them as agreed in the commitment. Since forfaiting is without recourse, the exporter has no further interest in the financial aspects of the transaction and it is the forfaiter who must collect the future account receivables due from the foreign importer (or the issuing bank).

Once the payment risk has been passed to the forfaiter, the exporter obtains funds in return for the receivables (or bills of exchange). The forfaiter has two options: to keep the receivables (or bills of exchange) until the maturity date, or to sell the receivables (or bills of exchange) again on without recourse.[32] Figure 12.5 shows the typical process flow for international forfaiting.

12.5.3 Advantages/Disadvantages of International Forfaiting[33]

International forfaiting could have the following advantages to the exporter:

- the exporter can eliminate non-payment risk by the foreign importer as the forfaiter purchases receivables "without recourse";
- the exporter can offload foreign exchange risk;
- if interest rate rises, the fixed interest rate could prove inexpensive.

International forfaiting could have the following disadvantages to the exporter:

- the cost for international forfaiting is normally very high, and often higher than commercial lender financing;[34]
- the option fee is epayable even if the forfaiting facility is not taken up;
- the commitment fee is payable at the outset and a penalty would be charged if the receivables are delivered late;
- if the interest rate falls, the fixed interest rate could prove expensive;

---

[31]US Department of Commerce/International Trade Administration (2012c), p. 23.
[32]Palmer (1999d), p. 104.
[33]Ibid., p. 103.
[34]US Department of Commerce/International Trade Administration (2012c), p. 23.

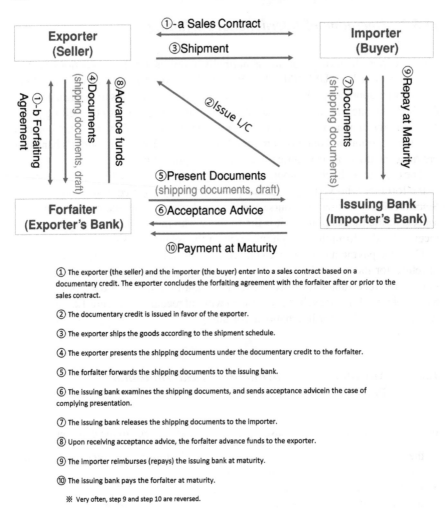

Fig. 12.5 Process flow of international forfaiting

- international forfaiting is normally offered to an export transaction with documentary credit transaction or with payment guarantee;
- the funds are advanced to the exporter only after acceptance advice by the issuing bank (or the confirming bank) is received
- international forfaiting is normally limited to medium and long-term export transactions over USD100,000.

References

Bishop, E. (2006a). *Finance of international trade* (p. 132). Oxford, U.K.: Elsevier.

Bishop, E. (2006b). *Finance of international trade* (p. 138). Oxford, U.K.: Elsevier.

Bishop, E. (2006c). *Finance of international trade* (p. 137). Oxford, U.K.: Elsevier.

Donnelly, M. (2010a). *Certificate in international trade and finance* (p. 125). Ifs School of Finance, Cantebury: U.K.

Donnely, M. (2010b). *Certificate in international trade and finance.* (p. 26). Cantebury, U.K.: Ifs School of Finance.

Grath, A. (2014a). *The handbook of international trade and finance* (3rd ed., p. 142). London, U.K.: Kogan Page.

Grath, A. (2014b). *The handbook of international trade and finance* (3rd ed., p. 145). London, U.K.: Kogan Page.

Jimenez, G. C. (2012). *ICC guide to export/import: Global standards for international trade.* (4th ed., p. 142) Paris, France: ICC Publication No. 686.

Palmer, H. (1999a). *International trade and pre-export finance* (2nd ed., p. 21). London, U.K: Euromoney.

Palmer, H. (1999b). *International trade and pre-export finance* (2nd ed., p. 99). London, U.K: Euromoney.

Palmer, H. (1999c). *International trade and pre-export finance* (2nd ed., p. 107). London, U.K: Euromoney.

Palmer, H. (1999d). *International trade and pre-export finance* (2nd ed., p. 104). London, U.K.: Euromoney.

Sang Man Kim. (2010). A comparative study on a supplier credit and a buyer credit in international transactions of capital goods. *International Commerce & Law Review, 48,* 129.

Sang Man Kim. (2017). World shipbuilding industry and export credit insurances for ship exports: Focusing Korea's export credit insurances. *International Journal of Applied Business and Economic Research, 15*(10), 268–269.

US Department of Commerce/International Trade Administration. (2012a). *Trade finance guide: A quick reference for US exporters* (p. 15). Washington D.C., USA: US Department of Commerce.

US Department of Commerce/International Trade Administration. (2012b). *Trade finance guide: A quick reference for US exporters* (p. 21). Washington D.C: US Department of Commerce.

US Department of Commerce/International Trade Administration. (2012c). *Trade finance guide: A quick reference for US exporters* (p. 23). Washington D.C., USA: US Department of Commerce.

Willsher, R. (1995a). *Export finance: Risks* (p. 66). U.K.: Structures and Documentation, Macmillan Press, Basigstoke.

Willsher, R. W. (1995b). *Export finance: Risks* (p. 37). U.K.: Structures and Documentation, Macmillan Press, Basingstoke.

Chapter 13
Finance for Overseas Construction

13.1 Introduction

Overseas constructions are normally so huge and complex that tremendous amounts of funding is required. An overseas construction project requires longer-term financing than traditional commodities. This is because the amount of time it takes for an overseas construction project to pay for itself is considerably longer than for consumer goods.[1] This amount of time, known as the capital goods cycle, extends into years. It may take considerable time before enough products can be produced for it to pay for itself. Most of the loans are not short-term roll-over credits, but long-term credits. In many cases, syndicated loans rather than single loans are provided.[2]

Moreover, some of the importing countries are developing countries and are politically and economically unstable. Accordingly, the financing mechanism for an overseas construction project is crucial to a successful outcome. This is the primary reason why we need to understand financing mechanisms for overseas construction projects.

As there are many parties involved in overseas construction financing, which is generally international financing, there may arise various disputes and legal issues. Therefore, understanding the legal aspects of the financing for an overseas construction project is also required.

As an overseas construction project involves considerable amounts of funding, the owner (the employer), particularly if he is in a developing country, cannot or will not finance the undertaking out of his own resources. The owner normally requires that the financing mechanism be provided by the contractor.

There are various financing mechanisms available for an overseas construction project, some of which are combined. These include supplier credit/buyer credit, project finance, export credit insurance (or export credit guarantee), syndicated loans,

---

[1] Venedikian and Warfield (1996a), p. 20.

[2] In a syndicated loan, two or more financial institutions provide loan: Fight (2004), p. 1.

S. M. Kim, *Payment Methods and Finance for International Trade*,
https://doi.org/10.1007/978-981-15-7039-1_13

independent guarantees (or demand guarantees, standby letters of credit), official development assistance (ODA),[3] government-backed export loans etc.

13.2 Supplier Credit and Buyer Credit

Financing mechanisms are classified into a supplier credit and a buyer credit according to who is responsible for providing finance.[4] In a supplier credit, the supplier (or the exporter) is responsible for providing finance, while in a buyer credit the buyer (or the importer) is responsible for providing finance. In every project (but not limited to an overseas construction), funding will be provided by one of these two financing mechanisms.

A supplier credit is quite opposite to a buyer credit with regard to the parties to the loan agreement, if any. In a supplier credit, the supplier (or the exporter) will be the borrower in a loan agreement, while the buyer (or the importer) will be the borrower in a buyer credit. A supplier credit and a buyer credit have respectively their own advantages and disadvantages from the respective parties' perspective. The selection of financing mechanism depends on financing conditions such as funding cost, the buyer's and/or supplier's financial conditions, the importing country's political risk etc.

The following section will give a more detailed explanation, as well as deeper analyses of supplier and buyer credit, analysing the advantages and disadvantages for all the parties (the exporter, the financial institution, and the importer) respectively.

13.2.1 Supplier Credit

13.2.1.1 Concept and Operation

A supplier credit means a financing scheme in which the supplier (or the exporter or seller) is responsible for providing the funds.[5] In a supplier credit, the exporter (the seller or supplier) extends a credit to the importer (the buyer) as part of an export contract.[6] Export credit insurance cover for this transaction may be extended to the exporter. In a contract for sale of goods, the seller provides the funds required to manufacture or to procure goods, and in a construction contract, a contractor provides

---

[3]Official development assistance (ODA) is the resources made available to developing countries by official agencies, including state and local government, for the purpose of promoting economic development and social welfare of those developing countries. ODA is also very useful financing for an overseas construction project.

[4]Stephens (1999d), pp. 73, 110, Willsher (1995a), pp. 66–78.

[5]Stephens (1999a), p. 110; Willsher (1995b), p. 75, Sang Man Kim (2017), p. 268.

[6]Stephens (1999a), p. 110, Willsher (1995b), p. 75; Sang Man Kim (2010a), p. 130.

the funds required to complete construction. When a supplier credit transaction arises in a mid and long-term transaction, the importer normally makes downpayment from 5–30% of the contract value.[7]

In a supplier credit, the contractor (or the exporter) borrows the funds necessary for the performance of the overseas construction contract with his own credit. After completing overseas construction, the contractor (or the exporter) gets paid from the employer (or the importer) on a deferred installment payment basis. The contractor (or the exporter) will, in many cases, require, in security of payment by the employer (the importer), a payment guarantee from the employer's parent company or a financial institution.

With the payment from the employer (or the importer), the contractor (or the exporter) repays the loan to the lender (or the financial institution). Even where the contractor (or the exporter) does not get paid from the employer (or the importer), they have to repay the loan with their own funds. Therefore, the contractor will be exposed to non-payment risk by the employer (or the importer) and also bear the obligation to repay the loan. With export credit insurance (or export credit guarantee), the contractor can mitigate the non-payment risk.

Figure 13.1 illustrates the typical process flow of a supplier credit.

As the contractor (or the exporter) borrows funds from a financial institution in a supplier credit, the contractor (or the exporter) will be a borrower and the financial institution will be a lender. In a supplier credit, the contractor (or the exporter) and the financial institution will be the parties to the loan agreement.

In a supplier credit, the contractor (or the exporter) will be required to assign the right to payment (or the account receivables) and/or the promissory notes issued by the employer (or the importer) to the financial institution (or the lender).[8] Although the employer (or the importer) is not a party to the loan agreement, the financial institution (or the lender) directly claims the payment from the employer (or the importer) when the right to payment is assigned to the financial institution (or the lender).

13.2.1.2 Securities

The financial institution (or the lender) requires securities when it decides the exporter's credit is not satisfactory. The main securities required by the financial institution are as follows.

A. Corporate guarantee.

The financial institution (or the lender) requires a corporate guarantee by the parent company, which is the simplest security. The financial institution (or the lender) will require an independent guarantee (or a demand guarantee) rather than a traditional guarantee (or a suretyship, an accessory guarantee). In an independent guarantee

---

[7]Bertrams (2013a), p. 39.
[8]Willsher (1995c), p. 76.

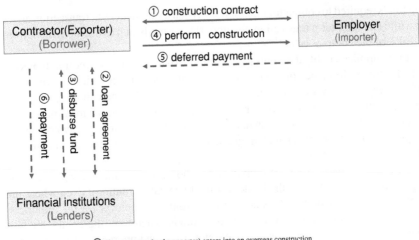

① The contractor (or the exporter) enters into an overseas construction
contract with the employer (or the importer), in which the employer
(or the importer) pays the contractor (or the exporter) on a deferred
payment basis.

② The contractor (or the exporter) enters into a loan agreement with the
financial institution (or the bank). The contractor (or the exporter)
borrows funds necessary to perform the overseas construction
contract from the financial institution (or the bank) with its own
credit.

③ The financial institution (or the bank) will disburse funds in installments
to the contractor (or the exporter) in accordance with the
performance of the construction.

④ The contractor (or the exporter) then performs the overseas
construction contract by using the funds.

⑤ After completing overseas construction in accordance with the
overseas contract, the contractor (or the exporter) gets paid from the
employer (or the importer) on a deferred payment basis. The
employer (or the importer) will pay with the revenues from the
operation of the overseas construction project.

⑥ The contractor (or the exporter) repays the bank with the payment
from the employer (or the importer).

Fig. 13.1 Process flow of a supplier credit

(or a demand guarantee), the guarantor undertakes to pay as a primary obligor not
a secondary obligor upon demand by the beneficiary,[9] while the guarantor, in a
traditional guarantee, is the secondary obligor and requires breach or failure under
the underlying transaction.[10] However, these days a parent company is reluctant to
provide such a guarantee.

---

[9] Bertrams (2013b), p. 11.
[10] Kurkela (2008), p. 12, Willsher (1995c), p. 76.

B. Assignment of the right to payment.

The contractor (or the exporter) is required to assign the right to payment to the financial institution (or the lender) as security for the loan. Then, the contractor (or the exporter) assigns the right to payment (or the account receivables) and/or the promissory notes issued by the employer (or the importer) to the financial institution (or the lender).[11] In this case, the employer (or the importer) will makes payment directly to the financial institution.

C. Export credit insurance policy

The contractor (or the exporter) is required to assign an export credit insurance policy to the financial institution. In this case, export credit insurance cover will be a condition precedent to the loan disbursement or to the effectiveness of the loan agreement. An export credit insurance policy will help the contractor (or the exporter) to obtain the funds from the bank easily.[12] Many countries have established export credit agencies to promote exports through various support mechanisms, including export credit insurance or guarantee.[13] The main aim of export credit agencies is to promote their exports by protecting exporters against commercial risks of the importer and political risks in the importing country.[14] When the commercial risks of the importer and the political risks in the importing country are not acceptable, the financial institution will require the contractor (or the exporter) to purchase export credit insurance and to assign the insurance policy.

13.2.1.3 Advantages and Disadvantages of Supplier Credit[15]

From the exporter's perspective, the advantages and disadvantages of supplier credit are as follows:

- It is comparatively easy for the exporter to borrow funds on a supplier credit basis for its good credit rating. Generally an exporter that won a contract for industrial plant export, overseas construction, or shipbuilding export will have a good stable financial condition. Therefore the exporter can borrow the funds required to perform export contract easily from a financial institution. The exporter surpasses the importer in negotiating the contract price for it provides finance.
- However, the exporter is paid on via a long-term deferred payment method. After the exporter completes its contract obligation, the importer may willfully raise a claim to deduct payment or to reject payment. Furthermore, the importer may become insolvent or bankrupt, in which case the exporter can not receive payment.

---

[11] Willsher (1995c), p. 76.

[12] Venedikian and Warfield (1996b), p. 2.

[13] Ray (1995), p. 1.

[14] Bishop (2006), p. 100.

[15] Supposition: The exporter is a company with a good credit rating, and the importer is a company with a poor credit rating located in a developing country.

- During the performance of the contract, the loan is added to the exporter's balance sheet as liability (debt). After performance of the contract, the contract value is added to the exporter's balance sheet as asset (account receivable). Thus the debt on the balance sheet increases, and the liability ratio rises, which results in the aggravation of the financial structure.
- The key to success for an exporter is to obtain securities to mitigate the risks. The securities are mortgage on the object, export credit insurance, guarantee by a bank or a parent company, etc.

From the importer's perspective, the advantages and disadvantages of supplier credit are as follows:

- The advantages of a supplier credit for the exporter are the disadvantages for the importer, and vice versa. In a supplier credit, the importer is somewhat free from non-performance risk by the exporter for the importer makes payment only after the exporter performs the contract.
- In a typical overseas construction contract, the importer (or the employer) makes an advance payment of 5–30% of the contract price to the contractor (or the exporter).[16] The importer can get rid of the non-refundment risk of downpayment by way of an advance payment guarantee issued by the financial institution at the request of the exporter. Furthermore the importer requires a performance guarantee issued by the financial institution. In the event the exporter fails to perform the contract, the importer can make a demand under the performance guarantee as well as under the advance payment guarantee. As the exporter provides finance, the exporter can surpass the importer in negotiating the contract price, which may result in an increase of the contract price.

From the financial institution's perspective, the advantages and disadvantages of supplier credit are as follows:

- The financial institution provides loan to the exporter in a supplier credit, and to the importer in a buyer credit. Which credit is more beneficial to the financial institution depends on the specific credit conditions of the exporter and the importer, and on the terms and conditions of the loan agreement. Where the exporter has a sound credit rating, the loan in a supplier credit is considered to be more secured. Where the exporter has its principal place of business in the domestic area, establishing securities is easier. Therefore, the financial institution does not require high spread in a supplier credit.
- When the repayment term of the loan is long term, the financial institution tends to require securities for an event of default, such as assignment of the receivables under the export contract, assignment of the export insurance policy, etc. In rare cases the financial institution purchases the receivables 'without recourse' and

---

[16]See "FIDIC–Conditions of Contract for EPC/Turnkey Projects" Article 14.2:
"The Employer shall make an advance payment, as an interest-free loan for mobilization and design, when the Contractor submits a guarantee in accordance with this Sub-Clause including the details stated in the Particular Conditions."

with a high rate of discount, in which case the exporter is free from any kind of non-payment risk at all.

13.2.2 Buyer Credit

13.2.2.1 Concept and Operation

A buyer credit means a financing scheme in which the buyer (or the importer) is responsible for providing the funds.[17] A buyer credit is an arrangement in which the supplier (or the exporter, the seller) enters into a contract with the buyer (or the importer), which is financed by the buyer (or the importer).[18] Such arrangements are frequently used to finance capital goods or projects on a medium or long-term basis.[19] A buyer credit is a loan or credit extended by the financial institution directly to the buyer (or the importer).

The exporter enters into a contract with the importer, which is financed by means of a loan agreement between the lending bank and the importer. In a contract for sale of goods, the importer shall provides the funds required to procure the goods by the exporter. In an overseas construction contract, the employer provides the funds required to complete the construction. The loan on a buyer credit is a tied loan, which should be used for a particular export contract. In practice, the funds are disbursed directly to the exporter in accordance with the performance of the contract.

A buyer credit has two mechanisms: a direct loan and a relending facility. A direct loan is given directly to the importer, and a relending facility is given to the bank in the importing country, and that bank gives the loan to the importer. A buyer credit is common in project finance, a method of raising long-term debt financing for major projects through "financial engineering", based on lending against the cash flow generated by the project alone.[20]

An export credit agency in the exporting country provides export credit insurance cover to the lender (or the financial institution), and the exporter is paid by the loan by the performance of the contract.[21] In an overseas construction contract, the contractor is paid by the loan on a progressive payment basis. A buyer credit benefits the seller as the seller gets paid in full on delivery of goods or on completion of construction, and also benefits the buyer as the buyer is able to obtain medium and long-term finance.[22]

---

[17]Willsher (1995a), p. 66, Stephens (1999b), p. 73, Sang Man Kim (2010b), p. 129, Sang Man Kim (2017), p. 268.

[18]Stephens (1999b), p. 73, Willsher (1995a), p. 66.

[19]Stephens (1999b), p. 73, Willsher (1995d), p. 67.

[20]Yescombem (2002a), p. 1.

[21]Stephens (1999b), p. 73, Willsher (1995d), p. 67.

[22]Donnelly (2010), p. 136.

Interest on the loan accrues during the drawdown period (or construction period in an overseas construction contract) and is typically payable during the drawdown period. However, these days, especially in project finance, the interest during the drawdown period (or construction period in an overseas construction contract) is capitalized for the borrower for the importer does not make any profit during construction.

Even if the contractor (the exporter) fails to accomplish the construction (contract), the borrower (the employer) has to repay the loan disbursed. Once the construction is completed, the importer makes revenue by operating the project. And the borrower (the employer) repays the loan (principal and interest together) with the revenue. The interest can be paid either at a floating rate such as Libor plus spread, or at a fixed rate such as CIRR (Commercial Interest Reference Rate).[23]

Figure 13.2 illustrates the typical process flow of a buyer credit.

As the employer (the importer) borrows money from a financial institution in a buyer credit, the employer (the importer) becomes a borrower and the financial institution becomes a lender. The employer (the importer) and the financial institution become the parties to the loan agreement. Where the employer (the importer) lacks credit-worthiness, the financial institution purchases export credit insurance and charges an insurance premium to the employer (the importer). Typically, an export credit agency in the exporter's country covers the loan agreement. In some cases, the parent company of the employer (the importer) borrows money from the financial institution.

13.2.2.2   Securities

A financial institution requires securities when it decides the borrower's (the employer or the importer) credit rating is not satisfactory. The main securities required by the financial institution in a buyer credit are as follows.

A.   **Corporate guarantee.**

The financial institution requires a corporate guarantee from the parent company of the borrower (the employer or the importer). This is the simplest security. However, these days parent companies are reluctant to provide corporate guarantees. Especially in project finance, the sponsor which is the parent company of the project company, does not provide a direct payment guarantee to the financial institution.

---

[23]CIRR (commercial interest reference rate) is a fixed interest rate published monthly by the OECD. CIRR represents the lowest interest rates for each of the major currencies at which official export credit agencies may officially support credits of over two years' maturity.

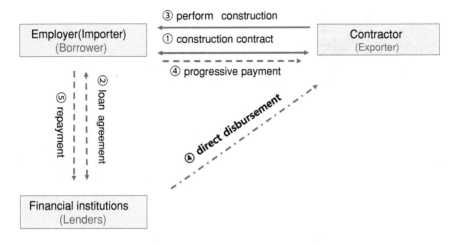

The general procedure for a buyer credit in an overseas construction project is as follows;

① The contractor (the exporter) enters into a construction contract with the employer (the importer), in which the employer pays to the contractor on a progressive payment basis.

　※ In progressive payment terms, the contractor is paid in proportion to the performance of construction. In an overseas construction contract, the contractor is normally paid monthly. Every month the employer checks the performance and issues a certificate. And the contractor is paid with the submission of certificate and invoice. Finally, at completion of the construction, the contractor is paid in full.

② The employer enters into a loan agreement wi th the bank.

③ The contractor (the exporter) performs the construction.

④ The employer (the importer) pays the exporter on a   progressive payment basis with the loan. The bank disburses the loan to the importer. In fact, the bank disburses the funds directly to the contractor (the exporter).

⑤ Once the contractor (the exporter) completes the construction, the employer (the importer) repays the bank with the revenues from the operation of the project on a long-term installment basis.

Fig. 13.2 Process flow of a buyer credit

B. **Export credit insurance (Export credit guarantee)**

The financial institution purchase export credit insurance (export credit guarantee) that is provided by the export credit agency in the exporter's country. Generally, the importer pays all the costs related to export credit insurance (export credit guarantee).

C. **Performance guarantee**

The financial institution requires a performance guarantee (or bond) for the completion of construction, and requires the employer (or the importer) to assign the performance guarantee to it or to nominate it as a beneficiary under the performance guarantee. The financial institution also requires a concession from the host country, long-term off-take contract, etc.

13.2.2.3 Advantages and Disadvantages of Buyer Credit[24]

From the exporter's perspective, the advantages and disadvantages of buyer credit are as follows:

- The exporter (the contractor) is normally paid on a progressive payment method in a buyer credit, in which it receives full payment on or before the completion of construction (the performance of the export contract). Therefore, the exporter is not exposed to non-payment risk. As the exporter receives payment on a progressive payment basis or 100% downpayment, it enjoys the same satisfaction as cash payment. The exporter does not need to borrow funds to perform the export contract. After the exporter performs the export contract, the margin (operational profit) only is added to balance sheet as an asset, which results in the decrease of liability ratio and the improvement of financial status. As the exporter's finance structure improves, the borrowing cost afterwards will go down.
- As the importer provides finance, it surpasses the exporter in negotiating the contract price, which may result in a reduction of the contract amount. Furthermore, the exporter is obliged to provide a bank guarantee such as an advance payment guarantee (Ap-bond), and a performance guarantee (P-bond). The importer (the employer) requires that the export credit agency in the exporter's country provide export credit insurance (export credit guarantee) cover for the financial institution (or the lender).

From the importer's perspective, the advantages and disadvantages of buyer credit are as follows:

- In a buyer credit, the importer (the employer) can surpass the exporter in negotiating the contract amount to reduce the contract price. Where an export credit agency provides export credit insurance (or export credit guarantee) cover, the importer can borrow funds with long-term credit and low spread.

---

[24]Supposition: The exporter is a company with good credit rating, and the importer is a company with poor credit rating located in a developing country.

- However, the importer is exposed to the non-performance risk by the exporter. The importer should must repay the loan to the financial institution (or the lender) even though the exporter fails to perform the contract. To mitigate non-performance risk by the exporter, the importer, normally, requires a payment guarantee (Ap-bond) and a performance guarantee (P-bond) issued by the financial institutions.
- Where the exporter fails to perform the export contract, the importer shall makes a demand call under the advance payment guarantee (Ap-bond) and the performance guarantee (P-bond). With the payment from these guarantees, the importer recovers what it paid and damages caused by the exporter's failure. A loan agreement may stipulates a so-called "Isabella clause"[25] in order to obligate the importer to repay regardless of the performance of the contract by the exporter. The importer's financial structure gets worse for as its liability ratio rises.

From the financial institution's perspective, the advantages and disadvantages of buyer credit are as follows:

- As the importer has is in a poor financial condition in general in the buyer credit, high spread is applied to the loan. Especially, in project finance, the financial institution requires extremely high spread. To mitigate risk, financial institutions cooperate to provide loans on a syndicated loan basis. In many instances, the term and risk go beyond the willingness of one bank to carry so that several banks act as a syndicate in financing large projects with long term.[26]
- Furthermore, the financial institution requires securities for the importer's default as well as for political risk in the importing country. One of the most preferred securities is export credit insurance (export credit guarantee) by an export credit agency in the exporter's country, for export credit insurance (export credit guarantee) covers not only commercial risks but also political risks.

13.3 Project Finance

13.3.1 Concept

Project finance may be used for as a financing mechanism in an overseas construction project. Recently, the project finance mechanism has been popular in a huge overseas construction projects. As the sponsor is not willing to bear the project risk, they establish a project company that is designed to bear the project risk.

Project finance can be defined as a financing mechanism under which the lender makes a loan based on future cash flow generated by the project alone.[27] Project

---

[25] An "Isabella clause" in a loan agreement means that the borrower's obligation under the loan agreement is independent from, and is not affected by, the supply contract.

[26] Venedikian and Warfield (1996c), p. 21.

[27] Yescombe (2002a), p. 1; Gatti (2008a), p. 2, Vinter (1998).

finance differs from "financing projects" as the project may be financed in various ways.[28]

In a project finance, it is not a pre-existing company but a newly established company, commonly called as 'a "project company" or a "special purpose company" ('SPC')' that borrows funds from the lending banks. The sponsor does not provide a guarantee for the repayment by the borrower, and the recourse to the sponsor is limited.[29] Moreover, there is little mortgage on the real property. In this respect, there is a widespread belief that project finance is too risky to fund. Project finance requires a complete understanding of the legal, commercial and political background to the project. The lending banks look at the cash flow and viability of the project as the security for repayment rather than the general creditworthiness or financial strength of the borrower (the SPC).[30]

Project finance for natural resources was first developed in the Texas oil fields in the 1930s, boosted by oil price rise.[31] Project finance for public infrastructure was developed through so-called private finance initiatives ("PFI") of in the UK from early 1990s, and thereafter increased worldwidely in the mobile phone networks in late 1990s.[32] Project finance dramatically increased from early 2000s in the fields of energy/power, infrastructure, and oil and gas. For instance, the global sector share in 2009 was[33]: energy/power (35%), infrastructure (28%), oil and gas (22%), telecom (6%), petrochemical (3%), mining (3%), and industrial (3%).

Figure 13.3 illustrates the typical process flow of a project finance transaction.

Lending banks evaluate and analyse completion risk, resource risk, operating risk, market risk, currency risk, and political risk. After analysing the overseas construction project, lending banks enter into a loan agreement with the borrower. Generally, financial advisors play a substantial role in concluding project finance by analysing the project and preparing "preliminary memorandum information" (PIM)' to solicit lending banks and export credit agencies. Where a project can be proved self-financing, export credit agencies may cover the risks of the project itself rather than take only the political risk of the sovereign government in whose country the project is being carried out.[34]

---

[28] Yescombe (2002a), p. 1.

[29] Hoffman (2009), p. 4.

[30] Stephens (1999c), p. 104.

[31] Yescombe (2002b), p. 6.

[32] Ibid.

[33] (2011/12) "Dialogic Global Project Finance—Full Year 2012", *Project Finance Magazine* 317, p. 84.

[34] Willsher (1995e), p. 85.

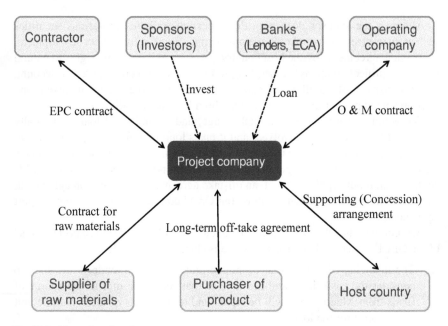

Fig. 13.3 Flow of project finance

13.3.2 Features of Project Finance

Project finance differs from conventional corporate finance. Project finance is based on future cash flow from the operation of the new project, while conventional corporate finance is based on a company's asset and credit rating. Project finance is financed for a new project not an established business.

A borrower is not a pre-existing company, but a newly established company which is commonly called as a "project company" or a "special purpose company" ('SPC')'. A project company has no business record or credit rating. Thus, the borrower (or the project company) does not have asset enough to repay the loan. The primary source of repayment of the loan is the cash-flow from the operation of the new project, not the asset of the borrower. The lenders rely on mainly on future cash flow of the project.

The sponsor (the parent company of the project company) does not offer guarantee to the lenders for the repayment by the borrower. Recourse to the sponsor is very limited (or in many cases there is no recourse at all), and thus project finance is called "limited recourse finance". Therefore, project finance requires a complete understanding of the legal, commercial, and political background to the project. The lending banks look at the cash flow and viability of the project as the security for repayment rather than the general creditworthiness or financial strength of the borrower (the SPC).[35]

---

[35]Stephens (1999c), p. 104.

Although the sponsor does not offer a guarantee, there are various securities such as guarantees for completion of construction, licenses for project development, concession agreements by the host country government, ownership rights to natural resources, project company's asset, long-term off-take agreement, escrow account, etc. The risks must be allocated equitably between all the parties involved, and well-organized project finance allows for a high level of risk allocation.[36]

The volume of a project is normally huge, and a syndicated loan is normally required. Many parties are involved, and it takes long time for a project finance to be completed. Project finance involves various agreements or contracts other than a loan agreement, such as an engineering, procurement and construction contract (EPC contract), an input supply contract, an off-take agreement, a concession agreement, an operating and management contract (an O&M contract), a government support agreement, etc.

According to the OECD's "Arrangement on Officially Supported Export Credits" of the OECD provides that, project finance is characterized by[37]:

(a) The financing of a particular economic unit in which a lender is satisfied to consider the cash flows and earnings of that economic unit as the source of funds from which a loan will be repaid and to the assets of the economic unit as collateral for the loan.

(b) Financing of export transactions with an independent (legally and economically) project company, e.g. special purpose company, in respect of investment projects generating their own revenues.

(c) Appropriate risk-sharing among the partners of the project, e.g. private or credit-worthy public shareholders, exporters, creditors, off-takers, including adequate equity.

(d) Project cash flow sufficient during the entire repayment period to cover operating costs and debt service for outside funds.

(e) Priority deduction from project revenues of operating costs and debt service.

(f) A non-sovereign buyer/borrower with no sovereign repayment guarantee (not including performance guarantees, e.g. off-take arrangements).

(g) Asset-based securities for proceeds/assets of the project, e.g. assignments, pledges, proceed accounts;

(h) Limited or no recourse to the sponsors of the private sector share-holders/sponsors of the project after completion.

13.4   Syndicated Loans

Generally, an overseas construction project is so huge and complex that no single bank would have the capacity to lend the entire loan on its own. Some banks are reluctant to solely bear the risk arising from making huge loans, and others have

---

[36]Gatti (2008b), p. 3.

[37]See Appendix 1: Eligibility Criteria for Project Finance Transactions, I. Basic Criteria.

difficulty in supplying huge amounts of money. The desire to spread the risk has given rise to the syndicated loan agreement under which a group of banks each commit to contribute a proportion of the loan under the syndicated loan agreement between lending banks and borrower. Therefore, syndicated loans are more common than single loans (or bilateral loans) in large overseas construction projects.

A bilateral loan is a loan between a borrower and a single bank.[38] A syndicated loan (or "syndicated bank facility") is a loan that is provided to a borrower by multiple banks.[39] "International syndicated loan" is "a facility for which there is at least one lender present in the syndicated whose nationality is different from that of the borrower"."[40]

In a syndicated loan, two or more banks make a loan to the borrower on the common terms. There is usually one bank that takes a leading position in making part of the credit, and syndicates the rest to other interested banks. A syndicated loan is a much larger and more complicated version of a participation loan. There are typically more than two banks involved in a syndication. The parties to a syndicated loan are normally the borrower, the arranger bank, the lending banks, and the agent bank.[41] A syndicated loan is arranged and structured by the arranger bank(s), and is managed by the agent bank(s).[42] The arranging bank(s) will be normally the agent bank(s) in a syndicated loan.[43]

Under a syndicated loan, each lender should receive pro rata payment and should be treated equally. In order to preserve the principle of equality between members of the syndicate, some syndicated loan agreements attempt to cover these possibilities by providing that if a participant receives any payment, by set-off, benefit of security or otherwise, in a greater than pro rata proportion it will purchase proportions of the other participants' quotas or otherwise make such payments to the other participants as are necessary to establish pro rata receipts.

There are is a pari passu clause and a negative pledge clause in a syndicated loan agreement to prohibit the borrower from discriminating syndicate lenders. In normal syndication, all the lenders sign the loan agreement directly or through agents expressly on their behalf, and the obligations of lenders under the syndicate loan agreement are several. Each lender is responsible for its own commitment only, and is not responsible for the commitment of other lenders. In other methods of syndication, the leading bank is the only lending bank under the loan agreement but then arranges for other lenders to participate in the loan, usually without their knowing the borrower. In this case, the participants are not the parties to the loan agreement. Therefore, the participants are not responsible for the commitment under the loan agreement.

---

[38] Wood (2008a), p. 93
[39] Fight (2004), p. 1.
[40] Blaise (2004), pp. 77–78.
[41] Wood (2008b), p. 94.
[42] Fight (2004), p. 1.
[43] Ibid.

References

Bertrams, R. F. (2013a). *Bank guarantees in international trade* (4th ed., p. 39). Netherlands: Kluwer Law International, Hague.

Bertrams, R. F. (2013b). *Bank guarantees in international trade* (4th ed., p. 11). Netherlands: Kluwer Law International, Hague.

Bishop, E. (2006). *Finance of international trade* (p. 100). Oxford, U.K.: Elsevier.

Blaise G. (2004). The syndicated loan market: Structure, development and implications. *BIS quarterly review* December, pp. 77–78, www.bis.org/publ/qtrpdf/r_qt0412g.pdf.

Donnelly, M. (2010). *Certificate in international trade and finance* (p. 136). Cantebury, U.K.: Ifs School of Finance.

Fight, A. (2004). *Syndicated lending* (p. 1). Oxford, U.K.: Elsevier.

Gatti, S. (2008a). *Project finance in theory and practice* (p. 2). London, U.K.: Academic Press.

Gatti, S. (2008b). *Project finance in theory and practice* (p. 3). USA: Academic Press, Burlington.

Hoffman, S. L. (2009). *The law and business of international project finance* (3rd ed., p. 4). USA: Cambridge University Press, New York.

Kurkela, M. S. (2008). *Letters of credit and bank guarantee under international trade law* (2nd ed., p. 12). USA: Oxford University Press, New York.

Ray, J. E. (1995). *Managing official export credits: The quest for a global regime* (p. 1). Washington D.C., USA: Institute for International Economics.

Sang Man Kim. (2010a). A comparative study on a supplier credit and a buyer credit in international transactions of capital goods. *International Commerce & Law Review, 48,* 130.

Sang Man Kim. (2010b). A comparative study on a supplier credit and a buyer credit in international transactions of capital goods. *International Commerce & Law Review, 48,* 129.

Sang Man Kim. (2017). World shipbuilding industry and export credit insurances for ship exports: focusing korea's export credit insurances. *International Journal of Applied Business and Economic Research, 15*(10), 268.

Stephens, M. (1999a). *The changing role of export credit agencies* (p. 110). Washington D.C., USA: IMF Washington.

Stephens, M. (1999b). *The changing role of export credit agencies* (p. 73). Washington D.C., USA: IMF Washington.

Stephens, M. (1999c). *The changing role of export credit agencies* (p. 104). Washington D.C., USA: IMF Washington.

Stephens, M. (1999d). *The changing role of export credit agencies* (pp. 73, 110). Washington D.C., USA: IMF Washington.

Venedikian, H. M., & Warfield, G. A. (1996a). *Export-import financing* (4th ed., p. 20). USA: John Wiley & Sons, Hoboken.

Venedikian, H. M., & Warfield, G. A. (1996b). *Export-import financing* (4th ed., p. 2). USA: John Wiley & Sons, Hoboken.

Venedikian, H. M., & Warfield, G. A. (1996c). *Export-import financing* (4th ed., p. 21). USA: John Wiley & Sons, Hoboken.

Vinter, G. (1998). *Project finance* (2nd ed.). London, U.K.: London Sweet & Maxwell.

Willsher, R. (1995a). *Export finance: Risks, structures and documentation* (pp. 66–78). Basingstoke, U.K.: Macmillan Press.

Willsher, R. (1995b). *Export finance: Risks, structures and documentation* (p. 75). U.K., Basingstoke: Macmillan Press.

Willsher, R. (1995c). *Export Finance: Risks, structures and documentation* (p. 76). Basingstoke, U.K.: Macmillan Press.

Willsher, R. (1995d). *Export Finance: Risks, structures and documentation* (p. 67). Basingstoke, U.K.: Macmillan Press.

Willsher, R. (1995e). *Export finance: Risks, structures and documentation* (p. 85). Basingstoke, U.K.: Macmillan Press.

Wood, P. (2008a). *Law and practice of international finance* (p. 93). London, U.K: Thomson Reuters.

Wood, P. (2008b). *Law and practice of international finance* (p. 94). London, U.K: Thomson Reuters.
Yescombe, E. R. (2002a). *Principles of project finance* (p. 1). London, U.K.: Academic Press.
Yescombe, E. R. (2002b). *Principles of project finance* (p. 6). London, U.K.: Academic Press.

Chapter 14
Export Credit Insurance or Guarantee

14.1 Introduction

Export credit insurance (also referred to as "export insurance", "export credit guarantee", or "trade credit insurance") was initially introduced to support exports.[1] Export credit insurance is a sort of 'export "export credit' credit" that includes export credit guarantee, export credit insurance, direct credit/financing, refinancing, and interest rate support.[2]

An institution operating export credit programmes is called an export credit agency ("ECA"). Many countries have established ECAs to promote exports through various supports.[3] The main aim of ECAs is to promote their exports by protecting exporters from the commercial risks of importers, and from the political risks of an importing country.[4] Most ECAs are either government departments or public corporations, but some are private companies.[5] Many ECAs operate either export credit insurance or export financing, while some operate both export credit insurance and export

---

[1] Stephens (1999a), p. 1, Sang Man Kim (2017), p. 264.

[2] OECD (2018):

Chapter I General Provisions

5. Scope of Application

The Arrangement shall apply to all official support provided by or on behalf of a government for export of goods and/or services, including financial leases, which have a repayment term of two years or more.

(a) Official support may be provided in different forms:

(1) Export credit guarantee or insurance (pure cover).

(2) Official financing support:

– direct credit/financing and refinancing, or

– interest rate support.

(3) Any combination of the above.

[3] Ray (1995a), p. 1.

[4] Bishop (2006), p. 100.

[5] Stephens (1999b), p. 9.

S. M. Kim, *Payment Methods and Finance for International Trade*, https://doi.org/10.1007/978-981-15-7039-1_14

financing. Export credit operated by an ECA on government account is called "offi-cially supported export credit",[6] and those ECAs are called "official export credit agencies".[7]

Officially supported export credits began in 1919 by with the UK's Export Credit Guarantee Department (ECGD),[8] and the International Union of Credit & Investment Insurers (the Berne Union) was formed in 1934.[9] Officially supported export credits became by the 1980 s significant instruments for facing up to competition abroad.[10] Official export credit support plays an enhanced role in periods of economic uncer-tainty, for instance, during the period of the global financial crisis of 2008, through filling the gap where market capacities are temporarily limited,[11] and also promotes national exports.[12] Official export credit could be granted to the exporters who cannot provide collaterals (securities) for export financing to commercial banks.[13]

Official ECAs do not aim at making a profit,[14] but do aim at supporting exports. Normally, export credit insurance programmes charge less lower premium than the commercial entities because they are operated for non-commercial purpose or by the public body in order to support exports.

While official export credit support promotes national exports,[15] they have brought the concern that they may distort the fair competition in international trades.[16] Although official export credit supports (export financing, export credit insurance) were accepted by the World Trade Organization (WTO) (formerly the General Agree-ment on Tariffs and Trade), many official export credit supports have been imposed of countervailing measures by the importing countries, and many of these measures have been filed at the WTO Dispute Settlement Body by the exporting countries.

Post-Second World War, ECAs were offering and guaranteeing longer-term loans and in 1955 the Organization for European Economic Co-operation (OEEC) (the OECD's predecessor organization of the Organization for Economic Co-operation and Development (OECD)) requested governments to discontinue artificial aids to exports, including export credits. In respect of government export credit insurances or guarantees, this included the charging of insurance premiums otherwise than in

---

[6]Stephens (1999c), pp. 98–99. It is also called "public export credit": see Peter and Thomas (2006), p. 400.

[7]Stephens (1999a), p. 1, Murray (2010a), p. 441.

[8]The ECGD has been operating export credit under the name of the UK Export Finance (UKEF) since September 2, 2013. The website is at https://www.gov.uk/government/organisations/uk-export-finance.

[9]Berne Union (International Union of Credit & Investment Insurers) website: https://www.berneunion.org/.

[10]Ray (1996), p. 2.

[11]Janet (2009), p. 35.

[12]David and Clara (1997), p. 414.

[13]Yehuda (1986), p. 275.

[14]Murray et al. (2010b), p. 443.

[15]David and Clara (1997), p. 414.

[16]Roberto (2010), pp. 611–632, Filip and Gerda (2000), p. 6.

accordance with sound insurance principles (i.e. lower than is appropriate to the costs and extent of the risks covered).[17]

In 1978, the OECD prepared the "Arrangement on Guidelines for Officially Supported Export Credits"[18] to provide a framework for the orderly use of officially supported export credits and to provide for a level playing field (whereby competition is based on the price and quality of the exported goods and not the financial terms provided) and to working to eliminate subsidies and trade distortions related to officially supported export credits.[19] The Arrangement is a soft law and a "gentlemen's agreement".[20]

14.2 Functions of Export Credit Insurance (Or Guarantee)

Export credit insurance (or export credit guarantee) principally protects exporters from the risk of non-payment.[21] Export credit insurance (or export credit guarantee) significantly reduces the non-payment risk associated with an export transaction by providing the exporter conditional assurance that payment will be made even if the foreign buyer is unable to pay.[22] With export credit insurance cover (or export credit guarantee cover), exporters can protect their foreign receivables from various risks that could result in non-payment. Export credit insurance (or export credit guarantee) is one of the key security devices employed by the exporter.

As export credit insurance (or export credit guarantee) covers the risk of non-payment in international trades, banks are willing to finance for the transaction. Export credit insurance (or export credit guarantee) programmes are very useful for facilitation of trade finance in combination with various trade finance. When export credit insurance (or export credit guarantee) backs exporter's foreign receivables, commercial banks are willing to lend against assets otherwise excluded from the borrowing base.[23] Accordingly, an understanding of export credit insurance (or export credit guarantee) is often very essential to trade finance, in particular, for exporters with low credit.

Export credit insurance (or export credit guarantee) is issued in favor of exporters or their banks.[24] When an exporter can obtain export credit insurance (or export

---

[17]OECD (2011), p. 20.

[18]In January 2004, the title was changed to the "Arrangement on Officially Supported Export Credits".

[19]Ray (1995b), p. 2; OECD, "Arrangement on Guidelines for Officially Supported Export Credits": see Chap. I.1 Purpose.

[20]OECD (2011), pp. 7, 20.

[21]See UKEF website www.gov.uk/guidance/export-insurance-policy; see US EXIM Bank website www.exim.gov/what-we-do/export-credit-insurance; US Department of Commerce/International Trade Administration (2012a), p. 19.

[22]US Department of Commerce/International Trade Administration (2012a), p. 19.

[23]See US EXIM Bank website www.exim.gov/what-we-do/get-financing.

[24]Willsher (1995a), p. 80.

credit guarantee) for exports, the exporter can offer credit payment terms (or longer payment terms) to the foreign buyer.[25]

Export credit insurance (or export credit guarantee) basically provides protection against the non-payment risk. Export credit insurance (or export credit guarantee). It normally covers both commercial risks (such as insolvency of the buyer, bankruptcy, or protracted defaults/payment delay) and certain political risks (such as war, terrorism, riots, revolution, currency inconvertibility, foreign currency transfer restriction, expropriation, and changes in import or export regulations) that could result in non-payment. Furthermore, when export credit insurance (or export credit guarantee) backs exporter's foreign receivables, commercial banks are often willing to lend to the exporter with favorable terms against foreign receivables otherwise excluded from the borrowing base.[26]

Export credit insurance (or export credit guarantee) promotes exports by giving a variety of advantages to exporters. The key functions of export credit insurance include reducing non-payment risks, offering competitive payment terms, increasing exports with reduced non-payment risk and competitive payment terms, creating easy and accessible trade financing solutions, etc.[27]

However, export credit insurance (or export credit guarantee) does not cover physical losses or damages to the goods, which are covered by commercial insurances such as cargo insurance, marine insurance, fire insurance, casualty insurance, etc.[28] The exporter will not be indemnified when the non-payment is attributable to the non-performance of the underlying contract by the exporter, such as delivery of defective goods, discrepancies of the documents in a documentary credit transaction.

The Berne Union[29] set out the "Berne Union General Understanding",[30] which regulates the starting point of credit, length of credit, minimum downpayment, and installment. One of the main purposes of the Berne Union is to work for the international acceptance of sound principles of export credit insurance and the establishment and maintenance of discipline in the terms of credit for international trade. The General Understanding defines "short term credit" as "up to and including one year", "medium term credit" as over one year, and "long term credit" as "over 5 years".[31]

---

[25] Jimenez (2012), p. 110.

[26] See US EXIM Bank website www.exim.gov/what-we-do/get-financing.

[27] US Department of Commerce/International Trade Administration (2012b), p. 28.

[28] Murray et al. (2010b), p. 443; US Department of Commerce/International Trade Administration (2012a), p. 19.

[29] The Berne Union is an international not-for-profit trade association, representing the global export credit and investment insurance industry. The Berne Union was founded in 1934, and now has 85 members—government-backed official export credit agencies, multilateral financial institutions, and private credit insurers from 73 countries. See the Berne Union website http://www.berneunion.org/.

[30] Berne (2001).

[31] III. Definition of Credit Periods for Goods and Services
The Berne Union defines Credit Periods as follows:–
(a) Short Term Credit
Up to and including one year's credit.

As the Berne Union General Understanding restricts the length of credit of consumer goods to within two years, medium and long-term export credit insurance is applicable to exports of capital goods such as industrial plants, overseas constructions, and shipbuilding exports.

14.3 Main Types of Export Credit Insurance (Or Guarantee)

14.3.1 Overview

There are various types of export credit insurance (or export credit guarantee) operated by ECAs. The main basic types of export credit insurance (or export credit guarantee) would be a supplier credit insurance, a buyer credit insurance, a short-term export credit insurance, a medium and long-term export credit insurance, an export bond insurance, and an investment insurance.[32] The terms of a specific export credit insurance (or export credit guarantee) differ from ECA to ECA,[33] although the basic concepts are similiar.

A supplier credit insurance protects the exporter from non-payment by the importer. The exporter purchases a supplier credit insurance cover against the non-payment of their export. The buyer credit insurance protects the lender (the bank) from non-repayment by the borrower (the importer). The buyer credit insurance is usually used in medium and long-term credit transactions.[34]

Within the Berne Union, a short-term export credit insurance (or short-term export credit guarantee) is defined as insurance (or guarantee) for exports with repayment terms of less than one year–, and most often considerably less than this:—30, 60, or 90 days are standard, and a medium and long-term export credit insurance (or medium and long-term export credit guarantee) is defined as insurance (or guarantee) for transactions with tenors longer than one year (often three, five, seven and up to around ten years), typically in support of capital goods exports and large infrastructure projects.[35] An investment insurance covers risks associated with direct foreign investment.

A short-term export credit insurance is used in a transaction of consumer goods, while a medium and long-term export credit insurance is used in a transaction of

---

(b) Medium Term Credit

Over one year's credit. A formal division between Medium and Long Term Credit does not seem necessary, however, if this was required by any Member, then:

(c) Long Term Credit

should be regarded as over 5 years (i.e. Medium Term being up to and including 5 years).

[32] Stephens (1999d), pp. 8–11.

[33] Willsher (1995b), p. 81.

[34] Stephens (1999e), p. 10.

[35] Paul (2018a), pp. 5–6.

capital goods such as overseas construction, ships, industrial plants, etc. A short-term export credit insurance is usually used in a type of a supplier credit insurance. An export credit guarantee for pre-shipment finance (or a working capital loan guarantee) and an export bond insurance would also fall within export credit insurance (or export credit guarantee).

For instance, the Korea Trade Insurance Corporation (K-Sure), a Korean ECA, operates a short-term export insurance, and a medium and long-term export insurance. A short-term export insurance covers risks of non-payment of export proceeds in an export transaction due to political or commercial risks in transactions with less than two years of payment period. Short-term export insurance is the most frequently used insurance product among various export insurances.

A medium and long-term export insurance covers risks of non-payment in an export transaction due to political or commercial risks in transactions with more than two years of payment period. The K-Sure operates two types of medium and long-term export insurance; a medium and long-term export insurance (supplier credit), and a medium and long-term export insurance (buyer credit). A medium and long-term export insurance (supplier credit) is for an export transaction based on a supplier credit. 'Medium and long term export insurance (supplier credit)' It is selectively used as a security in an export transaction of capital goods (e.g., industrial plant, overseas construction, shipbuilding), while. Short-term export insurance' is used in an export transaction of consumer goods. Medium and long term export insurance (supplier credit) covers risks of non-payment by an importer in an export transaction due to political or commercial risks, the payment term of which exceeds two years. A medium and long-term export insurance (supplier credit) is typically considered more important than short-term export insurance for, as the payment term is longer and the risks are thus higher. A medium and long-term export insurance (supplier credit) enables a financial institution to provide a loan to an exporter against long-term receivables, for it is accepted as a security for the loan.

In 2017, the volume of total insured amount of by a short-term export credit insurance (or short-term export credit guarantee) by all Berne Union[36] members was USD 2,088 billiont. The volume of total insured amount by mid/long-term export credit insurance (or mid/long-term export credit guarantee) was USD 179 billion. And the volume of total insured amount of an investment insurance was USD 64 billion.[37]

---

[36]The Berne Union is the "International Union of Credit & Investment Insurers".

[37]Paul (2018b), p. 4.

14.3.2 *Short-Term Export Credit Insurance (Or Short-Term Export Credit Guarantee)*

14.3.2.1 Overview

Short-term export insurance covers risks of non-payment of export proceeds in an export transaction due to political or commercial risks in transactions with less than two years of payment period. As set out in the previous section, with a total volume of USD 2,088 billion in 2017,[38] this is the most popular among export credit insurances (or short-term export credit guarantees). The volume of total insured amount of a short-term export credit insurance (or short-term export credit guarantee).

A short-term export credit insurance (or short-term export credit guarantee) provides cover against non-payment by a foreign buyer, and covers political risks in an importing country. Although the specific procedures or flows of a short-term export credit insurance (or short-term export credit guarantee) varies on a according to the respective ECA, the very basic flows could be as follow:

Figure 14.1 illustrates the typical process flow of a short-term credit insurance transaction.

14.3.2.2 Supplier Credit Bills and Notes Facility

UK Export Finance (UKEF) provides the supplier credit bills and notes facility for an export transaction based on a supplier credit. This facility provides a guarantee to a financial institution (or a lender) to cover payments due under bills of exchange, or promissory notes, purchased by the financial institution from a UK exporter. The exporter will have received them in payment for capital goods and/or services supplied to an overseas importer.

Figure 14.2 illustrates the typical process flow of a supplier credit bills and notes facility.

14.3.3 *Medium and Long-Term Export Credit Insurance*

14.3.3.1 Overview

Basically, a medium and long-term export insurance (or mid and long-term export credit guarantee) covers risks of non-payment in an export transaction due to political or commercial risks in transactions with more than two years of payment period. A

---

[38]Ibid.

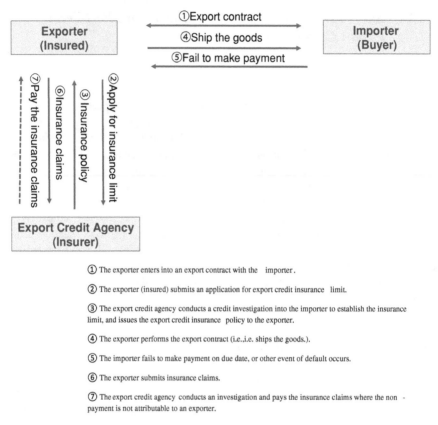

① The exporter enters into an export contract with the importer.

② The exporter (insured) submits an application for export credit insurance limit.

③ The export credit agency conducts a credit investigation into the importer to establish the insurance limit, and issues the export credit insurance policy to the exporter.

④ The exporter performs the export contract (i.e.,i.e. ships the goods.).

⑤ The importer fails to make payment on due date, or other event of default occurs.

⑥ The exporter submits insurance claims.

⑦ The export credit agency conducts an investigation and pays the insurance claims where the non - payment is not attributable to an exporter.

Fig. 14.1 Process flow of short-term credit insurance

medium and long-term export insurance (or mid and long-term export credit guarantee) is provided in an export transaction of capital goods (e.g. industrial plant, overseas construction, shipbuilding)

There could be two types of medium and long-term export credit insurance programmes: a medium and long-term export credit insurance (supplier credit), and a medium and long-term export credit insurance (buyer credit). There could be a medium and long-term export credit insurance (pre-shipment) other than those two insurance programmes. A medium and long-term export credit insurance (pre-shipment) covers the risks associated with the impossibility of the export after concluding an export contract, but it is very rarely used.

While a medium and long-term export credit insurance (supplier credit) covers the risks of non-payment to an exporter by an importer, a medium and long-term export credit insurance (buyer credit) covers the risks of non-repayment to a lender bank by a borrower (normally an importer). An exporter will be an insured under a medium and long-term export credit insurance (supplier credit), while a lender bank will be an insured under a medium and long-term export credit insurance (buyer credit). A

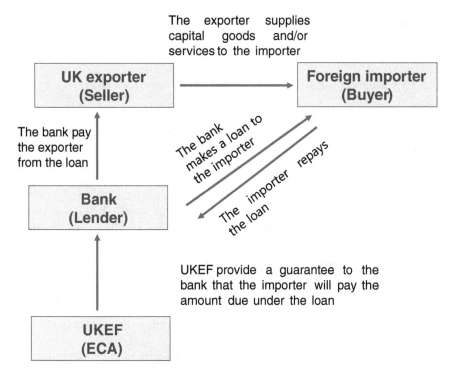

The exporter supplies capital goods and/or services to the importer

UK exporter (Seller) ──────────────▶ **Foreign importer (Buyer)**

The bank pay the exporter from the loan

The bank makes a loan to the importer

The importer repays the loan

Bank (Lender)

UKEF provide a guarantee to the bank that the importer will pay the amount due under the loan

UKEF (ECA)

Fig. 14.2 Process flow of a supplier credit bills and notes facility[39]

medium and long-term export credit insurance (buyer credit) is also called a "buyer credit insurance".

14.3.3.2 Medium and Long-Term Export Credit Insurance (Supplier Credit)

A medium and long-term export credit insurance (supplier credit) covers the risks of non-payment to the exporter by the importer. In a supplier credit, the exporter can borrow funds with favourable terms and conditions by assigning a medium and long-term export credit insurance (supplier credit) policy to the lender bank.

The exporter's credit rating in a supplier credit, is also replaced by that of the ECA providing the medium and long-term export credit insurance (supplier credit) where the insurance policy is assigned to the lender bank, and the lender bank will thus charge a lower interest than otherwise.[40] A medium and long-term export credit insurance (supplier credit) enables the exporter to reduce the funding cost. Thus, the exporter will be able to offer the importer very favourable payment terms, such as

---

[39]UKEF website www.gov.uk/guidance/supplier-credit-financing-facility
[40]Murray et al. (2010b), p. 443.

longer payment terms, lower interest rate for deferred payments, etc., which will give them a better chance to win the export contract.

14.3.3.3   Medium and Long-Term Export Credit Insurance (Buyer Credit)

A medium and long-term export credit insurance (buyer credit) covers the risks of non-repayment to the lender bank by the borrower (normally the importer). A medium and long-term export credit insurance (buyer credit) policy or a buyer credit insurance policy by an official ECA is, in the international financial market, treated as equal to the payment guarantee by the government. Therefore, in a buyer credit, the importer's credit rating is replaced by that of the ECA providing export credit insurance. If a medium and long-term export credit insurance (buyer credit) policy is provided, the lender bank will charge a lower interest than otherwise.[41]

Therefore, a medium and long-term export credit insurance policy contributes to reducing the funding cost. In a buyer credit, the exporter's ability to arrange a medium and long-term export credit insurance (buyer credit) policy is very essential. When an official ECA in an exporting country agrees to issue a medium and long-term export credit insurance (buyer credit) policy, the company in that exporting country will obtain priority in a bidding.

As Fig. 14.3 below illustrates, a medium and long-term export credit insurance (buyer credit) for an export contract (or an overseas construction contract) normally proceeds as follows:

14.3.3.4   Medium and Long-Term Guarantee

The medium and long-term guarantee (by the Export-Import Bank of the United States (US EXIM Bank)[42] helps US exporters secure competitive financing for foreign buyers. It guarantees long-term financing (generally up to 10 ten years) to creditworthy foreign importers. It is generally used for financing purchases of US capital equipment and services.

The medium and long-term guarantee is unconditional and transferable. It covers local costs up to 30% and ancillary services (e.g. financial, legal or bank fees) may be included. It helps foreign importers get competitive long-term financing that might previously have been unavailable otherwise.

As the medium and long-term guarantee is an officially supported export credit programmes, it requires that:

I.   the guarantee covers only the US content;
II. products must be shipped from the US to a foreign importer;

---

[41] Ibid.

[42] See US EXIM Bank website www.exim.gov/what-we-do/loan-guarantee.

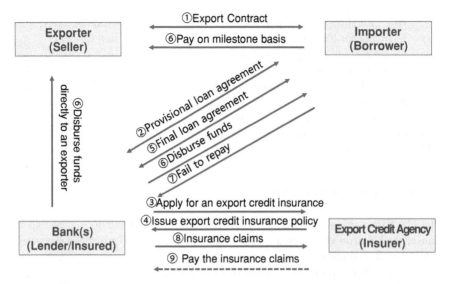

① The exporter enters into an export contract (or an overseas construction contract)   with the importer. In many cases, the exporter applies for a letter of intent to the ECA prior to submitting a bid or concluding a contract.

② The bank(s) and the importer conclude a provisional loan agreement.

③ The bank(s) applies for a medium and long-term export credit insurance (buyer credit) to the ECA

④ The export credit agency evaluates the application, including the importer's creditworthiness, shipping market conditions, importing country's political risk, etc., and then, issues a medium and long-term export credit insurance (buyer credit) policy.

⑤ The bank(s) and the importer conclude the final loan agreement.

⑥ The bank(s) disburses funds to the importer according to the loan   agreement, and the importer pays to the exporter according to the contact with the funds disbursed. In practice, the bank(s) will disburse funds directly to the exporter.

⑦ In the event the importer fails to repay the loan to the bank(s),

⑧ The bank(s) makes insurance claims to the ECA

⑨ The ECA(insurer) pays the insurance claims.

Fig. 14.3 Process flow of medium and long-term export credit insurance (buyer credit)

III. like other US EXIM Bank programmes, the medium and long-term guarantee may be offered in certain countries and under certain terms. The US EXIM Bank periodically publishes the "Country Limitation Schedule"[43];

IV. exports exports of military or defense products and services (with some exceptions) are excluded.

The functions of the medium and long-term guarantee will be:

---

[43] The Country Limitation Schedule as of March 28, 2019 is available at www.exim.gov/tools-for-exporters/country-limitation-schedule.

(i).   risk mitigation for an export transaction with a particular foreign buyer;
(ii).   financing for foreign buyers of US capital goods and related services;
(iii). secure entry to emerging markets;
(iv).   longer repayment terms;
(v).   flexible lender financing options, backed by the medium and long-term guar-
        antee, for foreign buyers of US capital goods and related services for long-term
        projects as well as medium- term;
(vi).   coverage for 100% of commercial and political risks;
(vii). no limits on transaction size.

14.3.3.5 Buyer Credit Facility

The UK Export Finance (UKEF)[44] provides a buyer credit facility for an export
transaction based on a buyer credit. Under the facility, the UKEF provides a guarantee
to a financial institution (or a bank) that provides funds to an overseas importer (an
employer), so that capital goods and/or services can be purchased from the UK. The
loan agreement is concluded between the overseas importer (the employer) and the
financial institution. The UKEF provides an export credit guarantee to the financial
institution that the loan will be repaid by the overseas importer (the employer). The
UK exporter (the contractor) sells the capital goods and/or services to the overseas
importer (the employer), and the financial institution then uses the loan to pay the
exporter (the contractor) for goods and/or services delivered.

Figure 14.4 illustrates the typical process flow of a buyer credit facility.

14.3.4 Export Bond Insurance (Bond Insurance)

14.3.4.1 Overview

In the export of capital goods such as overseas construction, industrial plants, or
ships, a bond or a guarantee (e.g. performance guarantee, advance payment guarantee,
warranty bond, etc.) is normally required as a security for the exporter's performance
of the contract. There is a range of bonds or guarantees such as the tender guarantee
(or bid bond), the performance guarantee (P-bond), the advance payment guarantee
(AP-bond), the retention guarantee (R-bond), the warranty guarantee (W-bond), etc.
These bonds or guarantees are issued in favour of the importer by the financial
institution at the request of the exporter (the contractor).

The financial institution that issues such a bond or a guarantee shall pay to the
beneficiary (normally the importer) on demand in the event the exporter fails to
perform the contract or other event of calling occurs. The financial institution will

---

[44]See UKEF website www.gov.uk/guidance/buyer-credit-facility.

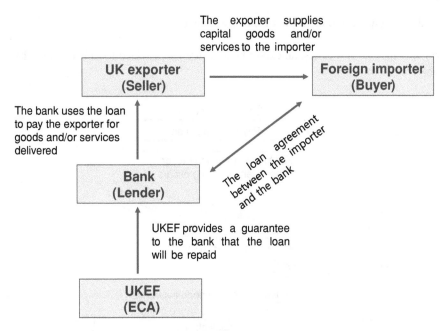

Fig. 14.4 Process flow of a buyer credit facility[45]

recourse to the exporter once they receive the demand for payment from the beneficiary. Therefore, a bond or a guarantee is, in practice, considered as the exporter's contingent liability. For this reason, the financial institution will issue a bond or a guarantee within the credit limit of the exporter, if not, they will request a security in return for issuance of a bond.

An export bond insurance protects the guarantor (the bank) against unfair calling and/or fair calling by the importer (the beneficiary), or the exporter against loss caused by unfair calling by the importer. The details of the export bond insurance vary from ECA to ECA. Some ECAs issue a bond or a guarantee instead of providing an export bond insurance. Some ECAs provide export bond insurances to guarantor banks, while others provide export bond insurances to exporters. Some ECAs cover only unfair calling, while others cover both of unfair calling and fair calling.

An export bond insurance policy is well accepted as a security for a bond, and facilitates issuance of a bond or a guarantee. When the exporter uses up its credit limits and is unable to provide a security, which occurs very often, an export bond insurance is essential for concluding the export contract (or the overseas construction contract). In many instances, the exporter applies to the ECA to provide the export bond insurance support prior to concluding the contract.

---

[45]UKEF website www.gov.uk/guidance/buyer-credit-facility

14.3.4.2 Operation of Export Bond Insurance

As the Fig. 14.5 illustrates, an export bond insurance provided for a bank normally proceeds as follows:

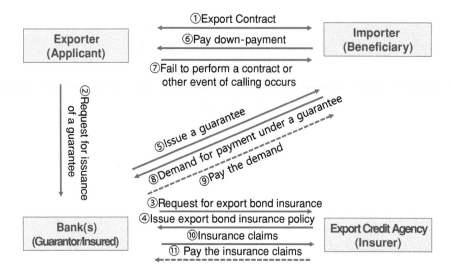

① The exporter (or the contractor) enters into an export contract (or an overseas construction contract) with the foreign importer (or the employer).

② The exporter requests the financial institution (or the bank) to issue a bond or guarantee.

③ The financial institution applies for an export bond insurance to the ECA In practice, the exporter submits the application form on behalf of the financial institution.

④ The ECAevaluates the performance competence of the exporter including the financial standing, and issues the export bond insurance policy.

⑤ The financial institution (or the guarantor) i ssues the bond (or the guarantee) in favour of the importer.

⑥ The importer pays downpayment, and progressive payments according to the performance of the contract.

⑦ In the event the exporter fails to perform the contract or other event of calling   occurs,

⑧ The importer demands for payment under the bond (or the guarantee) to the financial institution (the guarantor).

⑨ The financial institution (the guarantor) pays to the importer immediately upon receiving demand for payment.

⑩ The financial institution (the guarantor/insured), makes insurance claims to the ECA .

⑪ The ECA(the insurer) pays the insurance claims to the financial institution (the guarantor/insured).

Fig. 14.5 Process flow of export bond insurance

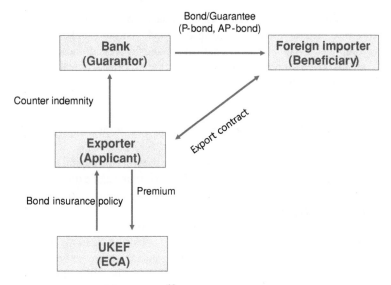

Fig. 14.6 Process flow of bond insurance[46]

14.3.4.3 Bond Insurance

The UKEF provides bond insurance for UK exporters, where the bank issues the guarantee (Bid-bond, P-bond, AP-bond, R-bond, or W-bond) to the foreign buyer (the importer) or the counter guarantee to the foreign bank. Bond insurance is an another name for an export bond insurance.

Bond insurance protects the exporter against loss caused by the "unfair calling" of the guarantee issued to the importer. Bond insurance also protects the exporter against loss caused by the "fair calling" of the guarantee due to certain "political events".[47]

Figure 14.6 illustrates the typical process flow of bond insurance.

14.3.5 Export Credit Guarantee (Or Working Capital Loan Guarantee) for Pre-shipment Finance

14.3.5.1 Overview

Most ECAs provide export credit guarantees for pre-shipment finance (or for export working capital financing). An export credit guarantee for pre-shipment (or a working capital loan guarantee) is offered to a lending bank as security for

---

[46]UKEF website www.gov.uk/guidance/bond-insurance-policy

[47]UKEF website available at https://www.gov.uk/guidance/bond-insurance-policy.

pre-shipment finance (or a working capital finance pre-shipment) necessary for purchasing raw materials, manufacturing the goods, and/or purchasing the goods from local suppliers. With an export credit guarantee for pre-shipment (or a working capital loan guarantee for pre-shipment finance), the exporter is able to increase their borrowing capacity considerably.

14.3.5.2   Working Capital Loan Guarantee for Pre-shipment[48]

The US EXIM Bank, an American ECA, operates the working capital loan guarantee for pre-shipment export working capital (or for performance of export transactions). The guarantee guarantees repayment for of a percentage of the working capital loan if the borrower (US exporter) defaults.

The working capital loan guarantee empowers exporters to unlock cash flow to perform export contracts and enables exporters to borrow more funds from financial institutions. The guarantee is a 90% loan-backing guarantee to a lender bank. With a working capital loan guarantee, financial institutions will be willing to provide loans to exporters by decreasing repayment risk. However, the US EXIM Bank does not replace commercial banks; it simply backs their loan and increases US exporters borrowing power.[49]

The working capital loan guarantee can be used for paying for materials, equipment, supplies, labor, and other inputs to perform contracts, for purchase of finished products for export, and for posting standby letters of credit (serving as Bid-bond, P-bond, AP-bond, R-bond, or W-bond). With an expanded borrowing capacity, exporters, in particular SMEs, are able to borrow more working capital. The guarantee can cover both multiple export contracts and individual contracts, and can guarantee both revolving and transaction-specific facilities. The guarantee requires no minimum or maximum transaction amount.

With the working capital loan guarantee, exporters can borrow more working capital, secure performance guarantees (Bid-bond, P-bond, AP-bond) necessary to win and perform export contracts, and increase their global competitiveness. The functions of the working capital loan guarantee are:

- flexible financing for large contracts;
- more attractive advance rates than conventional financing;
- obtain the line of credit quickly from a qualified lender;
- inclusion of otherwise excluded collateral in borrowing base;
- lower collateral requirements for bid bonds, performance bonds, or advance payment guarantees.

---

[48] See US EXIM Bank website Www.Exim.Gov/What-We-Do/Working-Capital; Www.Exim.Gov/ What-We-Do/Get-Financing.

[49] See US EXIM Bank website www.exim.gov/what-we-do/get-financing.

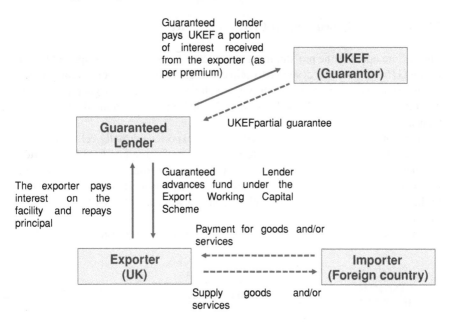

Fig. 14.7 Process flow of export working capital scheme for pre-shipment

14.3.5.3 Export Working Capital Scheme for Pre-shipment[50]

The UKEF operates operates the export working capital scheme for pre-shipment export working capital. Under the scheme, the UKEF issues a guarantee to a guaranteed bank at the request of a UK exporter.

A guaranteed bank pays the UKEF a premium for the guarantee with the interest received from the exporter. The exporter preforms an export contract with the funds advanced by the guaranteed bank (i.e. the exporter purchases raw materials to manufacture the goods, the exporter purchases finished goods from the local supplier). The exporter gets payment from the importer after performance of the export contract, and repays the loan with the payment received from the importer.

The export working capital scheme for pre-shipment finance assists UK exporters in gaining access to working capital finance both pre-shipment and post-shipment in respect of specific export-related contracts. The scheme enables UK exporters to borrow export loans in circumstances where their banks are reluctant to provide the full facility amount.

Figure 14.7 illustrates the typical process flow of an export working capital scheme for pre-shipment.

---

[50]See UKEF website.

14.3.5.4   Pre-shipment Export Credit Guarantee

The K-Sure operates the pre-shipment export credit guarantee. Pre-shipment Export Credit GThe guarantee is designed to help exporters where the exporters can produce the guarantee as security toward securing pre-shipment finance. The guarantee is very helpful, in particular, to SMEs that have difficulty in receiving trade financing from banks.

Once an export contract is entered into, an exporter normally relies on banks to secure loans to purchase raw materials and manufacture goods to be exported, but these banks normally require some type of security from the exporter. The pre-shipment export credit guarantee serves as security for the bank to advance loan to the exporter. The guarantee is well accepted as a security for such pre-shipment finance.

The process for the pre-shipment export credit guarantee is illustrated in Fig. 14.8:

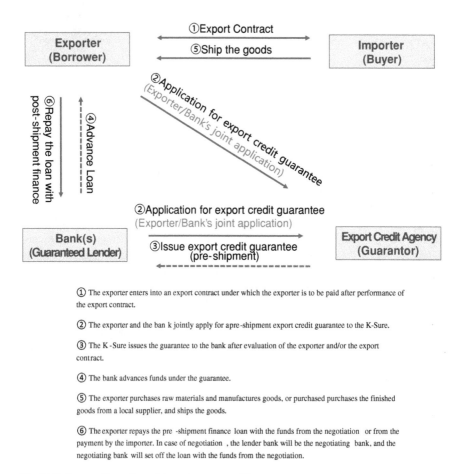

① The exporter enters into an export contract under which the exporter is to be paid after performance of the export contract.

② The exporter and the ban k jointly apply for apre-shipment export credit guarantee to the K-Sure.

③ The K-Sure issues the guarantee to the bank after evaluation of the exporter and/or the export contract.

④ The bank advances funds under the guarantee.

⑤ The exporter purchases raw materials and manufactures goods, or purchased purchases the finished goods from a local supplier, and ships the goods.

⑥ The exporter repays the pre -shipment finance loan with the funds from the negotiation or from the payment by the importer. In case of negotiation , the lender bank will be the negotiating bank, and the negotiating bank will set off the loan with the funds from the negotiation.

Fig. 14.8 Process flow of pre-shipment export credit guarantee

Where the exporter fails to ship the goods, the exporter repays the pre-shipment finance loan with his own funds. In the event the exporter fails to ship the goods, or fails to repay the pre-shipment finance loan, the K-Sure pays the bank and recourses to the exporter.

References

Berne, U. (2001). *Berne union general understanding.* 99654-RL, January.

Bishop, E. (2006). *Finance of international trade* (p. 100). Oxford, U.K.: Elsevier.

David, C. and Clara, C. (1997) The EU proposal for a council directive on export credit insurance: A critical evaluation. *Geneva Papers on Risk and Insurance – Issues and Practice*, p. 414.

Filip, A. and Gerda, D. (2000). Export promotion via official export insurance. *Open Economies Review*, 6.

Janet, W. (2009). Facilitating export credits. *Berne Union Yearbook, 34,* 35.

Jimenez, G. C. (2012). *ICC guide to export/import: global standards for international trade* (4th ed., p. 110) Paris, France: ICC Publication No. 686.

Murray, C., et al. (2010a). *Schmitthoff's export trade: The law and practice of international trade* (11th ed., p. 441). London, U.K: Thomson Reuters.

Murray, C., et al. (2010b). *Schmitthoff's export trade: The law and practice of international trade* (11th ed., p. 443). London, U.K: Thomson Reuters.

OECD. (2011). *Smart rules for fair trade: 50 years of export credits* (p. 7, 20). OECD Publishing.

OECD. (2018). *Arrangement on officially supported export credits.* (TAD/PG(2018)8).

Paul, H. (2018a). 2017 Year end data in review. *BU Spring Meeting Newsletter,* 5–6.

Paul, H. (2018b). 2017 Year end data in review. *BU Spring Meeting Newsletter,* 4.

Peter, E., & Thomas, U. (2006). Public export credit guarantees and foreign trade structure: Evidence from Austria. *World Economy, 29*(4), 400.

Ray, J. E. (1995a). *Managing official export credits: The quest for a global regime* (p. 1). Washington D.C., USA: Institute for International Economics.

Ray, J. E. (1995b). *Managing official export credits: The quest for a global regime* (p. 2). Washington D.C., USA: Institute for International Economics.

Ray, J. E. (1996). *Managing official export credits: The quest for a global regime* (p. 2). Washington D.C., USA: Institute for International Economics.

Roberto, S. (2010). Doha reform of WTO export credit provisions in the SCM agreement: The perspective of developing countries. *Journal of World Trade, 44*(3), 611–632.

Sang Man Kim. (2017). World shipbuilding industry and export credit insurances for ship exports: Focusing Korea's export credit insurances. *International Journal of Applied Business and Economic Research, 15*(10), 264.

Stephens, M. (1999a). *The changing role of export credit agencies* (p. 1). Washington D.C., USA: IMF Washington.

Stephens, M. (1999b). *The changing role of export credit agencies* (p. 9). Washington D.C., USA: IMF Washington.

Stephens, M. (1999c). *The changing role of export credit agencies* (pp. 98–99). Washington D.C., USA: IMF Washington.

Stephens, M. (1999d). *The changing role of export credit agencies* (pp. 8–11). Washington D.C., USA: IMF Washington.

Stephens, M. (1999e). *The changing role of export credit agencies* (p. 10). Washington D.C., USA: IMF Washington.

US Department of Commerce/International Trade Administration. (2012a). *Trade finance guide: A quick reference for US exporters* (p. 19). Washington D.C., USA: US Department of Commerce.

US Department of Commerce/International Trade Administration. (2012b). *Trade finance guide: A quick reference for US exporters* (p. 28). Washington D.C., USA: US Department of Commerce.

Willsher, R. (1995a). *Export finance: Risks structures and documentation* (p. 80). Basingstoke, U.K.: Macmillan Press.

Willsher, R. (1995b). *Export finance: Risks structures and documentation* (p. 81). Basingstoke, U.K.: Macmillan Press.

Yehuda, K. (1986). Insurance and risk management of foreign trade risks. *Geneva Papers on Risk and Insurance – Issues and Practice*, 275.

Index

CPSIA information can be obtained
at www.ICGtesting.com
Printed in the USA
LVHW021009041021
699444LV00001BC/33

9 789811 570414